"The best book I have rea

Iain Dale

"Oates takes you on an extraordinary journey from teenage rebellion, through the fight for African rights, to the top ranks of the British government. It's all the more extraordinary because the story is true – his is a life lesson that serendipity and courage can change things for good."

Laura Kuenssberg, former BBC political editor

"Unusually for a political figure, Jonny Oates has written about love: how it tormented him and how it healed him. Few in political life are as candid about the underpinning of what drives them. A gripping tale of escape and rescue, this is the story of the making of a liberal soul."

Gary Gibbon, political editor, *Channel 4 News*

"*I Never Promised You a Rose Garden* charts the unusual emotional and political journey of Jonny Oates. By turns tender, moving and funny, it is an unflinchingly candid story of teenage rebellion, of love and – above all – of heartfelt compassion. If anyone doubts that there is still a place in politics for exceptional, decent people, this is a book for you."

Nick Clegg, Deputy Prime Minister 2010–15

I NEVER PROMISED YOU A ROSE GARDEN

JONNY OATES

\B^b\
Biteback Publishing

This paperback edition published in Great Britain in 2022 by
Biteback Publishing Ltd, London
Copyright © Jonny Oates 2020, 2022

Jonny Oates has asserted his right under the Copyright, Designs and Patents Act 1988
to be identified as the author of this work.

Excerpt from Michael Buerk's 1984 Korem broadcast reproduced by kind permission of the BBC.
Excerpt from *Country of My Skull* by Antjie Krog published by Vintage, reprinted by permission
of The Random House Group Ltd.

Every reasonable effort has been made to trace copyright holders of material reproduced in this
book, but if any have been inadvertently overlooked the publisher would be glad to hear from them.

ISBN 978-1-78590-760-9

10 9 8 7 6 5 4 3 2 1

A CIP catalogue record for this book is available from the British Library.

Set in Minion Pro and Futura

Printed and bound in Great Britain by
CPI Group (UK) Ltd, Croydon CR0 4YY

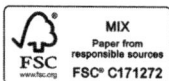

For David
who has lit up my life with happiness

And in loving memory of
Sylvia Oates and Mildred Hill

CONTENTS

PREFACE

This is the story of a journey which began in Addis Ababa during the famine of 1985 and ended in the Rose Garden of 10 Downing Street, twenty-five years later.

It is not a political autobiography – if you are looking for the history of the coalition government, you will have to look elsewhere. It isn't my life story either – there are too many important people missing from it and too many of my mistakes untold for that.

It is, rather, a journey through geographies and politics and emotions. A story about some of the things that happened to me on the way and of some of the people who helped ensure that I kept marching on.

The journey starts with a messed up fifteen-year-old boy embarking on the futile exercise of trying to run away from himself. That boy is me, but I found that to write about myself at that particular moment in my life with the degree of honesty that I wanted to, I needed to take a step back and view things through a more distant lens. Accordingly, I have written the opening chapters of the book, until I was found and rescued by Father Charles Sherlock, largely in the third person.

Many of the place names in Africa have changed since I lived there, so wherever possible I have used both the name as it was at the time and the modern name in current use. In the acknowledgements, I have referred to Prince Buthelezi by his royal title; however, during his time as

Home Affairs Minister, which coincided with my time in South Africa, Prince Buthelezi did not use his royal title, so I have generally followed this practice in the main text of the book.

The events retold here are as accurate as I can make them. They are drawn from a combination of my recollections, my diaries and the letters that I wrote home from Africa at different points over three decades, all of which my mother had preserved. Wherever possible, I have checked my recollections against outside sources and with others who were present at the time. The conversations that I record in the book are reconstructions from recollections sometimes dating back thirty years; they should not be regarded as verbatim records.

Finally, although all the facts are to the best of my knowledge accurate, I have changed the names of some individuals in order to avoid causing unnecessary embarrassment.

BBC News, Tuesday 23 October 1984

Dawn, and as the sun breaks through the piercing chill of night on the plain outside Korem, it lights up a biblical famine, now, in the twentieth century. This place, say workers here, is the closest thing to hell on earth.

Thousands of wasted people are coming here for help. Many find only death. They flood in every day from villages hundreds of miles away, dulled by hunger, driven beyond the point of desperation.

Fifteen thousand children here now; suffering, confused, lost. Death is all around; a child or an adult dies every twenty minutes. Korem, an insignificant town, has become a place of grief.

The relief agencies do what they can. Save the Children Fund are caring for more than seven thousand babies. Every day they weigh them on a sling then compare their weight with their height. By this rule of thumb, one in three is severely malnourished, starved to the point of death.

There's not enough food for half these people. Rumours of a shipment can set off panic. As on most days, the rumours were false; for many here there would be no food again today.

Two months ago, there were ten thousand people here; now the latest harvest has failed, there are forty thousand. There's nothing like enough food in the country; not enough transport to move it if there was.

Some of the very worst are packed into big sheds, seven thousand now, most apparently dying of malnutrition, pneumonia and the diseases that prey on the starving.

This three-year-old girl was beyond any help: unable to take food, attached to a drip but too late; the drip was taken away. Only minutes later, while we were filming, she died. Her mother had lost all her four children and her husband.

Those who die in the night are brought at dawn to be laid out on the edge of the plain.

Dozens of them; men, women and children, under blankets or bound in sack cloth for burial in the local custom.

This mother and the baby she bore two months ago wrapped together in death.

As body after body was brought down, the grief became almost tangible. By Korem's standards it wasn't a bad night; thirty-seven dead. Tomorrow there would be more; the day after, more still.

A tragedy, bigger than anybody seems to realise, getting worse every day.

Ethiopia is turning into the worst human disaster for a decade. A disaster begun by nature but compounded by man.

This is Michael Buerk for the Six O'Clock News in Korem, northern Ethiopia.

PART ONE

WHEREVER YOU GO

1

REMEMBERING

I was fourteen years old when I decided to run away to Ethiopia. Fifteen by the summer of 1985, when I actually made it to the Ethiopian capital, Addis Ababa. Why did I go? To save the world – at least that's what I told myself – but perhaps more prosaically and less originally, I was just running away from myself.

Twenty-eight years later. I am on an Ethiopian Airlines flight heading from Maputo in Mozambique to Addis Ababa. I am sat by the window in seat 2L. Next to me in seat 2J is the UK's Deputy Prime Minister, Nick Clegg. It's a very different flight from the last one I took to Ethiopia. Thirty thousand feet below me, the sun is setting over Africa and the darkness is gathering.

I try to imagine myself as that fifteen-year-old boy who sat on a different Ethiopian Airlines plane all those years ago, and I don't know if I should admire him or fear him. I do recall a few things from that original flight: the music channel stuck to country and western and Lynn Anderson percolating through plastic stethoscope-style earphones with the stark message 'I never promised you a rose garden'.

I remember excitement as well as fear – my first glimpse of Africa as the plane descended through the dawn. I remember seeing the straw-thatched huts dotting the rural expanse, and the beauty of the light on the land. I remember the sense of anticipation that I felt as an almost physical thing, a concrete experience that I can take out and examine.

And I think also of Father Charles Sherlock, who rescued me with his wisdom and kindness and who, by the remarkable coincidences of fate, is here in Addis now.

• • •

The official part of my visit to Addis passes in a haze. Transported from meeting to meeting with the Deputy Prime Minister, it is hard to follow where in the city we are rushing to and from. So much of it has changed, so much grown up in the past few years. But the scent of Addis still evokes memories: the smell of woodsmoke and diesel fumes and the ubiquitous eucalyptus.

At dinner at the embassy, before the DPM and the rest of the delegation catch their flight home, I am asked about that earlier trip to Ethiopia. As I describe how it came about, I see that journey, for the first time, through other people's eyes: as something romantic and brave – and I make the mistake of believing it.

I am staying on for the weekend for a reunion with Father Charles, so at about 10 p.m., Bill, one of Nick's protection team, comes in to tell me that a car is waiting to take me to the hotel where I stayed all those years ago. I am excited and nostalgic at the prospect of a weekend in the place that played such a significant role in my life.

After I have checked in, I head to my room. It is on the fourth floor and is pleasant and large; it seems little changed from three decades ago. I stroll out on to the small balcony to take in Addis in the cool night air. I look out at the lights of the city, and then down at the car park below me, and as soon as I do that, any delusions about a romantic and brave adventure flee into the night. I am, once again, that desperately troubled fifteen-year-old boy who has decided he has nowhere left to run. And so he is standing on a hotel balcony just like this one, perhaps even this one, and he is calculating – is that far enough to fall to ensure it will be a clean and merciful end?

2

BOLE AIRPORT, ADDIS ABABA

It's 7 a.m. at Bole Airport, Addis Ababa. The morning air that greets the passengers of the Ethiopian Airlines flight from London is fresh and cool, pregnant with the promise and threat of an African day. Among the passengers who descend the steps from the aircraft and cross the tarmac to the terminal building is a fifteen-year-old English boy who has run away from home.

It is either August 1985 or 1978, according to your choice of western or Ethiopian calendar. Either way, the brutal folk who make up Ethiopia's Marxist military dictatorship, the Derg, have been in power for eleven years. This fact is celebrated by lacklustre triumphal arches, which are strewn across the city, acclaiming the years 1967–78. In truth, there is little to celebrate. Haile Selassie, the Ethiopian emperor, who preceded the Derg, was overthrown for his failure to deal with a famine. Awkward, then, that eleven years on, Ethiopia is plunged into another, which the Derg, with its customary mix of brutality and incompetence, is handling even worse.

The boy has no money, except a battered £1 note, thirty birr in Ethiopian currency and the American Express card he has stolen from his father – and he has no idea what he is going to do now.

Inside the terminal building, there is lots of bustle. Ethiopia may be a Marxist-Leninist military dictatorship, but such is the scale of its grotesque and brutal failings that it has exacerbated a devastating famine and in doing so has, paradoxically, brought a degree of prosperity to the capital, its economy driven along by the aid workers, aid shipments and journalists who have been flooding in.

The boy goes and stands by the single luggage carousel and watches the suitcases go around. There is no obvious point to this activity. He doesn't have a suitcase himself; his only luggage is a small, powder-blue holdall with white handles, turning to grey, which he carried with him on the plane and which is now on the floor between his legs. Inside it are a few changes of clothes – three white T-shirts, three pairs of striped cotton boxer shorts, three pairs of socks – and a Book of Common Prayer.

Nevertheless, the boy stands there earnestly surveying his fellow passengers' baggage, because he has no idea what he is going to do next. Standing by the carousel allows him inconspicuous time to think, and to try to quell the panic that has risen in his stomach and is now clambering up his insides and constricting the muscles in his throat.

He stands very still and focuses all his energy on achieving a sense of calm; by this method he is able to withstand the rising panic and restore himself to a state of controllable fear. He decides that he must get himself into the centre of the city and track down the aid agencies, who he so misguidedly believes will be waiting with open arms, ready to embrace his altruistic offer of help.

He has not yet worked out that the aid agencies' demand for unskilled fifteen-year-old English boys is likely to be limited, or, let's be blunt, non-existent. In any case, inspired by the film *Gandhi*, he has a righteous certainty that if he wants to do something passionately enough, it will be possible to achieve the objective by sheer force of will and, if necessary, a little assistance from God. He is yet to learn the lesson that sometimes you can't make a thing happen by wanting it to – however hard you try and however much you pray.

He is about to learn that lesson – pretty brutally, in fact.

But for now, even if he has considered the possibility of rejection, he has discounted it. If necessary, Gandhi-like, he will walk to the feeding camps and just start to help out. How he will be of help, he has not considered. Surely his passion to save the world will be enough – what more could anyone ask?

Quite a bit, it turns out.

3

WILL

It is the first day in a new term. The boys, all freshly returned to school, are still excited to be back together after a summer away; still abundant in holiday stories and adventures. Not yet jaded by lessons and proximity to one another and short days and darkness. Autumn is making increasing forays, but today it is still warm enough to think the summer will last for ever.

A small group of friends are lying around at the edge of the meadows that run down to the river Kennet, screened by long grass, puffing on cigarettes, sharing out stories rich in exaggeration and embellishment. The warmth feels good and so does the scent of the grass and the camaraderie. Gradually, people drift off until there are just two of them.

One is a dark-haired boy, olive skinned, slight. He is propped up on an elbow while his friend lies on his back, his head cushioned by the bank and his rolled-up grey school jacket, staring at the clear blue sky and the waning sun. He seems in no hurry to move.

'Another smoke?' The dark-haired boy proffers a cigarette packet. His friend nods and the boy extracts one from the packet and hands it to him.

'So what happened, Will? You hardly got down to London at all.'

'You know, my dad. Usual stuff.'

His tone is resigned exasperation.

11

He places the cigarette in his mouth and strikes a match against the worn glasspaper side of the box. It skids along the surface ineffectually. He strikes again, this time on the upper part of the glasspaper, which is less worn. The pink-headed match fizzles desultorily into life. He coaxes the flame, his hand cupped around it, his face a picture of concentration as he brings match and cigarette together. He puffs on the cigarette rapidly to ensure it remains alight and then he lies back again and contemplates the sky.

After thirty seconds or so of silent contemplation, he says quietly, 'It's so frustrating. He just doesn't get me. He thinks everyone is a "bad influence". You're the only one he thinks is OK and that's only because your dad's a vicar and somehow that makes him think you are good.'

The dark-haired boy listens as Will looses his frustrations in his quiet gravelly voice. And although he is hearing him, he is seeing him more intently. He takes in his friend's brow, wrinkled now with his sense of injustice, his high cheekbones and soft, almost imperceptible freckles, his light brown hair flecked with the gold of the autumn sun. His green eyes intense and focused.

The boy feels a sharp stab of anticipation and excitement which turns rapidly to fear. He leans back into the grassy bank.

Will continues to talk out his frustrated summer, with his friend interjecting occasionally with sympathetic sounds to indicate he is engaged. Finally, he concludes with an exasperated sigh and gets to his feet, offering a hand to pull his friend up. 'Anyway, sorry to offload this shit on you. It's good to have you around. I missed you over the summer.'

It's a moment, a nanosecond of intensity, and then Will grins and breaks it. 'Come on, we better get back. See you tomorrow.'

He parts with an affectionate squeeze on his friend's shoulder and they head off in different directions.

The dark-haired boy crosses the narrow stone bridge over the river, but instead of turning right by the tennis courts towards his boarding house, he takes a left and heads along the grassy path by the riverside. He comes to a small gate and passes through it into a meadow. The trees alongside the river dapple sunlight onto the water, which dances in the flow.

At the end of the meadow is his thinking spot, a stile shaded by trees, with a long hedge to its right, running uphill alongside the meadow. Perpendicular to the stile on the left is the tree-lined bank of the river. If you sit on that stile, facing the direction of the town, all is lush greenery and sunlight and shade. It is the beauty of England.

It's where he sits and smokes and thinks. He never comes here with anyone, not even Will. It's the place where he tries to make sense of growing. Of the plunging, soaring, sinking ride of adolescence. Where joy and dread and shame and confusion are examined or ignored or driven into hiding.

Today, he comes to the stile to contemplate happiness. Two months of summer holidays passed and he saw Will only twice. Once in London and once at Will's home in the manicured suburbs of a provincial town. Will's absence pulled at him every day, dragging and sinking him. But now they are back together, and Will is as kind and thoughtful and troubled as the Will he constructed in his absence.

He has feelings for Will which he knows he must not entertain. So he threatens them and chases them away and lights another cigarette in the gathering dusk.

4

A BIBLICAL FAMINE, NOW IN THE TWENTIETH CENTURY

Why did I run away to Ethiopia? Why did I run away at all? Easy enough to answer the first question; harder to answer the second. I'll start with the easy bit.

On Tuesday 23 October 1984, I was home from school for the half-term holiday, lounging on a sofa in the sitting room of our new home, St Bride's Rectory in Fleet Street, as the BBC news played out on the telly. I wasn't paying too much attention, to tell the truth. And then, suddenly, I was.

There was something about the way in which the newscaster introduced the item that put me on alert. Her tone, sombre and subdued, her voice dropping as she introduced Michael Buerk's soon-to-be-world-famous report of the Ethiopian famine: 'Dawn, and as the sun breaks through the piercing chill of night on the plain outside Korem, it lights up a biblical famine, now, in the twentieth century. This place, say workers here, is the closest thing to hell on earth.'

The dispassionate urgency of Buerk's voice, the simplicity and economy of his language, overlaying harrowing footage of the dead and the dying, alerted the world to a human catastrophe, but it did more than that: it galvanised the world into action.

Michael Buerk knew how to use language, and he knew how to use silence too. The pauses in his commentary, as Mohammed Amin's footage spelled out the full horror of the suffering, were as powerful as his words. The silences demanded reflection; they insisted that we attend to what this meant, not just for the victims, but for ourselves as witnesses. 'This three-year-old girl was beyond any help: unable to take food, attached to a drip but too late; the drip was taken away. Only minutes later, while we were filming, she died. Her mother had lost all her four children and her husband...'

'Her mother had lost all her four children and her husband...' There was something about that simple statement that overwhelmed me. It was so relatable and so devastating. Tears swelled behind my eyes, and I clenched my jaw tightly, trying but failing to fight them back. Sorrow for loss; horror at the world that I saw through angry teenage eyes.

Those words and images from Michael Buerk's broadcast changed the world for me. I was not alone in feeling their impact. Millions of people saw the same images and had similar reactions. A total of 425 television channels around the world broadcast Buerk's report, and the sense of outrage that this biblical famine should be occurring amidst such plenty was harnessed and directed by Bob Geldof, lead singer of the Boomtown Rats, through Band Aid and Live Aid. Geldof was a rebel who had found a cause. Aged fourteen, I had found mine too.

These were days of excess, when European Community market intervention to stabilise agricultural prices led to grain and butter mountains piled high in European warehouses as the rains failed and grain stocks dwindled on the scorched plains of Ethiopia.

EC intervention stocks were not an abstract concept to me. Each day, my well-heeled schoolmates and I were fed on them. The school's refrigerators groaned with the weight of subsidised EC butter. Our breakfast tables were littered with half-pound packs, prominently stamped with the words 'EC Intervention Stocks: Not for resale', with the relevant EC regulation spelled out underneath.

In a desperate attempt to dispose of the grotesque mountains of excess, these stocks were handed out to charities, and – thanks to their charitable status – the most exclusive schools in the country were among the happy recipients. Subsidised butter fed to the richest people in the land while millions faced starvation.

Don't tell me there weren't things to be angry about.

The horror of the famine camp at Korem ignited a fury within me that was already smouldering. Natural teenage rebellion was now super-charged with a sense of righteous anger – the grotesque injustice of this famine was their doing; it was exactly what adults allowed to happen. Obsessed with imposing endless rules and restrictions on the rest of us, they were oblivious to the abjectly corrupt world that they had built.

That anger built in me over the following months as Bob Geldof cranked up the pressure in the face of the mind-numbingly slow reaction to the crisis. In December, the Band Aid single 'Do They Know It's Christmas?' was released to raise money to tackle the famine and received a massive response from the public, achieving the cherished Christmas No. 1 spot. Margaret Thatcher's tin-eared government insisted that VAT on sales of the record would not be waived, but they hadn't reckoned with Geldof and the strength of public opinion. Chastened, they backed down. By then I had clocked that politics had a lot to do with what happened in the world. It was a revelation that shaped the rest of my life.

Of course, I shouldn't pretend that my actions were fuelled purely by my rage at the injustice of the world. There were other issues too. I was a seriously messed-up teenager, looking for a cause through which to channel the anger and shame that I felt with myself, and if it hadn't been Ethiopia, doubtless I would have found something else.

I am not sure if anyone looks back at their teenage years and says, 'That was a great time to be alive.' Certainly, I don't. My rage was fuelled by the confusion and disorientation of adolescence, by my anger at feeling alone and different, and by an awakening sexuality which I feared, and which the world taught me to despise.

At fifteen, I was slight, dark haired, olive skinned, morose. Above all, morose. I looked older than my fifteen years; most of the time, I could pass for eighteen. I was taciturn, uncommunicative, locked inside myself – profoundly depressed. The depression arrived with my adolescence. It didn't leave until my late twenties. I am not talking here of feeling a bit down. I am talking about something very different. A sticky, suffocating web that is forever tightening around you, choking your sense of self-worth, feasting on your confidence. And however much you tear at it, you cannot rid yourself of it. So that, now, whenever you go to bed, you pray: 'Please God let me not wake in the morning.' And when you awake, it is with desperate sadness that another day has come.

That was me. That was how I lived my life. That was my prayer before I slept.

5

THE AIRPORT ROAD

The boy pulls himself out of his reverie. He has to work out how he is going to get from the airport to the city centre. On the plane, they had handed him an immigration card. Among other details, it demanded to know where he would be staying. This gave rise to his first misgiving. Obviously, he had no idea – he could hardly put 'feeding camp' – so he flicked through the in-flight magazine looking for hotel advertisements. There was only one, for the Hilton Hotel on what is now Menelik II Avenue, so he wrote that down. It turns out that the words he writes on this immigration card will prove very important to his life. But that is for later.

Right now, he has to negotiate the grim-faced immigration officials. He approaches the immigration desk warily. In turn, the immigration officials eye him suspiciously. A white boy dressed in faded denim jeans, a striped business shirt and an expensive-looking tuxedo jacket that once belonged to a now-deceased investment banker – but that is a whole other story.

The boy hands his passport to the official, who flicks through it until he finds the visa in Amharic script that fills an entire page of the old-style navy-blue British passport. He scrutinises it minutely but is unable to detect any flaws. Now he flicks to the photo page, where he finds a black-and-white photo of the boy, a year or two younger, staring intently into a camera lens, his dark-haired fringe a zig-zag admonition to an inexpert barber.

The immigration official's severe glance alternates between the photo and the boy standing before him, but again he can detect nothing wrong. The image is clearly of the boy. The boy has a visa issued by the embassy in London entitling him to enter the country. There is no reason not to stamp his passport and admit him, and eventually this is exactly what he does. But he seems uneasy about it. A few months ago, perhaps he would have challenged the incongruous presence of an unaccompanied fifteen-year-old boy at his immigration desk, but these days, with aid staff, journalists and the occasional pop star-turned-humanitarian flooding through the airport, the official contents himself with suspicious looks and grimly stamps the passport.

A cold sweat seeps through the boy's pores as he endures the immigration official's scrutiny, and the droplets are trickling down his back as he emerges from the airport into the light of an African morning. In the shade, it remains cool, but the sun is rising in the sky and already starting to heat up the day. The outside of the airport is populated by battered blue-and-white Ladas, which operate as a curious hybrid of bus and taxi. At a discreet and scornful distance from them are a fleet of sleek, beige Mercedes-Benz sedans which serve those with more expensive tastes and a greater desire to arrive in one piece.

The boy eschews these options and decides to walk. Needless to say, he has no idea of the distance from the airport to the city centre, nor has he considered how outlandish a mode of transport this will appear to the local populace – a white boy walking through the early morning streets. But he does know that he has very little cash and he needs to conserve it.

So he sets off down Bole Road towards the city. The first thing that he realises is that it is hot in the sun and a tuxedo jacket isn't the ideal attire for a summer's day walk in the Ethiopian capital. The next thing he notices is that he is attracting quite a bit of attention. The surprised looks from passers-by he steadfastly avoids, staring straight ahead and trudging determinedly forward. What he finds harder to ignore is the group of ragged and insistent young children who are gathering around him.

'Where you go, *faranj*?' demands one child, using the Ethiopian word for a white person, which the boy will hear very often during his time in the city.

'Carry bag?!' The tone manages to sound both friendly and aggressive.

He tells them he is going to the city centre, which elicits blank looks – he later discovers that Addis doesn't really have a city centre. He tries 'Hilton Hotel', which seems to mean more to them.

'We take you there.'

He isn't keen on this development. His head, right now, is overwhelmed by the trouble he has got himself into, and he wants his walking time to be quiet and to allow him to think. That is now out of the question, surrounded as he is by five or six children insistently vying for the right to carry his bag. The powder-blue holdall contains almost all the boy's belongings and he is naturally reluctant to give it up to anyone, least of all a bunch of fleet-of-foot children. So he tries to ignore them and to walk on in the hope that they will become bored of him and disappear.

He really understands nothing of the world and certainly nothing of the world of these children. They are not going to be put off; they are not going to get bored and head for home. They most likely have no home to go to except the street, and to them there is nothing the slightest bit boring about a white man in a tuxedo tramping through their city.

The constant cry of '*Faranj! Faranj!*', accompanied by an insistent tugging at his jacket to ensure his attention, is starting to get to him. Alongside that, the novelty and excitement of his first intercontinental flight and the sights and sounds and scents of his first day in Africa are starting to be replaced by the magnitude of what he has done. He is aware of the precariousness of the predicament he has placed himself in, and that awareness threatens to overwhelm him.

In this moment of weakness, he surrenders to the calling of the street kids. What has he to lose, he thinks. So he stops, unslings the bag from his shoulder and hands it to the child who has assumed leadership of this ragged band of demanding children. He is a boy of nine or ten, dressed in tattered red shorts and a washed-out grey T-shirt with small holes in the fabric around the neck and a large hole at the bottom, where the fabric has given way entirely.

The child takes the holdall solemnly and tries to sling it over his shoulder in the manner that the boy has been carrying it, but he is considerably smaller and it unbalances him. He staggers, unshoulders it and grins broadly. One of his fellows comes to his aid, and the two of them take hold of one of the bag's white handles each. In this manner, with the bag swinging between the two of them, they head towards the city with a processional seriousness of purpose.

Soon the other boys are squabbling for the right to a turn carrying the bag. But the chief street child and his comrade are not for sharing the task, which they have taken to with an impressive display of responsibility. And so this family of lost children continue their journey, the white boy, perhaps most lost of all, adorned in expensive western clothes in the midst of a gaggle of five or six raggedly dressed African children, the two bag carriers immediately before him, the others straggling around him.

The pavements on Bole Road – in as much as they exist – are pitted and potholed, the air is laden with the fumes of ancient Ladas and a tumour of fear is growing heavy in his stomach. Yet the boy cannot help being struck by the vibrancy which is all around, and now that he has conceded to the street children, he starts to look about him, to absorb the looks of surprise on the faces of those passing by, sometimes turning to suspicion, other times dissolving into smiles and giggles and muttered comments.

What might surprise people who had been to other parts of Africa – but does not surprise the boy, as he has never been outside Europe before – is that, aside from the children, no one has asked him for anything. Even they have only asked that they should be allowed to carry his bag, although, of course, there is an implied price in that.

Every now and then, other children join the throng, laughing and giggling and crying out – '*Faranj! Faranj!*' or 'Americaaan!' But they are swiftly pushed off by the praetorian guard who have claimed him as their own since he began this trek down Bole Road.

The distance he has to walk to the city is only four miles or so, but the boy does not know this. So he is walking slowly in the growing heat, acclimatising himself to the thinness of the air and the sense of adventure and fear that is heightening his senses. He is still wearing the heavy black tuxedo despite the rising temperature, and the sweat is starting to soak through a shirt which has already suffered through a summer's day in London, a flight across Europe and north Africa and now the beginnings of an African day. He would love to remove the jacket, but in it are his passport and wallet and he knows that if he takes it off, one of the children will insist on carrying it. Though they have carried his bag with a reverence and sense of responsibility more appropriate for a holy relic, he just can't risk his jacket disappearing into the back alleys that run off Bole Road. So he sweats some more and carries on.

As the journey continues and the morning gets later, so Bole Road grows increasingly busy. The Ladas are joined by buses, belching blue diesel fumes, and the pavements are now thronged with pedestrians, some striding purposefully towards their destinations, others gathered in groups on corners, waiting for lifts or buses. Bole Road is wide and straight and poorly made, the pavements worse. Running off it every few hundred yards are dirt alleys, leading to impromptu settlements of corrugated-iron roofs held up by mud walls. Some are evidently shops; others, homes.

Eventually, the road widens out into a huge open space. It is Meskel Square today; back then, it was *Abiyot* or Revolution Square. In one corner of the square is a vast red billboard displaying the faces of Marx, Engels and Lenin. Ethiopia – home to one of the oldest churches in Christendom – is having a new holy trinity imposed upon it, this time down the barrel of a gun.

At the top of Revolution Square, Bole Road is intersected by another expansive thoroughfare of two carriageways, each of three or four lanes, which climbs up a hill away to the right. Crossing this road is a hazardous undertaking, but it is nearly the end of the journey. On the other side, Bole Road gives way to Edget Behibret, now Menelik II Avenue, another wide road climbing the hill towards what was once the imperial palace. A few hundred metres beyond Revolution Square, the avenue crosses a river and then the two carriageways diverge around Addis Ababa Park. To the right is Africa Hall, the headquarters of the UN Economic Commission for Africa, in those days the only high-rise building in Addis Ababa, and beyond it is the Hilton Hotel, replete with uniformed guards standing to attention at its gates. No skyscraper, this, but still one of the highest buildings in Addis.

Fifty metres before the hotel, the children come to a stop. They do not seem keen to progress closer to the guards. The English boy assumes this is because they fear being chased away, but it suits him well. The senior child takes hold of both handles of the bag and presents it to the boy with a serious expression, underlining the significance of the undertaking he has discharged. The boy reaches in his wallet and extracts a ten birr note – this is one third of his total store of Ethiopian currency. To his surprise, the child's face darkens, his brow furrows and he pointedly pulls back his hand in shock. 'No, *faranj*! No birr! Doll-aaars, Dee-Marks.'

The boy is nonplussed. He does not have a wealth of experience of street children, or indeed any experience at all. But he can't help being surprised at the stricture of their currency regime, nor being slightly miffed that the pound sterling is not included in the menu of acceptable options. But as he surveys the faces of the other children, it is clear that they are all equally shocked and disappointed that their companion of the past hour and a half should attempt to pay them off in the debased local currency.

Naive as to the currency rules of the street, he has brought with him neither US dollars nor Deutschmarks, but he does have in his wallet, alongside the thirty Ethiopian birr, a solitary £1 note. He pulls it out and proffers it to the child, who takes it in his hand and scrutinises the small green bill carefully. 'Inglis?' he asks.

The boy nods and the child's face relaxes, mollified that he is at least now dealing in hard European currency, even if it does not meet with his exact specifications. Then the English boy points at the image on the note and says, 'That is the English queen.'

He doesn't know why he says that. Perhaps he thinks it will reassure the child as to the solidity of the currency. But the child just scowls up at him, either in incomprehension or in hostility, he is not sure which. Perhaps he has absorbed the Marxist rhetoric of the Derg and is appalled that the note in his hand is making him complicit in the hateful concept of hereditary monarchical succession – though to be honest that seems unlikely. In any event, the child stows the note in the pocket of his tattered shorts and turns away to deal with the throng of fellow street children who now surround him, chattering away, presumably demanding their cut.

The *faranj*, at last free of their attention, a circumstance he had fervently desired for most of the walk from the airport, now feels curiously abandoned, the company of the street children exposed as entirely transactional. He leaves them squabbling behind him and heads the final fifty metres up the road to the hotel. The walk has brought on a strong thirst and he is enticed by the thought of a Coke and some shade and perhaps a chance to wash in the hotel toilets.

As he approaches the hotel entrance, he hears a shout from down the street.

'*Faranj!*'

He turns and sees that the head street child, having settled his internal dispute, is grinning broadly and waving him farewell.

6

WILL

The late summer dissolves into the wet gloom of a drawn-out autumn term. Outside of lesson times, the boy wanders in from his boarding house a mile or so outside the main school, hoping to casually bump into Will. It is not the done thing to arrange times to meet; people just come over, and if you're around, you're around and if not, you're not.

And it's not an easy thing to find a specific person. It's regarded with suspicion to be looking for a particular person rather than the lads as a whole. So he might wander into a study where people are sat around on bean bags, chatting, teasing, joking. And once he has walked in, he is committed. Now and then, he might casually say, 'Anyone seen Will?' but not too often or people will make something of it. It will be a joke, but he won't feel it like that because somewhere buried inside him is the truth. So best not to be too specific and just hope he chooses the right study. Most times he doesn't. Then he must endure a half-hour gossiping and joking with the other lads and all the time thinking, I want to see Will. I want to see him so much.

Even if he is lucky and Will's there, he'll be with a bunch of other people. No real chance to be together. The best chance is to say, 'D'you fancy a smoke, Will?' and most times he'll say yes but most times some-one else will say, 'Hey, I'll join you. I fancy a smoke,' and then he'll feel an anger rising in him that he won't get to be with Will on his own, but he'll swallow it and go and have a smoke anyway.

And that's how he progressed through the autumn term towards the half-term break. Out of lessons, searching for Will. In lessons, cynical, distracted, a burden to his teachers. And in his solitary time, sitting on his stile trying to handle the headful of troubles bubbling and boiling inside his skull.

7

THE HILTON HOTEL, ADDIS ABABA

The boy nods a morning greeting at the guards who stand by a metal boom securing the entrance to the hotel grounds. He walks down the covered walkway and enters the cool darkness of the large hotel foyer. Generous leather armchairs populate the space. To the left is a large dark wooden reception desk and opposite it, the foyer lifts. Beyond the reception desk is a horseshoe bar and beyond that, doors on to the terrace and gardens.

One of the porters approaches him and offers to take his bag. He declines and strides purposely to the bar, where he orders a Coke from the elderly bartender. The man moves with a very exact slowness. Stooping to take a glass from under the bar. Crossing the bar to the ice bucket and picking out each cube one by one and placing it delicately in the glass. Finally, he extracts a Coke bottle and with great precision and deliberateness takes a bottle opener from his pocket and applies it to the metal cap. The process is mesmerising but agonising for the boy, whose thirst grows exponentially with every step of the tantalising procedure. Finally, the glass of Coke is set carefully before him. The elderly man smiles with his eyes, but his lips are impassive.

The boy takes his Coke out to the wide terrace and sits himself down to contemplate his position. Below the terrace, the hotel gardens spread out before him, and in the distance he can see the mountains that rise up to surround the city. From the trees below, exotic birdsong reaches the terrace, which at this time is still delightfully shaded and cool.

But the boy is not cool. He is hot and bothered. It has occurred to him that at this exact time the letter he posted to his parents from Heathrow Airport will be plopping onto the doormat of St Bride's Rectory in Fleet Street. He wonders who will open it. He tries to imagine their reaction when they discover he has not stayed the night at his friend Dan's flat in Kensington Church Street but has instead travelled to another continent, to a country in the grip of famine and civil war. Will their reaction be one of shock or anger or fear? And how will they respond to the story he has concocted to explain his departure? A story, he realises now, far from reassuring them that they are not at fault for his departure, is either so outlandish as to be entirely unbelievable or, if believed, so disturbing that it can only terrify them further.

He realises at that moment, drinking Coca-Cola in a shaded hotel garden, the entire magnitude of what he has done. He has lied and stolen from his parents. He is about to cause them untold heartache and anxiety, and he has absolutely no way back. Every bridge is burnt.

8

RUNNING

I suppose I might never have gone. Although I had worked up the idea in my head, even drafted a letter to my parents, I didn't have the money for a plane ticket to Ethiopia and I didn't see any practical way of getting it. Then, one morning, I went down to my dad's study and lying on his desk was his new American Express card – unsigned.

I didn't hesitate. I picked it up and put it in my pocket.

I walked up the steps from the study into the courtyard outside the house, my heart pounding inside me, then through the gate and out into Salisbury Square. I found a discreet spot by Fleetbank House and lit a cigarette. Fear and excitement (and nicotine) mixed together and made me light-headed. Now my plan was possible. More to the point, now I had no excuse not to put it into effect.

But time was of the essence. At some point my dad would notice his missing card. Not immediately, most likely – he was absent minded and would probably imagine he had mislaid it at first – but eventually he would realise. I couldn't risk any delay.

I went back into the house, picked up a pen and locked myself in the bathroom. I stared at the American Express card. On the front, it read MR J OATES – fortuitously, my dad shared the same initial as me and, like me, had no middle name. I turned the card over and signed it.

I now felt my actions were compelled. That, somehow, the card was a kind of sign from God that I must go; everything now flowed from that thought and dispelled all doubt from my mind. In that disturbed mindset, I picked up my passport and got on a bus to Piccadilly Circus. The Ethiopian Airlines office was based in Jermyn Street, and this is where I now headed to buy a ticket to Addis Ababa on my father's stolen credit card.

I don't remember too much about the next few days, except that it was only while buying the airline ticket that I discovered the need for a visa and vaccinations. The latter were swiftly arranged through a visit to the British Airways Immunisation Centre on Regent Street. The former was more problematic. Although my application was surprisingly never questioned – was it normal for fifteen-year-old English kids to apply on their own (or indeed at all) for an Ethiopian visa? – bureaucratic inertia took hold, lazing over my application as the time ticked ever closer to my departure. Finally, on the day before my departure, the visa was issued.

I was all set. Now all I needed was to buy the time to ensure I was safely on Ethiopian soil before my family realised I was gone.

On the day of departure, I slipped down the stairs from my room undetected and stashed my holdall in the downstairs bathroom, which was immediately inside the front door. Then I popped my head around the door of the sitting room, where my mother was reading. 'Mum, I'm going over to Dan's. I'll probably stay there tonight, OK.'

My mum looked up at her difficult teenage son and said, 'OK, have a nice time, and don't you two stay out too late.'

I closed the sitting room door, rescued my bag and jacket, walked down to Blackfriars Station and caught a Tube to the airport. As the train rattled its way through west London, I felt excited and scared.

At Heathrow, I posted a letter to my parents, checked in and, once I was through security, I called Will to say goodbye. Then I boarded the Ethiopian Airlines flight to Addis Ababa and left everything safe and known behind.

9

ALONE

On the terrace of the Hilton Hotel, the boy tries to rally himself from the feeling of despair that is threatening to overwhelm him. He pulls out a red-and-white packet of cigarettes from his pocket, extracts one and lights it. He pulls on it deeply, drawing in the rich cocktail of carbon monoxide and nicotine. He feels the hit reach his brain and the tensions start to relax as the nicotine distributes its dulling messages around his body.

He takes another draw and the tensions are released a little more. He feels better, but he knows the dangers of relaxing into lethargy and apathy. He has to have a plan. How could he just have come here all this way without any plan beyond arriving? How could he be so stupid? His eyes are stung by hot tears of childish rage. He sucks in some more smoke and tells himself to be calm. Please, he says to himself, please be calm. And he must have a plan. There is no point raging at his lack of one; now he must make one. So, slowly and deliberately, he does so. The first thing he will do is find a toilet and wash and change out of his striped business shirt and his day-old socks and boxer shorts. Then he will go in search of the aid agencies and offer himself as a volunteer.

He gets to his feet with a new-found sense of resolution. Inside the hotel, he asks the bartender to direct him to the toilets. He follows his pointed finger and sets off down the corridor, which runs off the foyer, behind the lifts. He enters the large men's room, which is mercifully empty. He places his powder-blue holdall on the floor of one of the cubicles and hangs his jacket on the back of the cubicle door. Then he unbuttons his shirt and slips it off his shoulders. It feels so good to be free of the sweat-stained shirt, but now he has to act rapidly before anyone else enters the room and finds him standing there half-naked.

He turns on the hot water and shoves a corner of his shirt under the tap, wrings out the excess of water, grabs the paltry bar of white soap from the basin and retreats into the cubicle to pull off the rest of his clothes. The shirt, grimy though it is, will have to serve as his flannel and towel. He rubs it vigorously over his body. Then with the dry half of the shirt he towels himself down. He stands momentarily naked in the cubicle, enjoying the sense of cleanliness and coolness, before reaching into his holdall and extracting a can of deodorant, a clean pair of boxers, a clean pair of socks and a plain white T-shirt.

He emerges from the cubicle feeling fresh and restored and smelling considerably better. He re-enters the hotel foyer with a renewed self-confidence and approaches the reception desk, where he asks if they can direct him to the offices of any of the aid agencies. The courteous, serious man on the reception desk is unsure about this question and calls his manager over. They debate the issue in Amharic for a moment or two but do not seem able to resolve it entirely. Gamely, the receptionist takes a piece of the hotel's headed paper and tries to draw a map; however, his manager's constant interruptions and corrections of his cartographic skills do not fill the boy with confidence. At last the process is completed and, finally satisfied though still looking unsure, the manager takes the map from his receptionist and hands it to the boy.

He thanks them in English and then asks them to tell him the Amharic word for 'thank you'. They smile, obviously pleased with the boy's enquiry, and both say together, 'A–MA–SE–GA–NA–LE–HU'.

'*Amisekanalo*,' the boy says, attempting inexpertly to copy the word.

They nod encouragingly.

'*Amisekanalo*,' he repeats.

They nod again.

Emboldened by their encouragement, he asks how he should say 'hello'.

'*Tena yistilign*,' the older man tells him seriously, giving him the formal Amharic greeting.

'*Canasterlyn*,' the boy says.

They nod indulgently at this rough approximation, perhaps not appreciating that he will boldly repeat this mispronunciation for the next thirty years of his life.

Taking the map, he slings his bag over his shoulder and heads towards the exit of the hotel.

'Sir,' calls the manager after him, 'will you be returning to the hotel?'

The boy considers this and then, unsure what else to do, says yes.

'We can keep your bag here, then, if you would like, sir.'

'Yes, thank you, that would be helpful,' the boy says.

The bag is not heavy, but it is an encumbrance, and he will be glad to be rid of it for a while, not least because of the demands to carry it which will inevitably ensue if he ventures onto the streets with it again.

The manager calls the bellboy from across the lobby, who takes the bag and returns shortly with a ticket for the boy. '*Amisekanalo*,' he says to the bellboy and then to the manager, feeling disproportionately moved by their small act of assistance.

Out on the wide street, he walks about fifty metres before pulling out the receptionist's map, his confidence waning in the bright sunshine and the unfamiliar afternoon heat. He has already attracted the attention of two young men sitting on the wall of the park opposite the hotel. His pause and obvious disorientation give them the opening they need, so they slip down and make their way across the street.

'Mister? Can we help you?' one of the young men asks him in accented but apparently good English.

The boy realises his error. Looking lost and out of place in this city is a homing beacon to those looking to beg or make a connection or simply break some boredom. He fervently wishes to get where he is going without accompaniment, but he realises that will now be impossible. 'Yes,' he says, explaining that he is looking for the offices of the aid agencies, naming one or two of the larger ones that they might have heard of. 'Do you know where they are?' 'Yes,' the young man says instantly but without a huge degree of confidence, and he takes the map from the boy.

Together with his companion, he consults the sketch carefully. They mutter in Amharic and then the younger of the two men exclaims loudly and definitely and the older shakes his head vigorously in agreement. He smiles and turns to the boy.

'Yes. We will take you. You will come with us. I am Tesfaye.'

'I am Bekele,' says the younger man.

The boy is encouraged by the new-found confidence of the men and decides that he could do worse than to have them as guides.

They look at him expectantly and he realises they are waiting for his name. He smiles and gives it to them. 'Jonny,' they repeat together. 'Come, it is this way.'

The three of them walk down the hill, side by side, and come to the main road at the bottom. After that the boy cannot keep track of much of the geography. The young men are busy telling him things and asking him questions. But eventually they come to a street – comparatively narrow, poorly made and running downwards off a main thoroughfare.

They come to a halt in front of a small compound. Inside the gate, a truck is being loaded or unloaded. His mind is blank, but there is someone he speaks to. He is not sure exactly what he says, except that he says he is here to help. The person is bewildered; harassed and stressed by his work, he finds it difficult to disguise his irritation. He has no use for someone like the boy, who is completely without skills.

The boy leaves the compound and returns to his guides. They can see he is disconsolate.

'No good?'

'No good,' he agrees.

'We take you to another.'

They consult the guard on the gate to the compound and then set off again with the boy in tow. But the reaction is the same at each agency – impatient dismissal from tense, overworked staff. It is only when they come to one of the American agencies that there is any different reaction. A square-jawed American has explained they have no need of volunteers and is just about to turn away from the boy when something strikes him. 'Say, how old are you?'

The boy is surprised by the question and is momentarily put off his stride. His pause is only very slight before he lies: 'Eighteen.'

But it is noticed by the man. 'You sure about that? This isn't a very safe country just to be wandering around in.' He says this kindly, but the boy is alarmed by his interest. He mumbles something, pushes his way out of the office and walks smartly out of the building. Rejoining his guides, he tells them he is finished with his business.

'Are you OK, Jonny?' Tesfaye asks the boy.

'Yes,' he says determinedly and strides purposefully ahead.

But he is not.

Tesfaye and Bekele sense that he is not in a mood for conversation, so they content themselves with walking in silence beside him.

As they turn onto the hill that leads up to the hotel, the boy realises that neither of the young men has asked him for anything, but he assumes they want some reward for their efforts. He is not sure how to broach this with them or how to explain that he now has only Ethiopian birr, his last £1 note having gone to the street kids.

He stops before the hotel and thanks them and asks them if he can help them with anything. They smile and he pulls a ten birr note from his wallet. 'I am sorry,' he says, 'I have no foreign currency.'

The young men seem much less concerned by this fact than the street children had earlier. They take the note without dissent. He is now down to twenty birr.

'We help you again later?' they ask.

'Maybe tomorrow,' he says.

Then he takes his leave of them and walks back into the hotel. The receptionist smiles at him in greeting and he tries to smile back, but the stress is gripping every part of his body, tightening itself around his sinews, and it is hard to master himself to respond.

He makes his way through the doors at the rear of the lobby on to the terrace and slumps in a chair. His stomach has fallen away, his eyes are smarting and every bone and muscle in his body is straining with stress. He sits in the chair paralysed by the ache of despair.

What has he done? What is he to do now?

The aid agencies could not have been clearer – some brusquely, others more kindly, but all categorically – you are no use to us, however noble you think your intent.

The boy sits there in the chair, overlooking the gardens, but he doesn't see anything and he doesn't hear anything except the pounding in his head.

What have you done?

By now the light is fading and the evening is coming, and he has no plan.

What will he do? Where will he sleep? He has next to nothing in his wallet except a gold American Express card crying 'thief' from his pocket.

And the only plan he ever had, the plan on which this whole reckless endeavour was predicated – that he would find his way to the aid agencies and they would embrace his noble-hearted intent – has just been brutally torn apart by the bemused faces and harassed irritation of the aid workers he has just seen.

The boy has been in Ethiopia less than twelve hours and the momentous scale of his stupidity is already entirely clear.

• • •

On his way up and down the road to the hotel, the boy has noticed that it crosses a bridge over a small culvert, and he wonders if he might be able to get himself out of sight there and gain some shelter to sleep under overnight. He will have to wait until it is fully dark before he can investigate properly, but it is at least a sort of plan.

The boy goes to the reception desk and reclaims his powder-blue holdall, which he takes with him out onto the terrace. He reaches into it and removes a small black book. He sits there with a cigarette in one hand and the Book of Common Prayer in the other and tries to find some words of comfort as he waits for the darkness to fall.

Finally, he decides that the streets may be quiet enough for him to execute his plan without detection. It is certainly dark enough. So he sets off again out the door of the hotel. The doorman points him to one of the beige Mercedes taxis that is drawn up outside, but the boy thanks him and declines. The doorman looks confused and attempts to remonstrate with him, but the boy walks on. At the entrance to the hotel compound – a boom gate – the two security guards who man it seem equally bemused by this white boy marching out of their hotel into the darkness.

'Sir?' one of them says urgently.

'Amisekanalo,' the boy says grimly and finally. Then he is gone into the dark, turning left down the hill towards the river.

Walking down the hill, it occurs to him that the obvious alarm of the guards at a guest walking out of the hotel into the night may not be an excess of caution on their part. It may be grounded in knowledge and experience; something he is precariously short of.

As he leaves the hotel behind and the darkness surrounds him, he realises that he is very scared indeed. It is not the temporary nervousness brought on by his immediate circumstances; it is a deep-seated fear of what he has done. Nevertheless, he keeps walking down the hill until the park to the right comes to an end, and to his left is an area of scrubland covered in spindly trees and, beyond them, a shallow river that is hardly more than a stream.

He looks about to ensure he is not observed and then steps off the pavement and into the bush, climbing gingerly down into the culvert. His mind is racing – What am I doing?! What am I doing?! – but he doesn't know what else to do. When he had observed the river on his earlier travels, he had thought to take shelter under the small bridge that supports the roadway overhead, but now he doesn't know what he was thinking; there is scarcely space for a small child, let alone a fifteen-year-old boy. So he hunkers down on the bank, hard up against the bridge wall, wrapping his arms around his knees and pulling them up to his chin.

A sense of aloneness and desperation overwhelms him. For the first time since he stepped off the plane at Bole Airport he can no longer master his emotions, and he begins to cry – quiet tears which flow in rivulets down his cheeks. 'Please help me, please help me,' he whispers under his breath and through his tears. Finally, after twenty minutes or so he is cried out. His tears are replaced by a cold sense of dread: that there is nothing to be done.

As he sits in this dreadful pose, he becomes aware of the sounds of the night around him. Every rustle in the scrubland now alarms him exponentially. In the distance he hears the sound of cars backfiring – or perhaps more likely in Mengistu's Ethiopia, shots being fired. He has no way of judging, for he has never heard a gunshot. He has lived a privileged life. This boy, the product of an upbringing in Richmond-upon-Thames and a private boarding school, is not well prepared for the revolutionary violence of the Derg.

Who knows how long he sits there? A few hours, perhaps – but eventually he pulls himself together. He cannot stay here. He will not sleep and if he lies down to attempt to, he will ruin the few clothes he has. He makes a resolution: he will give himself two days to try to find a way out of his situation; perhaps he can enlist the help of the young men outside the hotel. In the meantime, he will have to see if they can accommodate him for the night at the hotel.

He scrabbles up the incline from the riverbed, dusts down his jeans and brushes the dust from the tuxedo and then cautiously emerges from the scrubland and turns back up the hill to the hotel.

The guards at the gate are relieved to see him but suspicious. With his new-found resolution, he greets them: 'Canasterlyn.' Now they soften and smile, perhaps because he has bothered to attempt to speak Amharic, more likely in amusement at his mispronunciation.

Inside the hotel, the boy approaches the desk. Neither the friendly receptionist of the afternoon nor the manager are behind the desk. It is the night duty receptionist who peers back at him across the long wooden desk. 'I would like a room,' the boy says.

He hands over his passport to the receptionist, who copies out the passport number and other details onto a registration card with an agonisingly slow exactness.

If the receptionist is surprised that a young white man in a dusty tuxedo should be checking into his hotel at eleven o'clock at night, he is good at hiding it. Then again, the hotel is currently hosting Colonel Muammar Gaddafi and his female security detail on the top two floors and it may be that, in view of the eccentric demands of this delegation, the receptionist has determined that it is wiser not to display a capacity for surprise. 'And how will you be paying, sir?'

The boy produces his father's American Express card. The receptionist takes it and checks it against the passport. Satisfied that they are both in the same name, he produces a room key hanging from a heavy brass key fob.

His room, on the fourth floor, is clean and functional. The shower can only manage lukewarm water, which comes in dribbles rather than a torrent, and the soap is a tiny tablet, but it feels like heaven to be properly clean.

He dries himself off and climbs under the cool bed sheets. He's exhausted, but sleep won't come to him. As he lies in the bed staring at the ceiling above him, a knot is tied tight in his stomach, and fear and sadness are leaking around his body. He wonders what his mum and dad and brothers and sister are doing now, and he is overwhelmed by a sense of guilt and loss. He rolls over and buries his head in the pillow. Sometime in the early hours, sleep finally comes.

• • •

Years later, not many months before she died, I asked my mother what she felt when she discovered that I had run away from home. She didn't say much. Instead, she went to her room and pulled out a bulging blue ring-bound folder. In it were school reports, greetings cards and letters from later years when I was living in Zimbabwe and then South Africa. But at the top was the letter I had posted to my parents from Heathrow on the evening I left, and with it a photograph taken at the airport. A nervously smiling boy in a tuxedo, a blue striped shirt and a dark tie.

I find it hard to read that letter now; a bizarre mixture of quotes from Billy Joel songs – I wish that was the most shameful thing about it – and the Bible, wrapped around the web of fantasy I had spun to try to ensure my parents didn't feel they were at fault for my departure. If reassurance was my aim, the content of the letter couldn't have been better designed to achieve the opposite effect.

It's written on three sides of A4 paper. It starts off abruptly with an ill-judged quote from Billy Joel's 'Innocent Man'; there is no salutation, no 'Dear Mum and Dad'. Just Billy Joel proclaiming: 'Some people hope for a miracle cure, some people just accept the world as it is. But I'm not willing to lay down and die. Because I am an innocent man.'

And underneath, the stark sentence: 'By the time you read this letter I will be in Addis Ababa and heading for the famine camps.' Below that, I told a tale (otherwise known as a lie) about a close friend 'probably my best friend who you never met because you wouldn't of approved'

– although more accurately because he didn't exist – who had challenged me to go to Ethiopia with him to 'save the dying' but had died 'shortly before we got our papers together'.

For some reason I told my parents that this fantasy friend 'was a regular smoker of cannabis' and later felt the need to underscore this, describing him as 'a black kid, a rough kid, a dope smoker but … a good kid'.

And then I told them that I loved him.

I am not sure how I came to concoct this fantasy friend. I think he was an amalgam of Will (my actual best friend, who I was so absurdly and painfully in love with) and my sister's then boyfriend, a break dancer who was perfectly cast to be an adolescent's hero – he was mine, if nobody else's. But above all I needed to create a reason for my departure to avoid the truth.

The letter is really one long lie. Having concluded the description of my rather unconvincing 'best friend' by assigning an 'aura of goodness around him' and oddly comparing him to the then Bishop of Lichfield, Keith Sutton, I moved on to reassure my parents about my motives for leaving.

I made an agreement with myself that I would not go if I felt unhappy at home. I had to know that I was going 'cos I wanted to do something useful and not as an escape. And I know it's not. I love you both more than I could ever be able to describe. I am not running away. I am running to something.

Every word of that paragraph with the exception of the love that I felt for my parents was untrue. And if reassurance was my aim, the next paragraph chillingly undermines it. I asked my parents not to try to stop me; to ask themselves 'Whose life is it anyway?' The next two sentences are heavily crossed out, but I can still read them clearly, as my parents would have been able to: 'I make you this guarantee: If I am dragged back I WILL KILL MYSELF. Would I? I don't know but please don't try it out.'

The crossing out serves only to render the sentence more disturbing still.

I have read this letter a thousand times and yet every time I pick it up, I shudder with muscle-contracting shame at the callous concoction of lies and pompous precociousness that it contains; the self-righteous quotes and religiosity; the puke-makingly pious sign-off: not 'I love you' but 'God bless you'.

Above all, I feel shame at the fear and confusion it must have caused to my parents when they read it.

I am not proud of that letter. It is deeply fucked up. No question. But I also know why I wrote it. Because the alternative was to tell the truth. And I thought that would be much harder for my parents to deal with than the crazy nonsense I wrote to them.

That's how bad the truth was.

I was desperately unhappy. Unhappy at home and unhappy at school; angry at the world for all its stupidities, and confused by the adolescent hormones pumping around my body, causing me to hate myself and my sexuality. And, running through everything, this: I was in love for the first time in my life, and it was with a boy and I couldn't tell him – or even, really, myself.

Although even all this, I grant you, is no excuse for quoting from Billy Joel songs.

Sipping Coke on a hotel terrace 4,000 miles away in Addis Ababa, I don't think I had any real inkling of the impact it would have on my parents, nor did I know that two of my siblings, while shocked by the reality, were less surprised by the letter's content.

I discovered later that as I was making my preparations to leave for Ethiopia, my sister had come across the hiding place (to be fair, it was in her bedroom) where I had stowed my already drafted letter. She consulted one of my brothers, but together they decided that the letter was no more than the fantasy scribbling of an overactive adolescent imagination – a not entirely inaccurate conclusion – and, wishing to spare me embarrassment, she kindly placed the letter back where she had found it.

Now it was staring up at both of them accusingly from the polished dining room table.

My family were not alone in their state of anxiety. Sixty or so miles away, in a provincial city, a sixteen-year-old boy has just awoken after a sleepless night. The previous evening, he had answered the phone at home. It was his friend, calling from a payphone in the departure lounge at Heathrow Airport's Terminal 2.

'Will? It's me. I'm at Heathrow. I'm about to get on a plane to Ethiopia. I have to do something to help. I don't know how things will work out. I just wanted to say goodbye.'

Something like that. Truth be told, Will can't remember exactly what his friend said or what he said in response. He thinks he asked him if he was all right and that his friend said that he was, and that it was not convincing. But then the pips went, and through the urgent beeping his friend said, 'Bye, Will,' and then the line went dead.

10

ANGLICAN BETA KRISTIAN

The boy wakes in the morning light. His head is fuzzy and he feels unrested. It takes a moment or so for him to orientate himself to where he is, and as he does so, the fear comes back, crawling over him, pressing down on him, wrapping itself around his body. He rolls over on his side, pulls the sheet over his head and hunches himself into a foetal position. He lies there, gripped by the paralysing hold of depression and despair for an hour, perhaps two, before he finally bribes himself, with the promise of a cigarette, to rise from the bed.

He picks up his cigarette pack from the desk at the end of the bed, pulls on a T-shirt and a pair of boxer shorts and sits himself down on the small balcony which overlooks the car park. He lights a cigarette, drawing in the smoke and feeling the nicotine going to work.

He concentrates on pushing away the depressive paralysis and convincing himself that there is hope and purpose. The nicotine helps his resolve, but he understands that he has only eased the burden and the cloud hovers over him, ready to press down at any time. He needs a plan. He always needs a plan, and he never seems to have one. He decides that if they are around when he leaves the hotel, he will enlist the help of the two young men to try to see if there is an Anglican church in this city; perhaps through the church he can work out a way of helping.

He washes his shirt, his boxer shorts and his socks in the bathroom sink and hangs them on the shower curtain rail to dry. Then he pulls on the rest of his clothes and heads to the breakfast room, intent on fuelling himself for the day from the breakfast buffet, but the nicotine has suppressed his appetite and he manages only a black coffee and a somewhat stale croissant.

It is after ten when he leaves the hotel, and he is pleased to see Tesfaye and Bekele sitting on the wall on the opposite side of the road. It is not clear whether they are waiting for him specifically or whether this is simply their usual perch, but as soon as they see him they cross the road to meet him. The security guards at the gate look on disapprovingly but say nothing.

'Hello sir, can we help you today?'

'Yes, that would be great,' the boy responds. 'Is there an Anglican church here? Can you take me to it?'

Tesfaye looks unsure: 'Church?'

'Yes, Anglican church.'

Tesfaye and Bekele turn the matter over in Amharic at some length. Eventually, Tesfaye says, in his soft, reassuring voice, 'Yes, come with us, we will take you.'

They set off, turning right up the hill this time, until they reach the top and the ramparts of the presidential palace, once home to Ras Tafari, the Emperor Haile Selassie. The street they are on runs along a ridge above the city and the boy can see it sprawling out below, grand avenues contesting with mean alleyways.

As they walk, Tesfaye and Bekele chat amiably to the boy, asking him questions about England and often conferring with one another in Amharic on his responses. A few hundred metres after they round the curve of the palace wall, they halt at an entrance way to their right and Tesfaye disappears through it. The boy looks quizzically at Bekele, who says that that they will wait there until Tesfaye returns but offers no further information.

Tesfaye is gone for some time and the boy grows bored and irritable. He lights a cigarette and crosses the street to get a better view of the city below. The streets that run off this road are unmade and steep; the buildings, low and humble affairs with corrugated asbestos or iron roofs, some serving as shops, others as homes. The boy wonders what happens when the rains come: surely the street will turn into a torrent. The buildings look as if they have stood there some time, but then again, there have been no rains to speak of these past few years. The boy extinguishes his cigarette under the sole of his dusty suede shoe and crosses the road back to where Bekele is waiting.

Eventually, Tesfaye re-emerges and beckons Bekele and the boy to follow him through the gates. They emerge in a compound with an Ethiopian Orthodox church at its centre. 'Is this the Anglican church?' the boy calls doubtfully after Tesfaye. But Tesfaye is already striding across the compound. He leads them around the church and through an opening into a courtyard. An Ethiopian Orthodox priest rises from his haunches and greets the boy in Amharic. The boy responds inadequately and with forced politeness. Inwardly, he is furious with Tesfaye and Bekele. He has asked to be taken to the Anglican church because he needed the church; he saw it as his last hope. But instead they have brought him here to an Ethiopian Orthodox priest who has no English, and it is evident he is going to have to stay some time or cause great offence.

The priest takes his hand and indicates that he should join the group of men, possibly monks or other priests, who sit around a pot set up over a fire. The ancient priest sits next to the boy and holds on to his hand and speaks to him. The boy does not understand the words, but he sees the kindness in the wrinkles around the man's eyes and the wisdom in his face. He thanks the priest in English; he doesn't know for what, but his thanks are genuine.

Now Tesfaye and Bekele join them in the circle and seek to translate the priest's words. But the boy is irritated, finding less meaning in their stumbling translations than he had in the priest's unfamiliar words. After some time and considerable ritual, coffee is produced from beans roasted and ground before them. It is handed to the boy by the priest, who watches him as he raises the cup to his lips. The coffee is strong, bitter, grainy and good.

'Amisekanalo,' the boy says. And the old priest grasps his hand with bony fingers and looks at the boy with kindness in his eyes, though his face remains grave.

The others in the circle chatter in a low hum of Amharic. At last the priest speaks, this time in a clear strong voice, evidently to the others. Then he stands up and causes the boy to stand. He leads him a few yards away from the group and, taking both of the boy's hands in his, he addresses him quietly in Amharic. The priest is aware the boy does not understand his language but is keen to convey something to him even so. And the boy grasps this and though he does not know the words, he feels their meaning and he feels the kindness of the man and of an older, different Ethiopia.

The priest leads him back to the circle and speaks with Tesfaye and Bekele. They both rise and come to him and whisper that he must give some money to show appreciation for the kindness and hospitality of the church.

The calm that the priest had instilled in him immediately flees and he feels anger rise to the surface. He had thought he was receiving kindness, but now he sees he was being given an obligation. He is angry with the young men; they have brought him to the wrong place and now they are telling him he must pay for it. And he is down to his last few birr. Yet he knows there is no choice. So he reaches into his wallet and extracts some grimy notes, which he hands to Tesfaye, who in turn hands them to the priest, who nods his acknowledgement.

They leave the courtyard, cross the compound and exit on to the street, past impoverished women and elderly men who sit or lie around the entrance gate, seeking alms from the church. He ignores them in his anger, though he is not oblivious to their desperation, and marches out ahead of the young men, along the street and back towards the hotel. It occurs to him that Tesfaye and Bekele themselves will also be expecting money. Yet this is the first moment it has been obvious to him, and he feels another small fragment of himself chipped away. He is not a person: he is just a thing to be used, a source of grimy Ethiopian birr notes.

In his emotional immaturity, he does not consider that it is perhaps not unreasonable of the young men to expect some recompense for their efforts. After all, it is he who has asked for their help and why else would they bother to guide the boy around the city, however inexpertly?

They speed up their pace to catch up with him. He ignores them and marches on, crossing the road in front of the palace, marching along the ridge, turning right down the hill towards the hotel. He crosses the first carriageway to the park, then the second to the hotel side. Here, Tesfaye and Bekele catch up with him again.

They ask him why he is so angry. He stops and turns on them harshly, letting loose his anger and fear, telling them they have not taken him where he asked, accusing them of always wanting money from him, although this has been their first request (and in any event, it was for the church, not for them). They stand in front of him bewildered and offended by his anger, but perhaps they both notice the tears at the edges of his eyes. He pulls out the last notes from his wallet and pushes them into Tesfaye's hands. 'There, have it. It's all I have. I don't need you any more.'

He almost spits the words out in his childish rage, and then he turns and walks sharply away and into the hotel. Tesfaye and Bekele stand anchored to the spot. They do not understand the boy's anger. They have found it hard to follow his words, spat out as they were in his rapid staccato rage. He had asked to go to the church. They have no doubt about this, and they have taken him to the church; more than that, they have taken him to the priest. So why did he say they had taken him to the wrong place?

This is not just a confusion of language; it's a confusion of culture too. They asked him, 'Bēte kirisitīyan?' and he had replied yes, presuming that the young men were confirming that the Anglican church was a Christian church. But to them, this was not the question. They knew only the Orthodox church and the mosque. They have no idea of an Anglican church.

The boy enters the hotel. He is enveloped by his own anger and grief. He is heading to the end of his path. He knows that clearly now. How desperately he wants to turn around and head back the way he has come, but he no longer knows how. He ignores the greetings of the guards on the security boom. Head down, he crosses the hotel lobby and, despite its usual bustle, he feels a silence descend. A sense of total separation from all that is happening around him.

Inside his room, he closes the door behind him slowly and pushes it firmly shut. His world is steadily contracting. This room seems to be his life now. There seems no way out. A despair drifts down on him more profound than any he has felt before, filling up every cell in his body. Every one of his limbs feels heavy with it. His brain feels weighed down by it. Stopping him thinking, beyond the drumbeat of grief.

He walks out on to the balcony and looks down to the car park. The shade roofs of the carports stare back. He thinks, 'When I fall, will it be over?' The roofs, shading the cars, silently indicate that it may not. They would break his fall. He has a vision of falling and bouncing and then falling again. To the hot, hard ground. But in the boy's mind the vision does not end there. Instead, he sees himself staring back up to the balcony, still alive, feeling his limbs broken and useless. All of his failures consolidated in one final fiasco.

He moves away from the balcony, back into the room. He will have to find somewhere higher to fall from. He lights a cigarette, draws on it deeply, but the nicotine can no longer cut through his despair, even temporarily. He stubs it out less than half smoked. He shuts the door to the balcony. Pulls the heavy curtains shut. Removes his shoes and socks. Unbuttons his faded blue jeans and drops them to the floor, lacking the energy to fold them or even place them on a chair.

He takes two steps to the bed and lies down. At first, he lies on his back, staring at the ceiling. Then he turns on his side and finally onto his front. He buries his head in the pillows and cries.

And the horror of what he is going to do seeps into the pit of his stomach and rises in acidic fear. He is so afraid and so alone. And then the rage and pity: 'Why me, why me? Why, God, did you make me like me?' He burrows his head further into the pillows, presses his leaden limbs into the bed, as if somehow he might disappear into the mattress and be swallowed up. Eventually, like any child, he exhausts his tears and falls asleep.

• • •

The sound of a telephone rings around the boy's sleep. He is slow to recognise it, but the tone is shrill and persistent and eventually it breaks through. He reaches out his hand and grabs the receiver.

'Yes,' he says through sleep-dulled confusion.

'It is Tesfaye, we are in the lobby of the hotel. Why don't you come down and we will take you out for a nice evening.'

It is not clear what a nice evening would involve, but in any event the boy is confused and angry again. Why is Tesfaye pursuing him into the hotel? Disturbing his sleep. Awaking him to face his misery again. 'No thank you,' he says rudely and puts down the phone.

He rolls over and lies on his side, wondering if sleep will come back to him. After a fruitless half-hour of waiting, he concedes that it will not. He pulls on his T-shirt and jeans. Draws back the curtains and seats himself on the balcony.

He is calmer now. He is going to give himself one last shot. Tomorrow he will find the British Embassy and ask them if there is an Anglican church in Addis – as soon as the thought occurs to him, he cannot believe he did not think of it originally, instead of asking the young men. If there is an Anglican church here in Addis, perhaps they can point him in a direction where he can help. It's a plan of sorts and having a plan may get him through one more night.

He sits on the balcony in the cool Ethiopian night for perhaps three hours more, staring out at the quiet darkness, which is occasionally broken by the scratch of the wheel on his lighter flint and the small orange glow of the flame as he lights up another cigarette. His mind is still and contemplative, no longer racing. He smokes a last cigarette, returns to the room and tries to sleep again.

The morning comes eventually, but by then his brief optimism is gone. He wakes slowly, feeling his way into consciousness, his predicament piecing itself together gradually, step by step, in his mind. And when it does, dread glides along his stomach muscles, gripping at them, squeezing them, forcing the fear upwards. He swallows hard, trying to push it back to the pit of his stomach so it cannot succeed in rising up to suffocate him.

He knows he must get up, shake some energy into himself. But he feels paralysed, pinned to the mattress. Every one of his muscles as heavy as lead, his tendons tingle with stress. He rolls over, curls himself up, his arms pulled tight around himself. The intense physicality of mental ill-health.

'Please, please let me find a way out of this,' he whispers to himself. He lies there like that for some time, unable to summon the energy to break his paralysis.

Outside he can hear the calls of swallows and weaver birds. He imagines them in the sun-drenched gardens of the hotel on the other side of the heavy patterned curtains; a world away from this dark depression inside.

At last he manages to summon the energy required to break free of his bed. In the bathroom, he tries to make a dent in his lethargy. He stands determinedly under the shower and turns the faucet hard right to its coldest setting. The bracing chill of the water strikes his head, courses down his face. His brain registers the assault on his senses as the water reaches his shoulders, streams down his chest and back. It demands that his body move out of the flow, but he resists. His shoulders shudder, but beyond that he stands firm, counting the seconds to himself: '1,001, 1,002' … He aims to reach 1,045, but his resolve breaks at 1,020.

He spins the temperature selector away from cold, and milder water replaces the icy chill. His experiment is a success, temporarily at least. He towels himself dry, pulls on his clothes and yanks back the curtains. Glaring summer light gushes into the room, baffling his senses. He squints to allow his eyes to adjust, gathers up his wallet, cigarettes and lighter and steps out into the hotel corridor with new-found determination.

In the hotel lobby, he greets the concierge with false brightness – his life has taught him to be good at that by now – and asks him if he can order a taxi to take him to the British Embassy. He doesn't want to walk and take the risk (in fact, near certainty) of being commandeered by the young men again.

The embassy compound is on the very edge of the city and rises from Queen Elizabeth Street, now Comoros Street, into the hills beyond. There is a security post just inside the entrance way. The guard asks the boy his business, but it is not easy for the boy to explain. He wants to know if there is an Anglican church in Addis Ababa. The guard is non-plussed by this question: it is apparently not one he has come across before, and it is not one he has an answer for. He asks the boy if he needs consular services. Now it's the boy's turn to look nonplussed. He has no idea what consular services are, but he sees that he could get stuck here in mutual miscomprehension for some time. So he says yes, consular services are exactly what he wants. The guard points him up the hill towards the consular service buildings.

Inside the small waiting room, there are a few people ahead of him in the queue, but before too long he is called forward to the desk.

'Hi,' he says, 'could you tell me if there is an Anglican church in Addis Ababa?'

The British official looks at the boy curiously. 'Yes, there is,' he says, then pauses as if about to provide further details, but instead he asks, 'Are you a British national?'

The boy looks back at the official, frustrated at his failure to address the question. 'Yes,' he says impatiently. 'Could you tell me where the Anglican church is?'

The official ignores the question. 'Are you registered at the embassy?'

'No, I don't think so,' the boy replies tentatively.

'Well, you need to be in case anything happens. What brings you to Ethiopia anyway?'

A line of people has begun to build up behind him. 'I just want to find out about the church, can't you tell me?' The boy's voice is plaintive. It breaks a little at the edges.

'Yes, of course,' the man says, not unkindly, 'but first we need to get you registered. Do you have your passport?'

The boy is now not just frustrated by the questioning but afraid. Has the embassy been alerted to his runaway status? Is this man intending to apprehend him? 'No, not on me. Thank you. Don't worry,' he says and turns abruptly from the desk, pushing past the queue rapidly and out the door.

He marches swiftly down the hill towards the guard post, glancing over his shoulder, afraid of pursuit, but there is no sign of it. The official presumably has enough on his hands.

He acknowledges the guards and exits through the gates of the embassy compound. He has no idea where he's going, but he does not stop. Afraid of pursuit, he crosses the road, takes a left down one street, then a right into another. After a while, when it is evident that no one is attempting to follow him, he slackens his pace, and as he does so he realises that he doesn't know where he is. He has a vague idea that the hotel is somewhere down the hill to the right. But he also realises that he is more profoundly lost than any geographic awareness can help him with. He has used up his one last idea and the road has ended nowhere.

Why couldn't that person just have told him what he asked? That is all he wanted. The simple answer to a simple question. All his fear and self-pity and anger are coming together as he walks on, oblivious to all around him.

He pulls a cigarette from the packet in his pocket and flicks the wheel on the lighter flint. He stares into the small orange-and-blue flame before bringing it up to his cigarette. He holds the flame too long and feels its heat start to burn his thumb through the flint wheel.

He draws heavily on the cigarette. A childish rage of frustration and failure pricks his eyes with tears.

Eventually, he finds his way back to the hotel. It is still early in the day, perhaps eleven or twelve o'clock. As he heads down the hill, Tesfaye and Bekele observe him from the wall of the park.

They spring off it and cross the road to cut him off. He tries to increase his pace, but they intersect him just before the entrance to the hotel. This time they are not friendly. They are angry.

'Why don't you speak to us? We have shown you this place. We have helped you. You have given us nothing. You are bad person.'

They are aggressive and threatening, and though the hotel entrance is in sight, it is too far to shout or to run. And, more than that, the boy knows they have a point. He has shown bad manners. They have tried to help him and in return he has avoided them and insulted them.

But he has no pound or dollar notes, just a few remaining greasy Ethiopian bills. He opens his wallet and shows them it is all he has. They are not happy with his offering and do not hide it. 'You must go to the hotel and get more money. This is not good at all.' Tesfaye's soft reassuring voice is gone; now there is a hard, angry edge to it.

The boy feels crushed under the weight of all that has happened or failed to happen, and the onslaught of this anger is too much for him now. 'Yes,' he says quietly. 'OK.' But he knows that once he enters the hotel, he will not leave it again.

They stand and watch him menacingly as he walks slowly, defeatedly, past the security boom and into the building.

•   •   •

The boy walks the by-now-familiar route along the paved and partially covered walkway through the entrance hall to the reception desk, where he picks up his key. The energy and determination of this one-last-chance morning are gone. He is forlorn and defeated and it is in his every action and gesture. A boy with nowhere to go, who thinks he has no one to turn to.

If he only understood that a call to London, to his mother and father, would rescue him from this mess he has made. That there would be no anger, just a dam-burst of relief from their anguish, an outpouring of the love they have for him.

But he does not understand this at all.

He is a fifteen-year-old boy, who knows nothing of what it means to be a parent, has no conception of the love and hopes and fears that have been spent on him, invested with him and in him. If he did, he would not be planning to do what he is now about to do. He would not even contemplate it.

But he does not understand any of this. And, in reality, this disastrous failure of an Ethiopian misadventure is the least of his troubles. Because behind his desire to find salvation in helping others there are far darker and more insoluble troubles. Troubles of all shapes and sizes and colours, troubles that vie in his head for space and light and hearing. And one trouble above all that he cannot voice to himself, even in the most silent of nights. A heavy, dull cape of fear that presses upon his shoulders. Which he cannot shake off and which he will not reach out to, or touch or even acknowledge.

As the elevator reaches his floor, it is starkly clear to him what he must do. He no longer rages against it. He sees that, all other options having been reduced to one, it is no longer a matter of choice. The realisation gives him a brief thrill of terror. So it is going to come to an end. He is both calm and on edge as he alights from the lift. Instead of turning to the right to return down the corridor to his room, he turns to the left and exits through the heavy wood-and-glass door on to the stone steps of the fire stairs.

He climbs two flights of stairs. That should be high enough. But he has an urge to go to the top to ascertain the perfect place, so he climbs on another flight. His eyes are focused down towards the ground, calculating the height and speed and finality.

Back in his room, having found the right place, he considers the next few hours ahead. He needs to do two things before he takes the stairway. He will write to his family and he will write to his friend. He sits down at the desk and takes a piece of the bleached white Hilton Hotel letterhead and starts to write a mournful letter to his mum and dad and his siblings. His composure deserts him as he guides the cheap hotel biro across the paper and his straggly unkempt handwriting spells out his love for every one of them. Tears well in his eyes, but he continues to write until he is done. He seals the letter in a matching bleached white envelope and addresses it with the names of each of his parents and siblings. Then he takes up another sheet of paper and he tries to write to Will. But he finds that he cannot write another letter. So instead he writes, 'I am sorry.' And then with boldness and relief, 'I love you with all my heart and soul.' Then he signs the paper and seals it into an envelope marked 'Strictly Private and Confidential'. And he underlines 'Private and Confidential' in a shaky hand.

But the boy cannot go without hearing Will's voice one last time. He decides that he will call him. He owes him at the very least a goodbye. He picks up the telephone receiver from the table by the bed and explains to the operator that he wants to book a call through to a number in the UK. The operator takes the details and tells the boy that he will call back as soon as he has a line.

'How long will that be?' the boy asks.

'It is impossible to say, I am afraid, sir,' the operator replies. 'We are busy these days, it is not so easy to get an international line.'

The boy is frustrated but he simply says, 'Thank you, I understand, but please, I would appreciate if you can get me the line as soon as possible.'

It is hard from this distance to know what was going through his mind when he decided to place that call. How he rationalised the thought that he should telephone his friend nearly 4,000 miles away and tell him goodbye. What does he expect his friend's reaction to be? What would it be? A frantic, desperate voice begging the boy to come home, not to do anything stupid?

And what would the boy say? Would he repeat the few words he has already written to Will? And if he did, would Will realise the finality of what this goodbye meant? Would the boy's final declaration be followed by a slow replacement of the receiver on the hook in that bedroom in Ethiopia and a dull click speeding its way across 4,000 miles of telephone wire to his friend's ear? What then, as Will realised the magnitude of what was about to happen and of his powerlessness to prevent it? He would surely try to do something, but there would be nothing he could do, except live with that nothingness all his life.

How can the boy fail to understand this? How can he be planning to do something so callous? The truth is that the boy is beyond understanding now. There is no callousness in him. There is not a malign intent in his body. Just a desire to speak with the person he loves and tell him goodbye.

The boy sits down on the bed, puts his head in his hands and breathes deeply. After a minute or so, he swings his legs over, props himself up on the pillows and places his hands behind his head. And lying there on his back, he waits.

He tries to blot out the thought of what he is going to do next. It isn't hard at first; now he has made his decisions, his senses seem stuffed with cotton wool, dulling and resisting comprehension. But as the minutes tick on, fear starts to penetrate his consciousness. He tries to pray but he can't.

It is clear to him that he is going to do something terrible and that there is no way out of it. That he has tried every ruse to dodge it – even running all this way across the world – but that there is no dodging it any more. The bullet with his name on has been winging its way towards him for months and now it is so close at hand that he can feel the air that it disturbs.

He lies there, tense with waiting. Waiting for the call, waiting for the end.

11

'JONNY?'

There was a knock on the door. At first, the boy wasn't really conscious of it. The state he had wrought in himself was not conducive to interruption. But it came again, lightly but insistently. He called out from the bed, 'No room service. No thank you.'

But the knocking came again. Slowly and reluctantly, he got up off the bed, walked to the door and opened it. Instead of room service, he saw a sandy-haired white man who looked to be in his mid-thirties standing in his doorway. The sandy-haired man said, 'Jonny?'

• • •

I started to close the door.

Without aggression, but with firmness nonetheless, he placed his foot in the way. 'Jonny, my name is Charles Sherlock. I think I can help you. Can we have a chat and then if you tell me to go away, I will. I promise.'

It is the first time someone has spoken my name in days, and I feel a mixed sense of fear and relief, but I say nothing. I just let go of the door and walk back into the room. Resigned; defeated.

Charles Sherlock follows me. He sits on the chair, the small desk to his left. I sit down on the bed in silence.

Charles seems to cast a glance at the sealed letters on the desk. I am not sure whether he recognises what they mean. But his focus flits rapidly back to me.

He explains that he is an Anglican priest and that my parents have asked him to find me. He wants to help me, but he is not going to compel me to do anything. Whatever I decide he needs me to know how much my mother and father and sister and brothers love me and want me back home. His voice is earnest and friendly. There is nothing patronising or overbearing about him.

I remain silent, so he fills the space, speaking softly and reassuringly. He is telling me how easy it is to make mistakes – that we all do – smiling ruefully at the mistakes he has made – but they are just mistakes, that is all they are, and they are mostly easily fixed.

If a tone of voice and the skill of empathy can save a life…

The ring of the phone by the bed cuts through his words. I hesitate and then reach out to pick it up. It is the operator: 'We have a line to the UK for you, sir.'

I pause, and then I say, 'Thank you. But I no longer need it.'

•   •   •

It is early evening now, and at Charles Sherlock's suggestion we have moved downstairs to the hotel restaurant, where we are sitting over bowls of pasta and Charles Sherlock is cautiously winning my confidence. He does not tell me I must go home. He does not quiz me on the idiocy of my venture. He just tells me that things are going to be OK, shares his experiences with me and tells me about his life in Ethiopia. I feel a huge sense of relief and gratitude at the firm, gentle, reassuring kindness of this man.

He says that if I want to stay in Ethiopia for a while, that is OK, but I obviously can't stay here, at the Hilton Hotel. If I want, the Anglican chaplaincy will provide accommodation for a little while and I can observe the work they are doing caring for children orphaned by the famine and the civil war, through the Jerusalem Children's Homes, a joint venture with the Orthodox Church.

He doesn't push me to accept the offer. He suggests I should sleep on it and he will come and pick me up in the morning if that is what I want to do. Before he goes, he tells me that when people get themselves deep in despair, they often don't understand how much they are loved. He wants me to remember and be aware how very much my family love me and want me to be safe.

Then finally he says, 'Jonny, I can't make you do anything and I can't stop you doing anything. Your life is yours, not anyone else's. But I want you to think about the inconsolable loss your mum and dad and your brothers and sister would feel if you were gone, and I want you to realise that is because you are a far more precious person than you are prepared to believe right now.'

I have known this man less than three hours but I feel a bond of a lifetime, because I know that with his words, and his authoritative kindness, he has saved my life.

Despite this, in the foyer we part company with all the awkwardness of the English.

'Right, I'd better get back. Remember what I said, and I will be here to pick you up at 9 a.m. tomorrow.'

A brief handshake. A gruff adolescent mutter. 'Thanks.'

But no word I ever muttered was so heartfelt.

• • •

I watch Charles as he recedes from view down the entrance hall to the car park and, standing alone in the hotel foyer, I experience a sense of elation, a feeling that I have been saved, that an opening has been cleared and that the light is coming.

I return to my room, remove the letters from the desk and tear them slowly and deliberately into tiny pieces. Then I sit down on the bed and cry tears of relief.

12

FATHER CHARLES

It was Charles Sherlock who saved me. Who found me just in time, on what could have been the fateful day, just before the ring of the phone by the bed and that precise, Ethiopian-accented voice: 'We have a line to the UK for you, sir.' I suppose I should give some credit to the rudimentary nature of the Ethiopian telephone system, too. Had a line been available when I asked for it, that grotesque call would have been done, and when Charles came knocking on the door, I might well have been gone, climbing those stairs by the lifts.

Father Charles's arrival at that exact time was not just a matter of luck. It was also a consequence of his courage. As soon as my parents had contacted him via the Church network, he must have realised that the speed with which he found me might be vital, and that the one way to get a fix on where I was would be to view the immigration card that I must have filled in on entering the country.

That, of course, was easier said than done, as it meant persuading the immigration officials to open their records to him. Making such demands of the regime's officialdom might have been a risky thing to do, but that didn't put him off. He drove out to the airport immediately and cheekily demanded to see the arrivals cards. To his surprise, he found the officials very willing to help. The cards were all in dirty piles – it seems the officials never did anything with them – but among the mountains of cards, Charles managed to locate mine, with the crucial information that I was at the Hilton. He drove straight from the airport to the hotel, and that is where he found me.

But now, just the day after that heroic effort, Charles is going to have to save me again.

The lobby is busy when I emerge from the lift, my meagre belongings packed up in the powder-blue bag that is slung over my shoulder. Passengers from the early morning flights from Europe are checking in to the hotel; existing residents, predominantly journalists and aid officials, are setting out for the challenges of a new day amidst Ethiopia's bureaucracy and brutality.

I proceed to the reception desk to check out of my room. The staff are busy and harassed by irritable guests who have become impatient with all the form-filling. When it is my turn in the queue, I smile at the receptionist and wish him 'Canasterlyn'. He returns my greeting, but he is too pressed by the day to return the smile. I explain that I wish to check out and I proffer my (dad's) American Express card. He tells me I will have to wait while he prepares the bill, so I lean nonchalantly on the long wooden reception desk, unaware of the difficulty I am about to be in.

The receptionist returns with the bill, which is sizeable. Once more I proffer the credit card, which this time he takes. He pulls out a heavy credit card machine, placing the card in the frame and then slotting the light blue translucent carbon papers of the Amex voucher into the guides that hold it in place over my card. Then he brings the imprinting mechanism smartly across, back and forth, to make the carbon imprint of the card. He takes the card and the voucher out of the machine and then he retires to the back office. Through the door, I see him pick up a telephone, and my bloodstream floods with adrenalin.

I stand there transfixed, now I can see him speaking into the phone, his brow creasing. He seems to repeat a phrase twice, three times, increasingly agitated. Then, slowly, he replaces the receiver and advances towards the desk. I know what this means, what it can only mean. The adrenalin that has flooded my bloodstream demands that I run, or at least act in some way. But I cannot move. My body will not allow it. It knows, if my consciousness does not, that if running solved anything, I would be pretty much set by now.

The receptionist arrives back at the desk. 'Your card is refused,' he says, flatly but firmly.

My mind is racing through my response options but nothing computes. So I splutter a gibberish of indignant protest.

The receptionist is unimpressed. 'It is reported stolen.' His voice is flat and cold.

I am stunned. Surely my father would not have reported the card stolen knowing it was my only means of funds? But later I recall that I never told him I had taken the card so perhaps when he couldn't find it before I left he thought he had lost it and reported it as such, and the credit card company has subsequently determined it to be stolen after transactions have been posted to the card.

The receptionist seems to signal to someone or something behind me. I turn to see the security desk vacant behind me, abandoned by the officer, who right now is advancing across the floor towards me. I do not have any physical or emotional response left. But from my left a clear English voice says, 'Ah, sorry, a misunderstanding. I am paying this bill.'

The receptionist looks sceptical. 'No, sir, but the card is stolen.'

Charles smiles warmly back at the troubled receptionist and speaks to him in Amharic.

I don't know what he says. But he pulls out his wallet and extracts a credit card, which he places firmly on the reception desk. The receptionist shrugs and, retaining his troubled frown, takes the card and processes the transaction.

And once more I am saved.

The bill paid, Father Charles leads me outside, where we clamber into his car and set off on the short journey of a mile and a half or so to St Matthew's Anglican Church and chaplaincy.

Charles says nothing about the bill or the stolen credit card. He asks instead how I am feeling, with a gentle care that calms my swirling thoughts. He reassures me that I can get my bearings at the chaplaincy before I have to make any decisions. But, he says, when you are settled, we are going to have to talk about what comes next.

I am quiet in the car. I nod my acknowledgement and thank him in a small, distant voice. I am conscious of the great good fortune of meeting this kind man but conscious also of the failure that has brought me here. And I know that I am in danger of being overwhelmed in a moment by the swirling unfathomable misery that has misted up my life.

•   •   •

The Anglican chaplaincy is housed just off Queen Elizabeth II Street. It stands on a corner facing onto the paved road; a dirt road runs up the right side of the compound, lined with ramshackle homes. The chaplaincy is on high ground two or three metres above the street. We enter through a gate and up steps which rise between two high brick walls.

At the top of the steps is St Matthew's Church, the modest brick building that serves the small Anglican community of Addis Ababa. To the left is a single-storeyed tin-roofed building with a covered veranda at the front, opening onto a grass lawn. This is the chaplaincy which accommodates the two Anglican chaplains, Father Charles Sherlock and Father Colin Battell, who is currently on leave in England.

Charles leads me into the kitchen, where he introduces me to a warm, motherly Ethiopian woman, the housekeeper and cook for the chaplaincy, who wraps me in an embrace of smiles, and then to Gebre Egziabher, a young man in his late teens or early twenties who is training to be a deacon, and to Tibebu, a wheelchair-bound student of similar age who has been crippled by rheumatoid arthritis. I respond shyly to the warmth of their greetings. I have no idea what Charles has told them about me, but whatever it is, they seem happy to welcome me into this community.

Charles tells me that he has to go out on some visits. He suggests that I spend the afternoon acclimatising to my new surroundings but that when he returns, we will need to talk about my future plans.

• • •

Later that day, I am in the kitchen with Gebre Egziabher when Charles comes to find me.

We should talk, he says, and we go out on to the veranda, where the dusk is rapidly gathering. I am apprehensive and sit quietly in a wicker chair.

Charles, soft spoken, is, as always, clear but thoughtful in his words. 'I have spoken with your parents. They are so relieved that you are safe, and they send all their love. No one is going to rush you. You can stay here certainly for the next few weeks, but you must speak to them.'

I look down at my shoes and say nothing for the moment. How can I speak to them after what I have done?

Receiving no response, Charles leans forward. 'Jonny?'

I can't speak. My insides are scrunched up. I can't imagine what I will say to them. What they will say to me. So I stay silent, looking as firmly as I can at my feet.

Charles fills the space where my words should be. 'I understand that you are nervous, but you have no need to be. They are so glad you are safe. They just want to talk with you and tell you how much they love you.' Then, in response to my continuing silence, a firmer tone. 'Jonny, you need to make this call. It's the deal if you want to stay here.'

I raise my head from my shoes and quietly say, 'OK.'

The next day, Gebre Egziabher suggests we go for a walk with Tibebu so he can show me some of the city. I accompany them, but I cannot focus on the places Gebre Egziabher is showing me, my stomach is so churned up with fear at what I am going to say to my parents. Or, more to the point, what they are going to say to me.

In the evening, Charles finds me on the veranda. In his hand is a glass containing the slightest sip of Scotch. He proffers the glass. 'I brought you some Dutch courage.'

The Scotch is nothing in itself, it is literally a drop in the bottom of a glass, but it is much more than that. It is an appreciation of how hard I am finding the thought of speaking with my parents after all the heartache I have caused them. A golden sip of solidarity.

I remember that drink. Staring into it, puffing on a cigarette. I never liked Scotch, but I drank it anyway, in one swift slug that left my throat burning.

I don't really remember much of what I said to my parents. But I remember walking from the veranda to the room where the telephone was and sitting as I picked up the receiver, and then my parents' voices were travelling across the void between us: 4,000 miles of telephone cable, crackling and echoing with love.

The voices distort across the distance. Mum and Dad first, warm, anxious and eager to reassure: 'We want you home, but it's fine to stay there while you work things out. We just ask that you listen to Father Charles and follow his guidance.'

Then my siblings. My sister teasing me affectionately. My brothers warm and keen to know details about Addis. And then the call is over, and I breathe and return to the veranda, where Father Charles says, 'How did it go?' And I say, 'It was good,' and I mean it. I pause and then I say, 'Thank you.'

•   •   •

The next day, Charles took me to Addis Alem, where the Jerusalem Children's Homes had an orphanage on top of the hill that was briefly the site of Emperor Menelik's capital. I remember the couple who ran the home, two distinguished Ethiopians who received me kindly, and helping carry sacks of teff, the local grain, from the truck with kids from the orphanage, who were shy with me, as I was with them.

That's the last I remember of Charles in Ethiopia, until we met there thirty years later. He left the next day on his annual leave to England, to be replaced by a priest of a different order who had less patience for the self-indulgent teenager he found occupying his house on return from his vacation.

Charles Sherlock did not take a romantic view of my adventure, but he did not take an unsympathetic one either. He was practical and clear. Blunt that there was little use for an unskilled fifteen-year-old runaway in Ethiopia. But he was clear about something also. If you believe in something, don't give it up. Keep praying for it, but above all keep working at it and fighting for it. He told me kindly as he headed back to London for his annual leave, 'Go back home and learn and get some qualifications. In a year's time, less, the TV cameras will have forgotten about Africa. It's important that you don't.'

•   •   •

75

Father Colin Battell and I did not get along so well. He thought I was a drug addict. Not entirely surprising, given the tale I had woven for my parents. But beyond nicotine and the odd drink, I hadn't had much to do with drugs. The odd spliff here or there. But it had never done much for me, so I had stuck to the fags.

Above all, though, I think it was me more than anything that got to him. Whereas I think Charles understood me because he saw some of his own idealism, Father Colin saw nothing but a self-indulgent public schoolboy. And perhaps he was right.

• • •

Gebre Egziabher takes me with him when he goes out with Tibebu, wheeling him up and down the steep Addis hills in his wheelchair. It is hard to recall what we talk about, but we form a bond together. One late afternoon when Father Colin is out on business, Gebre Egziabher comes to me and says, 'Come on, let's go.'

'Where to?' I ask.

But Gebre Egziabher is conspiratorial rather than informative. 'No, let's just go now.'

So I shrug and follow him as he walks ahead rapidly, leading us through streets and alleys until we come to a low brick building. Inside is a long, dark room and there seem to be men slumped along the wall.

I pause nervously. Gebre Egziabher stops and comes back. 'No,' he says, 'come through here. We are getting beer.'

And he puts his hand on my shoulder and encourages me forward, past the slumped men and into another room where there is a makeshift bar. Gebre Egziabher orders beer for us both, which is flat and warm. It seems to have straw floating in it and tastes of something burnt. But I drink it anyway.

Gebre Egziabher turns to me and his voice takes on a very serious tone: 'Jonny, please, you must tell no one we came here,' he says. 'Father Colin will make me leave if he knows I have brought you here. So you must promise you will say nothing.'

I pledge this costless promise, but I am not really paying attention. I am thinking of the slumped smoking men in the outer room. 'Is it an opium den?' I wonder, but for some reason I don't ask. Instead I look at the brown liquid in front of me with straw floating on top of it, and I take another swig.

• • •

For the first few days, Father Colin largely ignored me. At the weekend, he announced he was taking me, Gebre Egziabher and Tibebu on a trip to Sodore, a resort south of Addis by the Awash River which had swimming pools and tennis courts, as I remember it.

Once Gebre Egziabher and Tibebu are settled by the pool, Father Colin suggests we go and have a talk. This is not a welcome prospect.

When we set out from the pool, I am unclear where we are going, perhaps to find a table where Father Colin can give his talk, so I leave the pool area barefoot, unprepared for the walk-and-talk that is about to ensue.

It is not clear whether Father Colin is oblivious to my bare feet or not, but he sets out on the walk-and-talk along a stony path beside the Awash River that is surely not designed for the barefoot walker. Perhaps it is meant as a penance; if so, it is definitely one that I won't forget. In practice, however, it seems counterproductive because I am so focused on avoiding the sharpest stones and on the growing pain in my feet that I pay very little attention to what Colin is telling me. The gist seems to be about my irresponsibility and self-indulgence and selfishness. None of them unfair points. In any case, it requires much less energy to concede them than dispute them. At one point, Father Colin asks me if I am taking drugs. I tell him truthfully that I am not. But it is clear that Father Colin is not convinced.

Our walk-and-talk continues for twenty minutes or more on a linear route alongside the river, and every step of the way I am thinking of my feet and the stones they will have to cross to get back. I consider drawing Father Colin's attention to my feet, but I conclude that this might make him even crosser than he already is with me, so I say nothing. At length, we turn, and each step becomes one step closer to stopping the pain.

The upshot is that Father Colin does not want me to stay. He tells me I must return home. I resent this and I resent Father Colin. But the reality is that I can't stay here – that I have been selfish and self-indulgent – and that it is time to go home. So perhaps it is just a question of timing and a tougher sort of love.

My goodbyes from St Matthew's are brief but heartfelt. The cook and housekeeper, who has mothered me in my few weeks in Addis, hugs me and presses on me a stack of *injera*, the sour flatbread that she knows I love. It is packaged in greaseproof paper and wrapped in foil, but I am unconvinced it will get through customs. Nonetheless, the tenderness of the gesture moves me, and I promise that I will share it with my family.

Gebre Egziabher and I shake hands and promise to keep in touch, but perhaps inevitably we do not. I say my farewell to Tibebu and then it is time to go. At that moment, Colin says, 'You haven't any presents for your parents. We must find you something to take them,' and he goes through the chaplaincy looking for something that will serve as a gift. He lights on an Ethiopian Orthodox cross and an elegant bowl, rather like a fruit bowl, which is ridged like basketwork, covered with fabric, but I think is in fact somehow fabric throughout. He tells me that one of the Emperor's granddaughters made the bowl in prison. I am touched by this thoughtful gesture and we part on better terms than we have enjoyed to date.

I don't remember the journey to the airport or much of the flight home. There was some of the fear I had felt when I boarded the flight the other way, but it was a different sort of fear, with none of the excitement that had spiked my trepidation on the way out. My dominant senses on this return flight were of failure and nervousness about how I would be received.

At Heathrow, the journey between the baggage hall and arrivals, where Mum and Dad are waiting, seems an impossible one to make. My heart stops. How can I explain myself? I pause before the customs channel, afraid to go on.

Finally, I step into the green channel and walk forward hesitantly, which I assume is what attracts the interest of the customs officer, who proceeds to dismantle my meagre possessions and study them in minute detail. He is heavily exercised by the Ethiopian coffee I have brought back – I am later told that this is because its strong aroma is often used as a cover for drugs – but remarkably he takes no interest in the stack of *injera*, which makes up a good proportion of the volume of my luggage. Finding nothing of interest, he directs me ill-temperedly to repack my bags.

And then that is it. There is no more prevaricating to be done. I walk out into the arrivals hall to face whatever music I have in store.

13

HOME

My parents, standing behind the barrier, look as anxious as I feel, but as soon as they see me their faces light up. I am hugged and kissed, amidst my mum's tears, and shown all the love that I don't deserve. My mind is a swirling mass of relief and guilt and shame. We go from the airport to a nearby hotel so they can have a chat with me before we return home. The journey there, though short, is an agony of anticipation for me. But I needn't have worried. Inside, they order coffee and tell me that all they care about is that I am back; that we should just treat my absence as if I had been away on a holiday and that I mustn't worry about anything. But if I want to talk about anything – anything – they are there for me. I mumble the best attempt at a thank-you that my surly fifteen-year-old self will allow and do my best not to cry.

Back home, my siblings tease me affectionately. It's good to be back with them. It's good to be home. It's good to have parents who hug you and love you, even when you have stolen and lied to them on a trans-continental scale. But despite all the goodness, nothing seems right. Because, despite travelling across continents and back, nothing has actually changed.

My headful of troubles is still bubbling and boiling and rumbling, with all the old ingredients jostling for ascendancy and some new ones now added for good measure, the most pungent of which is failure.

•   •   •

There is just deep, deep darkness now, and even with the loving and for-giving welcome from my parents and my siblings, I descend deeper into an abyss of shame and despair. I clam up, avoiding any contact that may lead to conversation and questions. I tell my mum and dad that I will not go back to my old school. My dad tells me I have to, that they can't afford anything else – I am by a quirk of fate a scholarship boy, and it will apparently be more costly if I stay at home and go to the local sixth-form college as I intend. But that's not his real reason. He wants me back at my old school because he thinks it will be the best thing for me.

Why doesn't he see the impossibility of the idea? How could I face anyone, how could I explain? And anyway, Will is there and how can I deal with that? It will break my heart. I cannot do it. I simply will not. My father says, 'Give it time. Think about it.' But I cannot think about anything. I just have this crushing mountain of despair on my back. And now I am itching and scratching and lethargic. My father takes me to the doctor, who diagnoses shingles and instructs that I must stay away from school. Relief, for now.

My parents are kind to me during this time, tolerant beyond belief. There are no raised voices, no demands for explanation. There is a care-fulness about their interactions with me; their love is obvious, but it is laced through with wariness born of fear. Fear of what I have done and what that means about what I might do. My siblings try to connect; they will wander out to where I sit in the church office, smoking and morose, and they will try to engage me. I will smile a tight smile and respond a word or two, but then I will be up on my feet walking, to another place where I can be on my own.

My father remarks on this to me after one occasion when my brother has gone to look for me and found me alone in the church office and I have hardly said a word to him but returned almost immediately to the house. 'Why won't you speak with your brother like you used to?' There is a quiet desperation creeping into his voice.

As the shingle sores fade and I start to recover my energy, my father tries again to persuade me back to school. Terry Rogers, my housemaster, suggests that I visit, just for a day. My parents enlist my friends, who call me and say, 'Why not, it can't do any harm and it would be good to see you.' So eventually, I allow my resistance to the day trip to weaken. I will go for a day. It will be good to see them, but that will be it. There is no way I am going back. It isn't possible.

So one day I take the Tube to Marble Arch and catch the long-distance coach to Marlborough. I sit by the window on the upper deck, my head resting on the pane, the glass cold against my face. My silver Walkman rests on my knee, my ears stopped up with orange foam headphones, blasting out Bob Dylan and Billy Bragg – no wonder I am depressed.

West London passes by, slow and clogged, and then, on the M4, somewhere beyond Heathrow, the traffic thins out and the orange double-decker coach breaks free of urbanity. I watch the fields flash past in the autumn light. My head, still resting on the glass, feels out the vibrations of the road. They comfort me, help me quell the anxiety, push back the panic that threatens to erupt as the miles between here and there steadily, unceasingly, contract.

The coach turns off the motorway and trundles along the A-roads, making its relentless way between fields and woodland, through small towns and villages, each one of which I know deeply as landmarks passed on many journeys to and from this place. I light a cigarette and pull on it in short, nervous tokes to steady my nerves, finishing it as the bus begins the climb over Savernake Hill before snaking down the other side, past Savernake Hospital and into the outskirts of the town.

My eyes take note of the petrol station and the Five Alls pub, the final staging posts before arrival. And then the bus is pulling up halfway down the wide high street, outside the low-slung building that houses the Polly Tea Rooms. I start down the stairs from the upper deck as the hydraulics hiss and seethe, pushing open the door.

It's a nice late autumn day, furnishing golden sunlight which softens the brick and grey stone of the buildings. The environment is familiar, but I am not comforted by the familiarity. My stomach is a mess of contorting muscles; spun around me is a cocoon of dreadful anticipation. Inside the cocoon, I feel quiet and disconnected, the world outside muffled and distant. Soon though, very soon, I am going to have to emerge from this cocoon and greet people and engage with them and answer their questions, and no doubt sometime I may even be expected to smile.

I sling my bag over my shoulder and walk slowly down the high street to the Merlin Hotel, where I am to meet my housemaster for coffee and a chat. I push open the door and walk in. Terry is there already, occupying a table near the window. Seeing me, he rises to his feet and advances in an energetic welcome. His face a picture of warmth, his crazy eyebrows raised to full mast. I am amazed that this man, whom I must have caused untold irritation to over the course of my school career, seems genuinely delighted to see me.

The cocoon around me dissolves and the noisy world intrudes again, so that despite the warmth of the welcome, I am confused and at odds. Terry seems to note my discomfort and tones down his approach, lowering his voice and taking the smile down from beaming welcome to sympathetic friendliness.

'Why don't we have a cup of coffee,' he says gently, indicating for me to sit down.

The next hour is a strange experience for me. Terry is warm and kind and reassuring: 'We are all very proud of you. What you did was very brave,' he tells me on a number of occasions. But I don't feel proud or brave, just bewildered that Terry should think me so.

It is clear that there are two narratives competing with one another: Terry's, which is that of a courageous boy motivated by compassion who set out on a brave, if flawed, expedition to help those less fortunate, and my internal narrative, which is of theft and failure, causing untold pain to my family.

Terry is all kindness and smiles. He says, 'I don't want to push you and you needn't decide today, but we would really like you to come back. People miss you a great deal.'

I am grateful for this kindness and I thank Terry and say something ambiguous about thinking it through, but the truth is I cannot conceive of returning to the school. How could I face all these people? It is hard enough for just this one day – but every day? The stress and tension sing through me. Terry seems to feel it. He looks intently at me and says, 'Don't make any decisions immediately. Spend the afternoon with your friends and then see how you feel.'

We walk down the road together towards the school. As we reach the school gates, the bells ring out denoting the end of morning lessons, and within seconds a torrent of grey-jacketed lower-school kids pour out of classrooms and head towards lunch.

Terry and I part here.

'Remember what I said. Take your time before you make your decision and call me if you want to discuss it further.'

He shakes my hand and walks off in the direction of the headmaster's lodge. I head up the steps between B House and C House into the courtyard. As I turn towards C House, I see Will, his face lit up in a wide smile: 'JO-NNEE,' he shouts and sweeps me up in an embrace. The smile is infectious and despite the emotions that are bubbling inside me, I cannot help but return it. Will steps back and looks at me and says softly, 'But are you OK, man?'

Before I can answer, I am being clapped on the back by Hank and Dan and Nicky and Harry and Emeka. 'Hey Jonny, you crazy fucker, good to have you back.' Nicky chuckles at me. We head across the courtyard and into the Norwood Hall, a huge 1950s hall laid out with tables and benches to serve 800 kids. The noise inside is intense, and I am peppered with questions from all sides as I stand with my friends in the lunch queue. Those who don't know me cast curious glances, perhaps aware of my exotic tale.

All is familiar but also changed. My friends no longer wear the grey of the lower school but have progressed into a variety of sports jackets, which are the mark of liberation for the upper-school boys. Rather more radically, girls have arrived this year, and it is clear from the air of tension that the boys are feeling out where they stand in this new environment, with the girls and with one another.

After lunch, we all head off to the island for a smoke and a chat. It's clear by now that I won't get any time alone with Will, and today I am glad of it. I don't think I could handle the intensity of my feelings. I prefer to pass the time in this unreal world of schoolboy banter. After a while my friends have to drift off to games or cadet training and it is time for me to catch the bus back to London. They walk me to the school gates and say their goodbyes, which are laden with the assumption that I will be returning to join them soon. I don't have the energy to tell them that I will not.

Then they are gone, and I set off up the high street to catch my bus. Outside the Castle and Ball Hotel, I bump into Jon Brown, a pale-faced, spiky-haired sixth-form student who doesn't have too much time for the rules. He is in the year above me and although I know him a little, from shared cigarettes every now and then, I have always been a bit in awe of him. So I am surprised by the warmth of his greeting. 'Hey Jonny, great to see you.' Jon's round face, as often sporting a scowl as anything else, is lit up by a smile. 'So when are you coming back?' he asks.

'I don't think I am,' I respond honestly for the first time that day.

Jon is silent for a moment. Then he says, with kindness etched through his voice, 'You should come back. People miss you. What else are you going to do anyway?'

'I don't know. Go to sixth-form college, I guess, although my dad doesn't want me to.'

'What's the point of going to a sixth-form college where you won't know anyone?'

That is perhaps the point – or, more precisely, the point is that no one will know me.

'Umm, I don't know, I'll think about it. Anyway, I'd better run to get the bus. Thanks. Good to see you anyway.' I am confused by this unexpected encounter and my words come out in a jumble.

'Well, think about it,' Jon says. 'It would be good to have you back.'

Back on the upper deck of the bus, I fish a cigarette out of the pack and as soon as we are beyond the high street and the jurisdiction of the school, I light it up, taking a long draw, leaning back into the seat and staring out into the late autumn dusk.

I am unsettled by my encounter with Jon, taken aback by his unexpected kindness and the intensity of his concern.

I have been so sure that I am done with that school; the one thing I knew was that I had to get away from it – from its privilege and its pain. But now I am not so certain. Maybe Jon is right. Maybe a new start would be even harder – and haven't I just spectacularly proved that running away from things doesn't solve them? Perhaps after all I should stick with what I know.

• • •

I returned to school sometime in October 1985. I had grown weary of fighting with my father over the issue, but above all my chance meeting with Jon Brown had changed my outlook. School would put me back with my friends and afford me greater freedom than I had at home, where my dad was keen to provide me with the benefit of his continuous advice.

The upper school that I joined on my return was very different from the school I had left at the beginning of July. My erstwhile roommate was gone: suspended for buying marijuana early in the summer term, he had been invited to not return when autumn came.

More significantly, there were girls in my year for the first time. They changed the atmosphere immediately. For one thing, the other boys started to wash. Perhaps more importantly, they shifted the atmosphere of the school in a direction that made it far more comfortable for me.

But none of this solved the problem that was at the heart of my unhappiness: the fact that I could scarcely acknowledge to myself that I was attracted to my own sex, and that I was in love with a boy who wasn't.

So while the school was much more my kind of place in those last two years I spent there, life still felt bleak for much of it.

Will and I resumed our strong friendship, and I continued to struggle with it.

The first night I was back, all the lads came over after evening study as a show of solidarity, and we sat and bantered in my small single bedsit and I tried to make light of the past months by spinning unconvincing stories of sexual conquest.

But the next day I had time with Will alone. We walked upfield from my boarding house and I had the first chance to talk to him properly. He gave me an exercise book which he had filled with his thoughts about life and about my disappearing act to Ethiopia. It was lost later, when I was working in South Africa, and I can't now recall much of its content, except that at the end he had written in light-blue washable ink, in his unmistakable curling script, three words: I love you.

When I read those words for the first time, I knew the thrill of being loved. But the thrill was short-lived. The intensity of our friendship might confuse things for me, but even then I knew in my heart that the love he had for me was not the same love I had for him. His care for me only made the reality harder.

Sometime during this year, my mum took me to see the musical *Les Misérables*. As Éponine sang of her unacknowledged love for Marius, I wallowed in the exquisite misery of it, casting Will as Marius and myself as Éponine. 'I love him but only on my own,' became my song, which I would sing softly to myself as I sat on my stile or walked back to my house after a smoke. Very lame, but very true.

The next two years passed in this pattern. My unrequited love occupied most of my thoughts outside the classroom, and the intense nature of my friendship with Will confused and at times deluded me. I started drinking unhealthily, climbing out the window of my room at study time and drinking alone in the village pub.

Nevertheless, the school was a much happier place for me than it had been before, and the new friendships that emerged helped give me strength. I found a soulmate in one of the girls in my house, Sarah, whose seriousness of purpose and love of books and theatre immediately connected with me. Two other girls, Becca and Kelly, also became important in my life, providing friendship and support and, together with Sarah, eagerly pricking my tendency to self-righteousness with gentle mockery whenever it raised its head.

I still have a picture that Kelly sent me, taken in her parents' house when we were both about seventeen. It shows the two of us deep in conversation – or, more exactly, it shows me clearly subjecting her to one of my impassioned monologues. On this photograph, Kelly had stuck a thought bubble above her head: 'Word in edgeways.'

Despite this happier environment, where I felt in many respects that I could be more of who I was, I continued to struggle with the truth that I would not acknowledge: that I was gay. In doing so, I caused hurt and confusions of my own.

This was not a great time to be an adolescent struggling with sexuality. The drumbeat of homophobia, driven by the tabloid press and the Conservative right, amidst the tragedy of the HIV/Aids crisis, was getting ever louder. It culminated in Section 28 of the 1988 Local Government Act, my belated eighteenth birthday present from the Conservative government. The Act made it an offence for local authorities to 'intentionally promote homosexuality or publish material with the intention of promoting homosexuality; or promote the teaching in any maintained school of the acceptability of homosexuality as a pretended family relationship'.

Opinion polling which had tested attitudes to homosexuality over the previous decades indicate that hostility to gay people reached its zenith at this point. It was not an atmosphere that lent itself to coming to terms with your feelings. And, lacking the courage of others, I didn't, and I drank to cover the gaps that left for me.

Some of my distress must have been obvious, because I remember one of the boys in my house, a prefect called Dave who I had always been friendly with but never particularly close to, came to my bedsit one evening to tell me he was worried about me and to ask if there was anything he could do to help. Like Jon's intervention, this touched me particularly because it was so unexpected; a random act of kindness that I have never forgotten.

I didn't forget, either, Father Charles's admonition to me before he left for the UK, to remember Africa and get my schooling done so I might be of practical help. One day during my A-level year, Terry Rogers called me into his study and told me he had heard of an opportunity for people in their year off between school and university to go and teach in Zimbabwe, and he asked me if I wanted him to put my name forward. I jumped at the chance.

The next time I saw Will, I told him excitedly of this opportunity, and to my delight he decided to sign up too.

And so the final A-level term came to an end and we all headed off on our different paths. I went back home and, after a short but important period as an intern for the Liberal MP Simon Hughes, I started a job in the accounts department of HMV to earn enough money to pay for my airfare to Zimbabwe.

Will came down to London at the beginning of that summer and we spent an idyllic day together, sunbathing and drinking by the bandstand in St James's Park before heading back to my house. My bedroom possessed only a single bed, but I was used to giving that up to guests and sleeping in my sleeping bag on the floor. We were both settling down, Will in the bed and me on the floor – I imagine I was moaning as usual about the hardness of the floor – when Will said, 'Why don't you sleep up here with me? There's space.'

My mind raced and I struggled to breathe, but finally I forced some words out of my mouth. 'OK, cool, if you don't mind.'

So I climbed into the bed. We lay back to back awkwardly, with one of Will's mix tapes playing Lou Reed's 'Perfect Day'. Soon, Will's breathing indicated he had fallen asleep, but I lay there awake, tense and amazed, cherishing the proximity to his sleeping body. Eventually, I must have fallen asleep, because I awoke to feel Will wrapping his arms around me.

PART TWO

FINDING MYSELF

14

ZIMBABWE

Early one Thursday morning in January 1988, an Air Zambia flight from London touches down in Lusaka. It is carrying an eclectic bunch of English kids who – with no more than A-levels to their name – are on their way to teach at secondary schools across Zimbabwe. Unqualified though we are, it is felt that we are ideally placed to impart wisdom to the students of Zimbabwe, by virtue of being both English and white.

As a model, it is not one that is followed today, but the motivation of Jim Cogan, the founder of Schools Partnership Worldwide, the organisation that has sent us, is noble. He wants privileged kids like us to understand that there is a world beyond ours, where lives are a lot harder, and he wants us to try to give something back to it. His initiative, started with nothing more than passion and determination, has become Restless Development, an inspirational organisation that now engages young people within Zimbabwe and the other countries where it operates, getting them involved in helping their own communities. A much better model, but one that would never have come into being without Jim's determination and vision.

And without that determination and vision I would never have got to Zimbabwe, and a key part of who I am would be missing, along with one of the most important friendships of my life.

The layover in Lusaka is long, eight hours in total, and there is not a lot to do in the transit lounge, so the twelve putative teachers, ten male, two female, spend it getting to know one another, playing cards and drinking suspiciously cheap Smirnoff blue vodka. Around 2 p.m. we set off to board an Air Zimbabwe flight to Harare, the path across the tarmac to the plane a little more zig-zagged for those who have hit the Smirnoff hardest.

At Harare Airport, we are met by Ken Anderson, a clergyman and chaplain at Peterhouse School, the Eton of Zimbabwe, set in the bush outside Marondera, about an hour's drive from Harare. But there is a problem. One of our group, my former schoolmate Dave, he of prefect rank and purveyor of unexpected kindness, is in trouble with the authorities on account of his camouflage backpack.

The possession of camouflage, except by the military, is illegal in Zimbabwe, and this is a particularly sensitive matter in a country that has only eight years before emerged from a brutal bush war in which white boys of our age were dressed up in camouflage and sent out to kill their fellow black citizens. Added to this, there is ongoing banditry from dissident former guerrilla forces, which has the government on edge. It may not help, also, that Dave is tall, blond and well built and would not look out of place at a military academy.

Ken has come to pick us up and take us back to Peterhouse, where we will stay the first few days before being assigned to our schools. But instead of heading out towards the school, he is ordered instead to drive us all to the Harare headquarters of Zimbabwe's Central Intelligence Organisation. The CIO, established under the white minority regime, has maintained its notoriety under Robert Mugabe. Ken, who I will later know as a calm and authoritative figure, is at this point nervous and agitated. The rest of us wait in the minibus outside CIO HQ as Ken accompanies Dave to whatever reception awaits him inside. This does not feel like an auspicious start to our time in Zimbabwe.

The light begins to fade before Ken and Dave emerge from the HQ. Dave has been let off with a reprimand and the confiscation of his backpack. Ken is still on edge and castigates Dave for his foolishness in arriving in Zimbabwe with an army surplus backpack: 'If you had had a South African or Israeli stamp in your passport, that would have been it, you would have been sent home and the whole scheme compromised.'

This seems unfair to me: no one has previously warned us about Zimbabwe's laws on camouflage and it seems unreasonable to expect us to anticipate this, but Ken's reprimand is born out of fear, which I later learn is the only sensible instinct when it comes to the CIO.

The delay has meant that our journey to Marondera is through the dusk and then the pitch-black night of the Zimbabwe bush, which must also be adding to Ken's agitation. As we head out of Harare, we can still see the landscape through the fading light. Huge grey stones balanced improbably on top of one another litter the bush to either side of the road, staring out at us through the gloom, until finally all is enveloped in darkness.

We spend a Saturday and Sunday at Peterhouse – whose students are absent enjoying their summer holidays – sleeping in the school dorms, being briefed by Ken on how we should approach our task, and eating the fantastic food that Ken's wife Polly serves up in their beautiful home. Then, deciding we are sufficiently acclimatised, Ken sends us on our way to the schools we will teach in. With two other boys, Joe West and Alan de Saram, I am assigned to teach in a school in rural Manicaland, 30km or so from the provincial capital of Mutare.

On the morning of our departure, we are up at 4.30 a.m. to pack, still nursing hangovers from a late night of farewell drinking games. After breakfast, Ken drives us to Marondera Bus Station, which is a cacophony of sounds and people and chaos. He finds the bus that will take us to Mutare, a few hours' drive to the south-east, and we watch nervously as our backpacks are stowed on the roof. Given that these contain our entire possessions, our nervousness is unsurprising but, as it turns out, misplaced. Ken reminds us of our instructions once we arrive in Mutare and then says his goodbyes.

The three of us, plus Adam, Lucy and Nick – three other members of the group, who will teach at a school on the other side of Mutare – clamber aboard the bus and make our way among the people and sacks of maize and chickens to the few remaining seats. Soon the bus is almost full to capacity, and the conductor leans out, puts his fingers to his mouth, lets out a piercing whistle of warning to any straggling passengers and then, content there are no more, pounds his hand on the side of the bus and hoists himself inside, pulling the door closed behind him. The bus jerks into life in a belch of blue diesel fumes and rocks and sways across the uneven ground of the bus station towards the security of the tarmac road to Mutare.

Inside the bus, there is the chatter of conversation in Shona, accompanied by curious glances and smiles at us, these six white youngsters – a startling sight, still, on a local bus. Outside, rich farming land flashes by before giving way to the bush. The road is good and the distance of little more than 200km passes by almost too rapidly. As we progress, the terrain alters and the eastern highlands come into view. We pass the Nyanga road and the bus starts to grind its way up Christmas Pass, the gateway to Mutare from the west. At the pinnacle of the pass, the road appears to pause on a plateau, with spectacular views to the right, before descending steeply towards the city, nestling in a bowl of the hills below.

The bus disgorges us in Mutare about 11 a.m. and we make our way to the nondescript Manica Hotel, where we are to await the headmaster of St James School, Zongoro.

The headmaster, Mr Manyumwa, does not arrive until sometime after lunch, by which time we have drunk a beer or two in a vain attempt to cure the hangovers from the night before. Simon Manyumwa is a small man sporting a grey-blue suit. A twinkle in his eye contrasts with a delicate, considered and serious face, which in turn gives way to the startlingly warm smile with which he now greets us.

We part from our three compatriots, who it turns out will not be so lucky with their headmaster, who fails to meet them at all, leaving them to set out for the school on their own, an endeavour that sees them lost and forced to camp out in the Vumba Mountains. Mr Manyumwa, by contrast, is the model of consideration. He has arranged for a lift in an ancient estate car to take us the 30km back over Christmas Pass and down the Nyanga road, which will bring us to the school.

We trundle along the road, the car straining and spluttering, past Old Mutare Mission, the site of the original city before the railway line from the Mozambique port of Beira forced relocation to the far side of the pass; on through the settlement at Manica Bridge, where a butchery, a government beerhall and a variety of shops cluster around the road, marking this out as the commercial centre of the district.

A few kilometres on from Manica Bridge is the smaller settlement of Zongoro. On the right-hand side of the road, up a gentle incline, is a bottle store with a polished concrete veranda on which stands a battered table football table. This bottle store will become important in our lives. It's where we get to know our fellow teachers and the male members of the local community, and it's where, sat with a bottle of Castle beer after school, legs dangling over the veranda, we have the best seats in the house for the spectacular sunsets that blaze across the horizon in this part of the world. To the left of the bottle store is Mr and Mrs Mwashita's grocery shop, which will become a store of warmth and kindness to us.

Beyond the shops, we turn off down a dirt road of sandy yellow soil. We bounce over the ruts for about half a kilometre until we arrive at a pristine white-and-blue school, with an entrance like a mini fort. Here, we disembark with our bulging backpacks. Mr Manyumwa puts his fingers to his lips and whistles, and two young men rapidly appear and greet us solemnly before being instructed to take our bags to the house that has been assigned to us.

Mr Manyumwa shepherds us up a path through a small maize patch to his house, a low-slung white bungalow looking down on the school. Mrs Manyumwa is there to greet us wreathed in smiles, and we take tea together before embarking on a tour of the grounds.

The school is pristine, a tribute to Mr Manyumwa's dedication and discipline. Through the arched, fort-like entrance is a courtyard with a garden laid out around paths marked out by white-painted stones that sparkle in the sunshine, and lead to the headmaster's office and a number of classrooms.

There is much to encourage us in the warmth of our welcome and the obvious care that is taken with the school, but there is one area of concern that is nagging at us. Mr Manyumwa is the headmaster of St James Primary School, and it is the primary school he is showing us around, but we are supposed to teach in the secondary school, and so far we can see no sign of it. We assume that this kindly headteacher just wants to show off his school first, so we do not question him on this matter, assuming he will show us in due time.

Our tour of the primary school complete, we walk back up the dirt road we drove down an hour or so before, towards another white bungalow with a green door and window frames and a small veranda with two steps up to it and a low wall around it. It is a modest but handsome place.

Mr Manyumwa whistles again and one of the young men who helped us earlier appears with a key. He opens the door and ushers us in. There is a main living space with two rooms off it and another room that must be entered externally. There is, not surprisingly, no electricity or water or indeed anything else. Just empty space and concrete floors and our three backpacks, which have been delivered here earlier.

Mr Manyumwa turns to us expectantly and asks, 'When will your furniture be arriving from England?'

There is an awkward silence. Then Alan ventures that we have no furniture. But, he says, wanting to end on a positive note, we do have sleeping bags. I join in with the reassurance as we regard Mr Manyumwa's crestfallen face. 'We will be fine. No problem.'

Joe, who is feeling unwell, remains silent.

Mr Manyumwa shakes his head, his brow furrowed in concern. 'Ahh, this is not a good thing!' And, despite our protestations, he promises he will find some furniture for us.

We all walk back out onto the stoop and Mr Manyumwa ceremoniously hands us the key and tells us he will leave us to get settled in.

Nonplussed by the expectation that we would have brought our own furniture and confused that there has still been no mention of the secondary school in which we are supposed to be teaching, it's Alan again who speaks up. He thanks Mr Manyumwa for the tour he has provided of the primary school but asks the question we have all been pondering: where is the secondary school?

Mr Manyumwa considers us thoughtfully. 'Ahh, that is a good question, Alan.'

He turns and gestures as if to indicate the school, but we can see nothing but bush as far as the horizon. And then he says, 'Yes. This is our challenge. It has not been built yet.'

15

WILL

Will never came to Zimbabwe. He called me one morning at my work at the HMV accounts department and said his dad said he couldn't go. It was never clear why, but the security situation wasn't good at the time and his father, having some knowledge of the region, may have felt it too risky a proposition. But there may have been other reasons too.

That summer night in my room in London, I had held my breath as Will wrapped his arms around me, but it was pretty immediately obvious that he was still asleep and this was an involuntary shift in his sleeping position, not the beginning of the fulfilment of my dreams. So I just lay there enjoying the sensation of his skin against mine, until sometime later he stirred and rolled away from me.

In the morning, we woke and dressed and went across the road to Luigi's café for a smoke and a coffee to help us with our hangovers. We sat on benches at a corner table. Will asked me awkwardly, 'You know, I woke up at some point in the night and we had our arms around each other. Did you know that?'

I should have said yes. I should have told him that he had turned to me and wrapped his arms around me and that yes, I had been awake, and I hadn't moved away because for me it was a magical moment. I should have told him the truth, at least in some form. But I didn't.

Instead I mumbled some unconvincing words of surprise. I probably went red at that point. Who knows?

Later that morning, Will headed back to his hometown. We were never really friends in the same way after that. I am not sure if that was because of me, or him, or perhaps it was because of both of us.

I think that night crystallised for me what I had always known: that Will was never for me and that despite all the love and care he had shown to me over the years, it was time to grow up and move on.

Perhaps he also had realised that my feelings for him went beyond the intense friendship we had shared since we were fourteen and felt it was time for him to move on too.

Or perhaps it was just that our paths diverged. I was working in London, raising money for my flight to Zimbabwe. He was still at Marlborough, and after I left to teach in Zimbabwe there were thousands of miles between us.

Whatever it was, although we saw each other once, or maybe twice, over the intervening years, it wasn't until thirty-two years later that we had our next meaningful conversation. A lot had happened to both of us in between.

16

BUILD IT AND THEY'LL COME

Simon Manyumwa's words hang in the air on the veranda. 'It hasn't been built?' Joe, Alan and I chorus in bewildered unison.

Mr Manyumwa delays his planned departure and sits down on the low wall that surrounds the veranda to explain the situation. It appears that the community has had the legal authority of the government to open a secondary school for some years but has been waiting in vain for the capital funds to enable construction. This appears to be a failure of both the Anglican Church and the government.

However, the government of Zimbabwe and the Anglican Communion haven't reckoned with the determination of Mr Manyumwa and Chief Mutasa, the influential traditional leader in the area. Ahead of their time, the chief and the headmaster have reversed the adage 'Build it and they will come' and tomorrow they intend to enrol a first year of entry to the new unbuilt secondary school. Their theory is that if they come, the government and Church authorities will have no choice but to build it.

Mr Manyumwa now explains to us that in addition to having no buildings, the secondary school has no teachers, except us. Tomorrow the students will arrive, and we will have 140 first-form pupils on our hands. But, he reassures us, we can share classrooms for now with the primary school. He is putting the best face on it and is practical and encouraging, but we can see he is embarrassed by the situation.

Having imparted his various bombshells, Mr Manyumwa takes his leave and strolls through the late afternoon sunshine back towards his house. Alan, Joe and I sit around the veranda looking at each other; we are all tired from the early morning start and hungover from the Sunday night drinking, and Joe is looking decidedly unwell. As such, we are none of us in the best state to defuse Mr Manyumwa's bombshells. We decide this is best left to the morning. In the meantime, we need to sort ourselves out.

Joe decides that he would prefer the room with its own entrance, so Alan and I take the two rooms off the main living area. By now the sun is starting to set, and very rapidly it becomes dark. We all have flashlights and we have been lent a precious oil lamp, which gives out a dull and smoky light. We sit on the floor and chat for a while and Joe shares some of his Hobnob biscuits, but in view of the fact that the new school term starts at 7.45 a.m. tomorrow, after not very long we decide to go to bed, which in reality means a sleeping bag on a rock-hard concrete floor.

• • •

I am lucky with my fellow housemates. Joe and Alan, while very different in character, are both thoughtful and decent people.

Joe is nineteen, the son of well-known actors Prunella Scales and Tim West. A fair-haired, bookish person, he has a paradoxical tendency towards obsessive exactness and vagueness, which in the initial weeks of our time at Zongoro drives me to distraction. Where I want decisions, clarity and action, Joe always seems to want more consideration and complexity. He's often in the right, and over time I come to recognise and appreciate his thoughtfulness and kindness, but the pressure of the situation we find ourselves in and my overly headstrong approach to life mean that he grates on me at first.

Alan is a more natural fit with my character. At twenty-one, he is the oldest and most mature of the three of us and takes a natural lead. He went to the same school as me, where his father was a housemaster, but he was three years above me and I have only very vague recollections of him there. He is with us here in Zimbabwe because he has left Oxford University, either for failing exams or for a misdemeanour that I can't now recall, or perhaps never knew. Red-headed with a straggly beard and irreverent sense of humour, he doesn't take himself or the world too seriously, and he has a natural scepticism about both my headstrong approach and Joe's otherworldliness. He is the anchor between us.

These early days at Zongoro are tough on the three of us. Joe is unwell – at first, we don't understand how unwell – and this adds to the strain of coming to terms with the fact that we are in sole charge of 140 pupils in a school which hasn't even been built. Not only do we have no other teachers to help us; we really don't have the first clue about what we are doing.

On that first day of school, we are up early with the light. It is midsummer in Zimbabwe and the heat of the day is already on us. We make a desultory attempt to wash with the bucket of river water that someone has kindly provided us with, and then we pull on crumpled shirts and jackets.

Morgan, the deputy headmaster of the primary school, comes over from his home a few yards down the dirt track and introduces himself. Together, we head down to the assembly area outside the primary school. Neatly uniformed pupils in burgundy skirts or shorts and cream-coloured shirts are streaming towards the school from all directions, chattering and laughing. As we encounter them, they greet Morgan respectfully and regard us with undisguised astonishment. If we meet their gaze, they turn away shyly and giggle together.

The assembly area is a large open space between what will become the three secondary school classrooms and the fort-like structure that houses primary school classrooms and serves as the entrance to the garden courtyard in front of the headmaster's office, around which further primary school classrooms are arranged.

There is a concrete dais, raised about two feet off the ground, running the width of the assembly area. It has a slight promontory at its centre which is where, during assembly, the headmaster stands, with teachers ranged on either side of him.

Mr Manyumwa is already in the assembly area talking with other primary school teachers who are milling around the dais. He greets us warmly and introduces us to the teachers who are with him. Then he instructs us that he wants the three of us to stand beside him on the dais when proceedings get under way, so that he can introduce us to the school.

A huge metal triangle, weathered rust-brown, hangs from a tree, and at a signal from the headmaster a stocky boy of twelve or thirteen strikes it three times with a metal bar to summon the pupils to assemble. The teachers mount the dais from the slightly raised ground to its rear and arrange themselves along its length. Joe, Alan and I go to stand by Mr Manyumwa as instructed.

When students and pupils are all in place, Mr Manyumwa gives another signal to the boy at the triangle. On this occasion he strikes the triangle only once and, at this, another boy standing by a tall white flagpole raises the Zimbabwean flag while we all stand to attention. The flag raised, the primary school music teacher then leads the pupils in a rendition of 'Ishe Komborera Africa' ('God Bless Africa'), Zimbabwe's national anthem at the time. It is stirring and beautiful, 500 children's voices ringing out with pride on this stunning sun-drenched morning in the African bush.

The formalities out of the way, Mr Manyumwa welcomes the children and introduces us one by one. In turn we step forward and thank the school for its welcome. There is no question that we are the absolute focus of attention, a sea of hundreds of faces staring up at this extraordinary spectacle, three white British teachers here in their midst in Zongoro.

After our introduction, Mr Manyumwa sets about giving instructions to the school. It is clear that he is a firm disciplinarian who demands good order. Today is set aside for enrolling pupils and collecting their contributions for the General Purpose Fund and the School Sports Fund; although education is in theory free, out-of-pocket contributions are required to keep the school in books and other resources. Mr Manyumwa warns them that if they don't have the money today, they must tell their parents to get it very soon because he will not allow children to remain in school unless they pay their contributions.

At the back of the throng of students, trying to make themselves inconspicuous, are a number of pupils who are not dressed in school uniform. They are unsuccessful in this gambit: Simon Manyumwa has spotted them and calls them to the front of the school. There they are made to stand while he calls up an immaculately uniformed boy of five or six whom he hauls up on to the dais and then extraordinarily picks up in his arms. He holds the boy up in front of the school describing each part of his crisp new uniform, with particular emphasis on his pair of smart new shoes. Then he dismisses the uniform-less students and sends them home in shame, warning them not to return until they are properly dressed.

The rest of the day is thankfully not too taxing. We enrol the secondary students under the direction of Mr Manyumwa, who collects the contributions, showing us how they must be carefully noted down in the secondary school ledger. A significant number of the students don't have the money, but it seems Mr Manyumwa is more tolerant of this than he is of non-uniformed pupils, because no one is turned away, although they are firmly admonished. In total we enrol 140 first-form students and, having done so, we divide them up into three classes: forty-four in Al's class and forty-three each in mine and Joe's. Forty-three names and faces to get my head around. It feels like I will never manage it. After an initial get-together with our classes, the students are dismissed. School proper doesn't start until tomorrow.

This is a relief as it allows us to relax and acclimatise to our new surroundings. Mr Manyumwa has sent a few of the secondary school students to the borehole, a kilometre or so away through the bush, on the other side of the river and the tarmac road. They return across the stepping stones, two of the students bearing plastic buckets of drinking water on their heads, which they bring to our house. A paraffin stove has also been procured for us, as well as some meat from the butchery in Manica Bridge, some vegetables and fruit – okra, tomatoes, bananas and mangoes – a loaf of white bread and a dozen eggs. Al cooks up the steak on the paraffin stove – quite a feat, given the limited heat it emits. The steak is pretty tough, but it's the first food, apart from Joe's strictly rationed Hobnobs, that we have had since lunchtime the previous day, so we wolf it down. We spend the rest of the afternoon trying to get to grips with the syllabus we will have to teach tomorrow.

The history syllabus is particularly challenging as it focuses on the emergence of early mankind, a period I have never studied. Each chapter in the book is followed by a series of questions to pose to the pupils after they have learnt this section of the syllabus. Most of the questions are obvious once you have read the relevant chapter, but there is one that stumps me. I re-read the chapter but can't find any further illumination, so I am forced to seek out the teacher's answer book, where the question is resolved definitively.

Q: 'What is the highest form of human development?' A: 'Socialism.'

If only I had known it was so simple.

Wednesday is the start of school proper. My class is assembled behind their desks when I arrive, and as I walk up the couple of steps and through the classroom door, I am met by a cacophony of wood scraping against concrete as my pupils push back their chairs and stand smartly to attention.

I walk to the heavy-set wooden desk at the front of the classroom, feeling nervous and apprehensive. I have absolutely no qualifications for this job, and the hopes of forty-three eager faces are invested in me, their futures to some degree at least dependent on my abilities. I feel completely overwhelmed, but there's no avoiding it. I will just have to pretend to be a teacher. I summon up all my memories of teacher-like authority and address the class.

'Good morning, class.'

'Good morning, Mr Oates,' they return in unison.

I signal to them to sit down, and the racket of chairs being moved returns. I remain standing and pick up a piece of chalk from the groove underneath the huge blackboard behind my desk, and I start to teach my first lesson.

We teach until the lunchtime break, when we wander back to the house. For lunch, we make do with tomatoes and hunks of bread torn off the loaf we were given yesterday. We should consider ourselves lucky; for most of our pupils, lunch is just a stick of sugar cane, which they chew on to sustain themselves through the day. For some, it is nothing at all. In the afternoon, we take the pupils for athletics until 3.30 p.m., although Joe, who has struggled through the morning classes, stays back at the house. He has been unwell since Monday and now is starting to sound pretty bad.

• • •

One afternoon after school finishes, we repair to the bottle store at the invitation of Morgan, known as 'Mandi', and a number of the primary school teachers, Stephen Mandikyana, Onni and Reuben. The bottle store is about half a kilometre from our house, across the sports field, then down a short but steep path to the shallow river and over the stepping stones before climbing another short but steep path to the tarmac road beyond. Once across the road, the store is not more than twenty metres up a dirt track. Castle or Lion lager and table football are on offer here, and, by the look of the motel-style rooms out the back, perhaps something more.

The bottle store stands on the higher ground that rises from the road towards the hills and mountains beyond. The veranda faces almost due west and is reached from the dirt track at the side; at the front there is a drop of about a metre from the veranda to the ground below. Most of the veranda is occupied by the table football table, but you can sit on the lip of it and dangle your legs and drink your beer. You enter the store through a doorway off the centre of the veranda; an outer metal gate and metal grilles on the windows secure the building's valuable contents when the store is closed.

Inside, pale blue paint is peeling from the walls, and straight in front is a tall bar, from behind which the barman will serve bottles of lager, cheap cane spirits and Chibuku, also known as Shake-Shake, a traditional sorghum beer, which you can buy in commercially produced cartons or from a great blue plastic water butt full of home brew at the back of the store.

If you go through the door to the left of the bar at the back, you pass into a store room which serves as a saloon bar and which is where Mr Manyumwa most often holds forth, preferring not to display his drinking habits to the rest of the community, where he is a man of authority with a reputation to protect.

Alan buys the first round of Castles and, as Mr Manyumwa is not with us and we are all too young to have reputations to protect, the six of us take our beers outside and sit with legs dangling over the side of the veranda, where we chat and watch the sun flame out in a glorious sunset behind the hills to the west.

We are on our third or fourth beer and darkness has fallen when the lights of a vehicle turning sharply off the road cause pandemonium: suddenly customers are sprinting, bottles in hand, towards the bush at the back of the bar. Alan and I are completely bewildered as our companions disappear at pace into the night, all except Mandi, who stays with us, loyal to the last.

The reason for the panic is apparent moments later, as a police vehicle screeches to a halt, its blazing headlights picking out the fugitives from justice heading into the bush, and khaki-clad officers of the Zimbabwe Republic Police leap out and head off in hot pursuit. The three of us sit there, Alan and I perplexed, Mandi resigned to the fate that he knows awaits us.

Unbeknownst to us, but not to Mandi, is the fact that a bottle store is an off-licence, a place that may sell alcohol to take away but not for consumption on the premises. The owners are breaking the law by allowing us to drink here, but we are also breaking the law by being here with open bottles in hand. There is no time for Mandi to make these explanations before one of the more senior officers is in front of us and placing us under arrest for illegal drinking.

There is a big kerfuffle to the rear of the bottle store as another officer pushes over the blue plastic water butt full of home-brewed sorghum beer. The barman watches disconsolately as the precious liquid cascades down the dirt track. Other police officers emerge from the bush with a few customers who have been too slow, or too drunk, to find a proper hiding place.

The police officer in charge orders us into the back of his vehicle, a pick-up truck adapted at the back with a low-slung metal roof and wire mesh sides. Mandi speaks to the officer in Shona and then in English, appealing to him that Alan and I are just a few days in the country and did not know the law. He is distinctly unimpressed and speaks sharply back to Mandi in Shona and signals us once more to climb into the back of the truck. I am resigned to meekly complying; my instinctive reaction is anyway to obey the instructions of a police officer, but added to that is the fact that I fear a white guy arguing the toss with a Zimbabwean police officer is not the wisest idea in a country so recently emerged from a racial civil war.

Alan, on the other hand, is not so easily cowed. He shakes his head and stands on his rights. He tells the officer that we had no idea that we were breaking the law, that we accept this is no defence against the offence itself, but that there is no need whatsoever to detain us. We are teachers at the school, there is no danger of us absconding and we will of course pay any fine or answer any charges if they are pressed.

There is a moment of silence when Alan has finished speaking in which the officer stares back at him, brow furrowed with anger, and I think Alan has misjudged this situation very badly. But Mandi takes the opportunity to fill the silence with his own appeal on our behalf and, eventually, the policeman relents. He instructs us to stay where we are and fetches his ticket book from the vehicle. He writes out our names laboriously and hands us each a ticket, solemnly warning each of us in turn that if we do not comply with its terms and present ourselves at the main police station in Mutare within a month to pay our fine, we will be in very serious trouble. Content with the strength of his admonition, he climbs back into the passenger cab and signals to his colleagues that it is time to leave.

Those of our fellow drinkers who failed to evade capture are not so lucky. They have already been herded into the back of the truck, and now the doors are slammed shut on them. The truck lurches down the steep, uneven track before turning left onto the road and roaring off into the night with the detainees. Morgan turns to us apologetically and dejectedly. The fine is Z$20 – a tenth of our month's wage.

It is not until the headlamps have disappeared down the road towards Manica Bridge that people start emerging from the bush. Stephen and Onni appear first. It is not clear where Reuben has got to; perhaps he has slipped through the bush back home. Stephen is grinning and laughing at the excitement and adventure of evading the cops; Onni is indignant at our stupidity in not running when they did and tries to tell us we are in the wrong. But his over-zealousness in this regard suggests that he is not comfortable with having abandoned us to our fate. Mandi says nothing, but the choice he made in staying with us is rebuke enough to Onni. From that day on I know that Mandi will be my friend, but I have no idea that it is a friendship that will become so important to me and last for more than three decades.

Over the first week at Zongoro, Joe gets steadily worse. On Thursday he is taken to Mutare General Hospital, but when he returns, he seems in no better shape and starts vomiting again. Joe has a very threadbare sleeping bag, so in view of his condition, I lend him the expensive, heavily padded bag that my mum bought me as a present before I left for Zimbabwe. As a result, I spend a very uncomfortable night sleeping almost directly on the solid concrete floor, but I take it as penance because at the start of the week I had rather doubted Joe's illness, ungenerously ascribing it to the result of a bad hangover from the weekend at Peterhouse and feeling resentful that the burden of teaching was falling largely on Al and me. Now it is clear beyond doubt that he has some nasty bug or food poisoning and that my resentments were entirely unfounded and unworthy.

On Saturday morning, we all go into Mutare, where Alan and I feast on steak, egg and chips at the Dairy Den diner on Main Street. Joe, having rallied a little over Friday night, now deteriorates further, so we agree he should stay in Mutare overnight and then get a bus to Ken and Polly's the following morning, where they can take care of him properly. Joe doesn't have sufficient cash on him, so I put the bill for his room on my dad's credit card, which this time, I have with his permission, for use in emergencies. I decide that this qualifies.

• • •

Some time later, I go to the police station to pay my fine. I am received with great good humour by a senior police officer, who takes my fine and stamps my admission of guilt form, before advising me that in future, if I see the police approaching the bottle store, I should hide my bottle or just run away.

He shakes my hand as I leave, still chuckling at the curiousness of this Englishman who chooses to teach at a school way out in the rural areas and doesn't have the basic common sense to run away from the law.

17

DEPUTY HEAD TEACHER

Mr Manyumwa comes to our house after lessons one afternoon in our second week, while Joe is still recovering in Marondera. He has an important issue to discuss with us. The Ministry of Education has informed him that they cannot provide a headteacher for a secondary school with only one year of entry. 'Therefore,' he says, 'one of you will have to be the headteacher and one of you the deputy.' For reasons of bureaucratic influence, it is apparently important to have both, notwithstanding that the school currently has a grand total of three teachers.

Nevertheless, Mr Manyumwa has some good news: the Ministry has agreed to provide us with two Zimbabwean teachers who will help reduce the strain of our teaching schedule immensely. Neither of us wishes to take on the responsibility of running a school when we have no qualifications even to teach in it, so after Mr Manyumwa leaves us, Alan and I toss a coin to determine who will take on the role, although, as he is a little older and definitely wiser, he is the obvious choice to take charge. Happily for the school, I win the coin toss, thereby escaping the poison chalice, and Alan is duly appointed acting headteacher, with me as his deputy. No one is ever quite clear as to the responsibilities of the deputy headteacher and how they differ from that of an ordinary teacher, but, critically, the title comes with an inkpad and a deputy head-teacher's stamp, and that is real power in 1980s Zimbabwe.

In due course, the arrival of the two Zimbabwean teachers is a massive relief. With five of us, we no longer have to teach a full timetable, and now the pupils will have the novel experience of being taught by two teachers who are actually qualified for the job. It is certainly to be hoped that their ability to teach Shona and agriculture is significantly greater than ours. We wonder why one of them is not appointed as the acting head, but we are told that no Zimbabwean teacher will take on the role because while it comes with extra responsibility, it does not come with additional pay.

The administration of the school is certainly not a small undertaking. Although we have only one year of entry, we have to face the same bureaucratic hurdles of other schools: the lack of books and equipment, the necessary engagement with both the Ministry of Education and the Anglican diocesan education authorities, and, last but not least, the delicate and complex issue of getting paid. For reasons I have never entirely understood, despite our lack of teaching qualifications we are here not as volunteers but as fully paid teaching staff on the payroll of the government of Zimbabwe. At least, in theory we are, but the practice of actually paying us appears considerably less compelling to the authorities than the theory.

In addition, there is a school that needs to be built, which necessitates Alan attending various conferences and meetings around Manicaland. The most important feature of which is the construction of new drop latrines, an urgent matter to ensure that the primary school toilets are not overwhelmed.

The issue of books and equipment is addressed by two routes, both involving our parents. Tim West, Joe's father, comes out to visit us in February, by which time Joe is fully restored to health and back with us, although it is never fully clear exactly what has caused his illness. Tim has a recent connection to the country, having played a cold-hearted security policeman in *Cry Freedom*, Richard Attenborough's film about the banned South African journalist Donald Woods, which was mostly filmed in Zimbabwe, some of it here in Mutare. As a result, he has formed a great affection for the place.

His visit is welcome for two reasons in particular: firstly because he is a warm and generous and funny man who takes an interest in all of us and is kind enough to stand us dinner at the Manica Hotel on a number of occasions, and secondly because he is concerned about the school and determined to help us out.

On the day he is due to return to the UK, he swings by the school on his way back to Harare. He has spent the morning at the Ministry of Education offices in Mutare, wrangling with officials for books for the school, and he has had some success. His hire car is loaded up with boxes of books, which are delightedly received by the students.

The second route is via my own parents. One of my tasks is to teach religious education. In one of my early lessons, as I try to teach the rudiments of St Mark's gospel from my battered King James Bible, one of the brightest and most engaging of our pupils, Simon Muchena, sticks up his hand in response to a question I have posed.

I duly call him, delighted by his enthusiasm. He stands, but instead of addressing the question, he looks directly at me and says, 'Sir, when you came to this country, we had our land and you had your Bibles. Now you have our land and we have your Bibles.'

I am a little taken aback by this. It is clearly a mantra that Simon has picked up from someone and is repeating, but he is doing so with considerable passion and conviction.

Of course, his premise is not strictly accurate. In the first instance, the real problem we both face is not that Simon and his fellow pupils have a surfeit of Bibles, but precisely that he doesn't have a Bible and nor do any of his fellow students. However, this seems a pedantic point to make, so instead I make a more pedantic one, pointing out that as I have only been in the country a few weeks and self-evidently still retain my Bible, this is an unjust charge to lay at my door. He redirects the charge to my father and grandfather, still not technically accurate, but I take his point and acknowledge the importance of his argument. Inwardly I am delighted by his willingness to challenge me. It's clear he is going to be one of our star pupils.

Simon Muchena's intervention underlines to me our continuing lack of books. Despite Tim West's helpful engagement with the Ministry in Mutare, which has provided us with some key textbooks, we are still very short in a number of areas. My dad is a clergyman, the Rector of St Bride's Church in Fleet Street, and I think it is time for his congregation to show some Christian charity, so I write to my parents to ask for help.

I tell them how kind and generous everyone has been to us, despite their lack of resources, and that we want to reciprocate. To date we have been buying things like science equipment and books out of our own money, but as we are yet to be paid, this is getting difficult. In particular, I highlight the fact that I am trying to teach St Mark's gospel and we have only two Bibles in the whole of the secondary school.

The following Sunday, my father gets up in his pulpit and tells his congregation that he is sure they will be as alarmed as he is to learn that his son – who as they know is not notably theologically accomplished – is currently responsible for the religious education of 140 young Zimbabweans. He fears that their alarm can only grow when they learn, furthermore, that his son is attempting this feat without any Bibles for his students. He implores them to help address this grave situation.

His appeal strikes a chord. The collective horror of the congregation at the idea that I should be responsible for anyone's religious education, let alone that I should be discharging that responsibility Bible-less, unlocks their generosity, and the money starts to flow in. My father forges a connection with an educational bookseller in Harare, and books and scientific equipment begin to arrive.

Even more importantly, he establishes a connection between St Bride's Church and St James Secondary School, Zongoro, which over the years will contribute to the education of scores of children as well as the construction and electrification of the school and the teachers' houses. Despite all the trials and tribulations that Zimbabwe has been through, the connection between St Bride's Church in Fleet Street and St James School in Zongoro endures.

18

FRIENDSHIPS AND PARTINGS

Baba Mwashita is the owner of the grocery store, which is just down the track from the bottle store. These are the two stores around which life revolves.

Baba Mwashita is a portly, prosperous-looking gentleman. His wife Mama Mwashita is, by contrast, slim and defined. Both are warm and welcoming to us. It is they who donate provisions to us in our first days. When we visit the store to thank them, Mama Mwashita tells us that her son is living in England and that while we are here in Zongoro, we are her children. Baba Mwashita nods sagely in affirmation.

I love this natural warmth and kindness. This immediate care for strangers despite them coming from thousands of miles away, despite all the differences of race and culture, despite the fact that until eight years ago, boys of a similar age and similar skin tone were bringing fear to this area as they tried to maintain racial supremacy through wanton violence.

Baba Mwashita is a figure in the community, and whenever we visit the store he is ready to share his wisdom and provide us with any advice we need. After school, I often find myself chatting with him on the veranda of his shop. Mama Mwashita is always eager to know how we are getting on, whether we have all we need, and keen to talk about England and her son.

Baba Mwashita is one of our few male acquaintances who does not attend the bottle store. He is a respectable man, a churchwarden and the primary school committee secretary. And, what's more, his wife is a formidable woman. These factors combine to explain his absence.

The local reverend, however, is less circumspect when it comes to frequenting our drinking spot. Perhaps he has decided that to do his job properly he needs to come to where us sinners are to be found. Certainly, he takes this ministration to the fallen seriously, for he is a regular visitor to the bottle store, although a less welcome one than Baba Mwashita would have been.

Since he has discovered that my father is a clergyman, and particularly since he has discovered that his congregation is willing to part with its money to help the school, the rotund reverend has been a constant thorn in my side. He believes that St Bride's should help him in his ministry. His first proposal is that they should provide him with a Land Rover. He not unreasonably makes the point that his work involves ministering to the faithful throughout a wide area and that without a vehicle his work is hampered.

I sympathise but explain that while the congregants of St Bride's may be willing to raise funds for children's education, I am less convinced that providing the reverend with a vehicle will be topmost of their priorities. The reverend listens gravely and a little sulkily and then he drops his bid for funds to less ambitious levels – what about two new chalices for the church? Again, I am unconvinced. But the reverend is one of those people who once you get stuck with him in a bar, you are lost. No one will come to your rescue, lest they become embroiled in his demands or subject to his admonitions.

After a few bottles of beer, his demands become more insistent and irritating. On one occasion, to distract him from his regular diatribe, I ask him about the curious habit of the schoolchildren. At midday every school day, the giant metal triangle is struck and immediately the students, without any instruction, push back their chairs and start reciting a prayer. The first time this happened, I was a little alarmed. I was in the middle of teaching a geography lesson, deep into the compelling subject of contour lines, when suddenly, despite the fact that I was in mid-flow, in unison, my class pushed back their chairs, stood up and started chanting.

I stood there by my desk astonished as the recitation went on. When they had completed it, they all sat down as abruptly as they had got to their feet. I asked them what this was and they told me it was a prayer they had said at midday every day since the first days in primary school. I at first imagined it was a Shona prayer, but as the days went on and I listened in a state of lesser astonishment, what I heard did not sound like Shona. The first line sounded like they were saying, 'Cassia Maria' – could I be mishearing 'ave' as 'cassia'? Surely they were not reciting the Hail Mary in Latin, here in a classroom, at an Anglican school, in the middle of the African bush? I was transfixed by this idea; it seemed like an amazing tradition, and I wondered where it had come from.

And so, desperate to distract the reverend from his supplications for Land Rovers and chalices, I asked him. He looked alarmed, as if the school had been caught out doing something wrong. He said he would stop it at once.

I remonstrated with him. I told him it was a great tradition and he shouldn't stop it. But he wasn't listening. He paused to ask me to buy him another beer, which I did, hoping it would mollify him; it did not. He simply warmed to his decision, his words becoming ever more passionate and more slurred, before he finally slammed his finished beer bottle down on the bar and stumbled out into the night. I was left forlorn that I had ever raised the subject.

Two days later, at midday, the huge metal triangle went un-rung, the prayers unsaid. I was horrified. I had ended a tradition that, who knows, may have gone back to the founding of the primary school in the 1920s. I went to see Mr Manyumwa, demanding that the prayers be reinstituted but, while sympathetic, he could not help. He reminded me that this was a spiritual matter and his authority merely temporal. The reverend was the man who had to be convinced.

At the next opportunity, I collared him. He listened to me carefully, but he was immovable. Then he started talking about his Land Rover again and I got the distinct impression that the only way the prayers would be heard again at St James School, Zongoro, was if the reverend took possession of the vehicle he so craved. As this was beyond my ability to achieve, I knew then and there that a quirky but wonderful tradition had just died at my hand.

●   ●   ●

One Saturday in early March, Alan, Joe and I trek into Mutare for some decent food. On our way home, we get a lift in the back of a pick-up truck, which is waved down near the hospital, on its route out of town, by the rotund figure of the reverend, who hauls himself into the back to join us. The reverend is sweating but sombre. He has come from visiting Baba Mwashita, who was taken to the hospital in the night, and he is returning with the news that Baba Mwashita has died. We are all shocked. Just yesterday, we had stood and talked with him at the door to his shop, and now he is dead.

When we arrive at Manica Bridge, just a few kilometres short of Zongoro, the large priest disembarks with a sprightliness that is usually alien to him; he is keen to make a hasty exit, it seems. As soon as he is safely down on the ground, he leans into the pick-up and tells us that we must pass on the news to Mama Mwashita that her husband is dead.

Alan argues with him, telling him this is not appropriate. This of all jobs is surely one for the reverend and most certainly not for three English boys. But the priest, though he looks shamefaced, is hurrying away. I call after him rudely, 'This is your job. You can't abdicate it to someone else.' If he hears me, he does not acknowledge it.

The pick-up truck pulls back on to the road and we head towards Zongoro, each of us furious and fearful about how we will break the news to the Mwashita family. In the end, we don't have to worry. The driver of the pick-up, who obviously has a greater sense of responsibility than the priest, takes on the difficult task himself. As soon as he pulls up, he gets out of the driver's cab and starts to walk towards the store to break the sad news. There must have been something about the way he carried himself, or just that fact that he was stopping and getting out, that made clear to the family the news that was about to be broken, because before the driver has said a word, Mama Mwashita emerges from the store, pauses a moment and then utters an ear-splitting scream of grief. Two women – her daughters? – hold on to her arms as she cries out, struggling and trying to throw herself to the floor, and all around her, the village erupts in despairing shouts and cries.

Baba Mwashita's body is brought the following day to lie in the church. I sit in my classroom marking books, with heavy rain hammering on the corrugated asbestos roof above me and thunder echoing around the hills, thinking of the shopkeeper, lying just a few yards away in the church. Although I have known the man only a matter of months, I feel a real sadness that he is gone.

A few days later, we all climb the steep paths to his home village, 5km into the hills behind his grocery shop. It is a sweltering day and we walk in a group with other teachers from the school. We arrive at the top of a hill, in an area of ground surrounded by maize fields, where the ceremonies are to take place. There is a sea of people already assembled, decked out in a plethora of colours: the blues and whites of the church uniforms, the loud colours of traditional shirts, and alongside these vibrant shades, the black and white of the clergy and the sombre suits of teachers and officials. We are told that a minister in the President's office is in attendance, such is the stature of this old man.

We find a space on a rise in the land where we can look down over the heads of the mass of people to where Baba Mwashita's coffin lies under a canopy, surrounded by his family and a coterie of ministers and other dignitaries. They speak in Shona, but their meaning is clear and the sentiments universal.

When the speeches are over, we line up to file past the coffin. As we get closer, it becomes clear that the coffin is open and as people are passing, they bend to kiss Baba Mwashita's temple. Joe realises this first and whispers urgently that he can't do it. Alan whispers back, equally urgently, that we have to, that not to do so would be utter disrespect. I have some sympathy for Joe: the prospect is not appealing to me either, not least because Baba Mwashita's body, to my certain knowledge, has now been three days in the heat of the bush. But Alan is right: given all Baba Mwashita's kindness, we cannot show disrespect in any way. When it comes to my turn, I lean into the coffin and brush my lips against his forehead. It feels cold and clammy, but otherwise there is nothing untoward. Joe follows me and, notwithstanding his misgivings, he, like me, overcomes them.

After we have shown our respects, we follow the throng of people and find ourselves standing amidst tall maize plants at the edge of a field that slopes upward. In front of us is the grave that has been prepared for Baba Mwashita's body. After all have paid their respects, the coffin is sealed and brought to the grave, and amidst the singing and the tears it is lowered into the ground, and the earth replaced. As the headstone is moved into place, the rain begins to fall, at first in large, single drops and then more persistently, a deluge of soft, warm tears mourning the dead, giving life to the corn.

• • •

One Saturday, we invite Mandi, his wife Alice and their two children, Leslie and Bridget, to lunch at ours. This is a momentous event in the de Saram–West–Oates household, the first social engagement we have hosted. It is made possible by the fact that we have purchased between us the great luxury of a two-ring Calor gas stove, and the community has provided us with a solid dining room table and two benches, made by the local carpenter.

Mandi and Alice are our closest friends in the community. We know Mandi best, because he is our companion of bottle store days and he has proved his care for us by remaining with us to face the music at the time of the police raid. Alice, his wife, is also a primary school teacher and is warm and welcoming to us, although I get the impression that she regards all of us, Mandi included, as slightly wayward children, sometimes to be indulged but always to be guided.

Alan and Joe often travel at weekends, but I tend to remain home, mainly because I am short of cash, and as a result I have got to know Mandi and Alice well and benefited often from their hospitality.

This Saturday lunchtime, Morgan, Alice and the children arrive at our house dressed in their best clothes, as I have agreed that I will do a photoshoot of the family together after lunch. We have swept and tidied the house and it is looking as spick and span as it is ever likely to. Alan is in charge of the cooking and is making a vegetable stew with rice. He is not happy with the blandness of his culinary offering, so he is busy adding spices to it while Joe and I entertain the family.

I have a bottle of champagne, which my friend Nicky gave me as a leaving present, and I crack it open in honour of the occasion. It has a picture of Charles and Diana on it, commemorating their wedding, which I don't think anything of at the time, but Mandi and Alice are interested in the royal couple, so after we have drunk it I give them the empty bottle as a memento, which they later use as a candleholder in their home.

Finally, Alan serves up the food. We all tuck in eagerly, but it is immediately clear that he has overdone the spices. The food is burning hot, almost inedible for adults, let alone children. Alan immediately apologises and urges the family not to eat it, he will make something else. But whether out of politeness or hunger, Mandi and Alice insist that the food is great and tuck into it. The children are not so sure, so Alice urges them on. Leslie, the older of the two, gives his mother a look that says, 'Are you nuts?' Alice gives a look back that says, 'Are you nuts enough to defy me?' And the children decide they are not and try to shovel this strange food into their mouths.

Their eyes are streaming and the youngest starts to hiccup, then suddenly slides off the bench, toddles a few paces across the floor to the door and, before her parents can ask her what she is doing, involuntarily pees on the hard, concrete floor. Mandi and Alice are horrified and so are we – not by what their youngest has done, but by the fact that we are the cause of it.

The champagne is probably wasted as an accompaniment to such a fiery concoction. And this is a shame because it turns out that it is very good champagne indeed. A year or so after I get back from Zimbabwe, Nicky and I are having a drink and he asks me urgently whether I still have the bottle. It seems like an odd question and I tell him no, it has been drunk. And then he asks me an odder one. 'Do you still have the empty bottle?'

I explain cautiously that I gave it away. It is clear that this is not a popular answer. 'Can you get it back?' he asks desperately.

I tell him that I doubt it because the last time I saw the bottle, it was being used as a candleholder in a house in rural Zimbabwe. But in any case, I ask, why is he so desperate for it?

So, Nicky explains. It turns out that I am not the only person who has removed things from their father without his permission. His generous leaving present to me was in fact an involuntary gift of his father. Nicky had procured it from his dad's wine cellar not realising its value and clearly without his permission. His father has now noticed its absence, and Nicky is in a tricky situation. It seems that it was a limited-edition bottle given to him personally by the royal couple, and as such it is of significant value to him sentimentally and possibly financially.

I contact Mandi to ask him if he still has it, not so much to procure its return, which seems impractical, but to alert him to its value. It seems, however, that when they moved into town, they parted company with it, I imagine gifting it to someone else, because few things that can serve a further purpose are thrown away in Zimbabwe. I cherish the hope that somewhere out there in the African bush that bottle is still serving as a candleholder, with the Prince's and Princess's faces gazing out on a Zimbabwean family as they go about their lives.

The lunch debacle could have been the end of our relationship with Mandi and Alice. Traumatised by our culinary haplessness and embarrassed by the peeing incident, it would have been hard to blame them if they had kept their distance. But in fact it strengthened our relationship, and it wasn't long before it was a subject of hilarity between us, particularly after a few beers at the bottle store. Though, wisely, the family never ate with us again.

19

APARTHEID SOUTH AFRICA

In no time, it seems the term is coming to an end and stretching ahead of us is the long Easter break. Towards the end of term, one of our pupils approaches me and asks if I will be travelling during the school holidays and if so whether I could visit his father in South Africa, whom he has not seen for many years. It seems impossible to refuse this request, although I have no concept of how far Johannesburg is, nor any real understanding of the volatile state South Africa is in.

A day or so after term ends, Alan, Joe and I set off for Harare. The first night, we meet up with a number of the rest of the SPW gang and spend a night drinking at an apartment owned by a relative of one of our fellow teachers. It's good to see the other guys, but I am keen to set off exploring Zimbabwe.

I get the train the following evening to Bulawayo, a gruelling eight hours to travel the 486km route, although at an average of 60km per hour, that's not bad; today, the journey regularly takes at least ten hours. I arrive around nine in the morning and kill time exploring the broad, handsome streets of Bulawayo. The city hall is gleaming white and bedecked with a huge banner celebrating the eighth anniversary of the end of white minority rule. Soon, it's time to catch the afternoon train on the next stage of my journey to South Africa, which will take me to Gaborone in Botswana via Francistown.

I arrive in Gaborone just before six in the morning and a friendly passenger gives me a lift into town. I repair to a seedy café for breakfast, which seems to be the only place open, and am shortly challenged to a game of table football by two young men who seem like they have not slept that night. I suspect a hustle, but you never know, perhaps they are just surprised at the sight of this white guy in their café and want to entertain him. I accept their challenge, not least because I worry about their reaction if I refuse, conscious that I am on my own in a city I don't know.

Sure enough, I win the game against my first opponent easily, the second then challenges me and again I win, although not quite so easily, and now the hustle begins. Bets are laid on the next game, which again I prevail in, and so on until I reach the limit of the money I have decided I am willing to be hustled out of, and I call time, saying I have to go but that as I won't take the challenge any further, I will pay out the bet. They accept the pay-out, but then my second challenger says, 'OK, but one last game – not for money, just for fun.'

I accept and he thrashes me 10–0. He grins broadly and reaches out his hand. 'You see!' he says and his friend laughs and slaps me on the back. I leave relieved that I have managed to exit with everyone's honour still intact.

I spend the morning in Gaborone, a small, pleasant town consisting principally of a wide thoroughfare with the National Assembly and government ministries at one end and Gaborone City Hall at the other, the kilometre or so between them populated by shopping malls and hotels. After collecting some money at the bank, I set off to hitchhike the 20km or so to the border with the Republic of South Africa.

A local goes out of his way to drop me at the border post and I progress the final few hundred metres to the RSA side on foot and get in line to have my passport stamped. The South African border official is black, which surprises me, but is perhaps supposed to indicate to visitors that South Africa is a more racially harmonious place than they might imagine it to be – which, of course, it isn't.

Just as the border guard is about to bring his stamp down in my passport, the man behind me calls out sharply, 'No, man!' As he does so, his hand shoots out from behind me to cover the passport page about to be stamped. 'You mustn't put an SA stamp in his passport, it will cause him all sorts of trouble. Rather, stamp it on a piece of paper.'

The border guard looks irritated at this unsolicited intervention in his work, but he complies, stamping a piece of paper which he secures into my passport with a paper clip and a warning. 'You must not lose this paper. They will want to see it when you leave. This is very important.'

And then, satisfied that I have understood, he hands me a small booklet on life in SA, a pocket-sized propaganda piece, attempting to convince visitors that SA is a haven of peace and racial harmony beside the chaos and disorder of its neighbours. The current state of emergency across the country tells a different story.

The man who has rescued me from the fate of an SA stamp in my passport is called Dave. He is a diamond merchant in his twenties who spends the week working in Botswana, returning at the weekend to his Afrikaans girlfriend, with whom he lives in Hillbrow, then an upmarket liberal district of Johannesburg, where the Group Areas Act, the law that underpins racial segregation in South Africa, has begun to fray at the edges.

Dave offers me a lift to Johannesburg, and somewhere along the road he stops to buy biltong and a case of Castle Beer, which we drink along the way. I don't know if it occurs to me that it is stupid and dangerous to sit in a car barrelling along the road to Johannesburg with a driver who is knocking back cans of lager as we go, but if it does, I decide to overlook it. Dave asks me about my plans in South Africa, and I tell him

I haven't decided definitely but I think I might pop down to Cape Town for a day and that I need to visit the father of my student. He laughs at the idea of my day trip to Cape Town.

'Do you have any idea how far Cape Town is from Johannesburg?' he asks, incredulous.

I confess that I don't. 'It's a fokken long way, that's how far. It's not a day trip, for sure.' Then he asks me where my student's father lives. I search out the slip of paper with his address and read it to him. This occasions another outburst, even more incredulous than the last. 'Jeez, man, you can't just walk into a black township. For a start you need a permit from the Bantu Affairs people, and then if you manage to get that and get to the township, they'll kill you, man.'

I discount the last warning. I have had similar from whites when hitchhiking, who have almost refused to let me out of their cars when I have asked them to drop me at Zongoro. Nevertheless, I concede to myself, South Africa is not Zimbabwe.

By the time we conclude the journey four or five hours later, remarkably still alive, we have consumed a lot of beer and Dave has offered me a place to stay for the night.

When we arrive at the apartment, our reception by Dave's girlfriend is much as might be expected. At first, she just appears astonished that he has come home drunk with a drunk house guest after a week away, but rapidly astonishment turns to anger. After giving me the coldest of quarter-hearted welcomes, she speaks sharply to Dave in Afrikaans and the two of them retire to the bedroom, where the full power of the Afrikaans language is detonated on Dave, in an explosion of anger that it is impossible not to follow, even though the language is foreign.

At first Dave attempts to argue back, but he is overwhelmed by the invective directed at him and his voice rapidly subsides and disappears from the exchange, save for a few subdued mutters of apology and abasement. I sit uncomfortably in their sitting room as the argument rumbles on in the bedroom. I would leave if I could, but I am drunk, it is late, and I have nowhere else to stay.

Eventually, Dave emerges chastened from the bedroom. His girlfriend does not. 'Come, man. Let's get something to eat.'

As soon as we are back on the street, I apologise profusely to him that I am the cause of such angst between him and his girlfriend. He waves them away. 'No, man, it's my fault. I should have known. But hey, that was a moerse row, no?'

Then he shakes off his subdued tone altogether and drapes his arm around my shoulder: 'Ons is twee dronkies!'

And he laughs uproariously at this deeply insightful observation.

After we have eaten, we head back to the apartment. By this time it is late, and we are even drunker. Happily, when we get back, there is no sign of his girlfriend, who seems to have retired to bed.

Despite my drunken state, or because of it, I decide it is a good idea to call my parents. So I ask Dave if I can make a reverse-charge call and get them to call me back. I duly place the call, but when they ring back and I go to pick up the phone, he motions me away and lifts the receiver himself. In response to my parents' request to speak to me, he drops into a strong Afrikaans accent: 'Nee, he is in die gaol!'

Dave thinks this is uproariously funny. It's fair to say my parents do not. Even I have my doubts. Dave hands the receiver to me, looking a little sullen at his under-appreciated humour.

I have no recollection of the conversation that I had with my parents, but I know it didn't go well. I then compounded their concern by failing to make contact with them again for another month, by which time they were desperate with worry that their son was wandering around southern Africa, drunk and in the company of who knows whom. This occasioned them to call Ken and Polly to express their concerns, a decision for which I later chastised them, in an imperious letter which is physically embarrassing to read today.

I slept a drunken slumber on the sofa that night and was woken early by Dave. 'Sorry, sorry, man, but you need to get up. We've got to go.'

He keeps his voice low, but his tone leaves no doubt that this is not a discussion. I pull on my clothes, clean my teeth and am hurried out of the apartment. Dave keeps repeating his apologies, but he says his girlfriend is too angry for me to be there when she gets up. He says he will drive me to a place where I can get a lift to Pretoria and, hungover like hell, he drives me a few kilometres out of the city and drops me on the side of the motorway, uttering further apologies as he takes his leave of me.

It is only later that I realise what a strange place this is for him to leave me. Not just because he has dropped me on the wrong side of the road, which means I will have to cross eight lanes of motorway carriageway to get myself in a position to hitch to Pretoria, but because there is a state of emergency in the country and standing alone beside a road is not necessarily the safest thing to do, as the truck driver who eventually picks me up is keen to underline. I sit in the cab between the driver and another guy, who I take to be his assistant. The driver is coloured, in South African parlance, and his assistant black – in apartheid South Africa, the Population Registration Act has divided humanity into four main race groups: white, black, coloured and Indian, each with sharply differing rights and privileges, including which jobs are open to them. It's not by chance, therefore, that the driver and his assistant have their respective roles. Nothing is by chance in apartheid South Africa.

They chat in a friendly way as we drive the 60km or so to Pretoria and then they go out of the way to leave me somewhere safer than they found me, dropping me just off the freeway where it runs into Pretorius Street, before continuing their journey north.

• • •

Pretoria in 1988 is an Afrikaans town, a white Afrikaans town; uptight, unwelcoming and super-charged with hostility. You can measure the hatred like humidity.

Hungover and depressed after the drunken night before, and cringing at the memory of that call to my parents, I am ill equipped to deal with Pretoria's Calvinist model of white supremacy.

At the Wimpy Bar, where I stop to grab some sustenance, all the tables in the outside area are taken. I spy an elderly couple at a table who are finishing up their meal. There is some space at their table, and they are chatting amiably to one another, looking like they might be someone's favourite grandparents. So I walk over to them and ask them politely, 'Would you mind if I sit with you at your table?'

The old man looks up from his conversation with his wife, his friendly eyes now black and cold, and for a moment he says nothing and then, simply, in harsh, accented English: 'I would rather sit with a kaffir than an Englishman!'

I stand there bewildered, holding my tray, my brain struggling to process his statement, which is so at odds with the demeanour of the two of them before I opened my mouth.

His wife looks uncomfortable but no less hostile. She says something to the man in Afrikaans and he shrugs and looks away from me. 'Kom,' he says to his wife. And they both get up and push past me, never varying the intense hostility with which they regard me.

I remain standing there a minute after they have gone, astonished and uncomprehending of what has happened. Then I sit at the vacated table. The hangover headache throbs inside my temples. I feel completely worn out and dispirited and, in the aftermath of this unexpected animosity, tears prick my eyes.

Later, I am to learn about the century-old hostility between the Afrikaans and British. About the Anglo-Boer War and particularly about the women and children taken from their homes by the British and concentrated into camps where they died in their thousands, of disease and malnourishment. The intention: to deny their menfolk the ability to continue the fight; the outcome: a deep and bitter anger in the Afrikaans people towards the British victors. It's not something they talked about much in my history lessons about the Boer War. Funny, that.

After I have eaten, I decide I will explore the city centre a little and I set out aimlessly down Pretorius Street. It is hot and my backpack is heavy, so, seeing a small park ahead, I decide that perhaps it would be worth stopping and making a plan before wandering further without objective. I cross the road to the park and search out a bench to sit on. As I lower my backpack from my back, I notice that the plaque on the back of the bench, which I had taken to be the sort of dedication to a deceased relative that is common in the UK, is something very different.

'Slegs Blankes', it reads, and underneath, the chilling English translation. 'Whites Only'.

I stand there and read it over again. I have seen these signs on TV news programmes about apartheid South Africa, but to be confronted directly with this banal but grotesque expression of racial segregation is something quite different. A shiver runs through me. I cannot sit there. I can't be a part of this, however passively. And so, although I know it is absurd and will make no difference to anyone, I back away from the bench, my eyes still transfixed by those four words, and then I stride away across the park to a point towards the middle, furthest away from any of the benches where I sit down cross-legged on the ground and try to process this fucked-up place.

Eventually, I decide it is beyond processing and I reach into my bag and fetch out my much-thumbed travel bible, *Africa on a Shoestring*, to check out the area. The first thing I need to do is find some cheap accommodation, so that I can dump my backpack and walk around a bit less encumbered.

I find an entry that looks OK about a ten-minute walk out of the city centre, but when I get there they tell me they are full and direct me to what I think at first is a cheap boarding house a few blocks away. After I check in, surprised to be asked how many hours I want the room for (all night, I say, perplexed and not yet fully comprehending), I discover it to be an incongruous cross between an old people's home and a brothel. I go up to my room and lie down on the narrow single bed with its fraying quilt and its grey sheets and decide to try to sleep off my hangover.

It's early evening when I awake, feeling marginally recovered. The room is hot and stuffy, so I get up and go downstairs. I peer into the lounge, which is populated entirely by old people, whom I do not fancy engaging with after my morning's encounter. Instead I think I will go in search of a cinema to kill some time.

I set out on foot back towards the city centre. On the way, I manage to lose myself and, seeing a group of three or four white boys of around my age at a street corner, I approach them to ask the way. They don't reply to me, but one of them speaks loudly to the other in Afrikaans. They both laugh and then the first one pushes me on the shoulder, continuing to speak Afrikaans in a mocking, interrogatory tone. Another pushes my shoulder from behind. The adrenalin kicks in and I lash out wildly in defence, and then I run for it as fast as I can, sprinting down the dark streets. The boys don't make chase. It seems they have had their fun.

By now I am completely lost but I am terrified of asking anybody on the street for directions, my encounters with locals having so far proved almost 100 per cent hostile. So I walk on, hoping I am heading back in the general direction of the boarding house, my cinema plans now discarded. I come across a cheap-looking Italian trattoria and decide this is as good a place as any to stop and ask for directions and get something to eat. Here, they are friendly and kind, and after a bowl of spaghetti, I am directed back to the boarding house, which it turns out is just a block or two away. I get into bed, although it is only around 9 p.m., and I sleep fitfully until the early morning.

I wake resolved that I have had more than my fill with apartheid South Africa. There is a bus in the evening which will take me to the Beitbridge border crossing and back into Zimbabwe. I kill time by visiting the Union buildings and St Alban's Anglican Cathedral, but most of the time I sit at the outside table of a café and read. The streets are quiet and sullen. A typical Sunday in Calvinist Pretoria.

Later, I try to get a local bus to the railway station, where the Beitbridge bus leaves from. But I am shooed away from the bus stop, which is apparently for non-whites only – 'Slegs nie blankes,' I am harshly instructed. In any case, there is no sign of a bus, so I decide to walk instead. It's dark by the time I reach the station and set about finding the place I must catch the bus from. The station is a handsome building, made ugly by the proliferation of apartheid instructions that seem to be affixed to every door and every bench.

I don't know whether I wait in the wrong place or whether the Beitbridge bus does not run on a Sunday, but by ten o'clock it's clear, even to a man of my Zimbabwe-learnt bus-waiting patience, that it ain't coming. It is too late to go and find accommodation on a Sunday night in Pretoria and, in any case, I don't fancy returning to the brothel/boarding house/old people's home, so I decide I will sleep here. I have my sleeping bag to keep me warm against the chill – it's not yet winter, but a night outside on the high veldt in April is not warm – and the bench of the bus shelter will have to serve as a bed.

I manage to doze off, but I wake an hour or so later from the cold. A few minutes afterwards, I see someone approaching in the uniform of the South African Defence Force. He is about my age and he has an uncanny resemblance to Will. He has missed his rendezvous with the unit he is supposed to be joining and now he is stuck, like me, in a city he doesn't know. We get chatting, and he tells me a bit about himself and his life in a small town to the north. He seems like a decent sort of person, eager to be friendly. Then we talk about where he is going.

He is a national serviceman, a conscript soldier on his way to the Angolan border, where SWAPO guerrilla forces are fighting for Namibian independence against the South African apartheid regime, which occupies and administers their country.

I express my horror that the government can force him as a conscript to go and fight their unjust wars. But he stops me cold.

'It's not like that, man. I want to go. If you believe in something, you must defend it. I believe in my country, so I must kill me as many Swaps as I can.'

He asserts this boldly but at the same time defensively. In the tone of a people who are sure they are right and so baffled and angered to find that they stand condemned by the world.

His words shock me, but most of all what shocks me is the realisation that he is not a monster; he is just another boy. I could have been him, except that he has grown up in the grotesque apartheid system, which has conditioned him to fear and hate those whom he does not know.

At some point he leaves, realising we have reached a point of mutual incomprehension. When the morning light comes, I get up and go in search of something to eat.

On Monday night, I finally manage to leave South Africa. This time I make sure of the bus timetable and book a ticket in advance. We leave Pretoria Railway Station around eight-thirty and trundle through the night, north through the Transvaal, to the border with Zimbabwe. I sit in a window seat, staring out into the darkness of South Africa.

The bus drops us off on the South African side of the Beitbridge border soon after sunrise and we proceed through the South African and Zimbabwean border checks on foot. As I board a bus on the Zimbabwe side which will take me on the first part of my journey back to the school, I feel immense relief to be back on Zimbabwe soil. I still have my notebook from that time, in which, after crossing the border, I wrote: 'I will never return to South Africa unless I can return to a free South Africa. A South Africa that has freed the blacks from oppression and hopelessness but also a South Africa that has freed the whites from their hatred and their fear.'

In 1988, that looked a long way off.

Back then, if you had tried telling the passengers of that bus that in two years' time P. W. Botha would be gone from the presidency, Nelson Mandela would be freed from jail and the ANC would be negotiating the end of apartheid with the National Party, they would have thought you were stark staring crazy and most likely sought urgent medical assistance.

It was simply an unimaginable thought. The only way it seemed that freedom would come to South Africa was via a protracted and bitter race war. For all the problems South Africa faces today, its transformation from apartheid state to multiracial democracy was a miracle.

My experience in apartheid South Africa left an indelible mark on me. When I returned to the UK, I immediately got involved with the anti-apartheid movement. It was the first society I joined at university, and when I was in London I would on occasion wander up from our home in Fleet Street to Trafalgar Square to sit on the upturned milk crates which served as seating for the non-stop picket outside the South African Embassy demanding Mandela's release.

The first time I attended, I was handed a signing-in book which had two columns: Name and Organisation. I looked at the names of the two activists manning the picket and saw next to their names the initials RCP and SWP, representing, respectively, the Revolutionary Communist Party and the Socialist Workers Party. I nervously scrawled the initials SLD, for Social and Liberal Democrats, next to my name and handed the book back to one of the picketers, who regarded the entry suspiciously, perhaps suspecting the creation of another rival socialist faction of which he had not previously been aware. He motioned for me to sit between him and his colleague on the milk crates and then he asked me about the initials. My explanation took him and his fellow picketer by surprise: it was clear they had not often encountered members of such a bourgeois party, and for the next few hours that I sat with them, they sought unsuccessfully to win my political soul for their respective and bitterly divided socialist factions. Every so often, when the ache to the bum of sitting on the crates became too intense, we would stand and chant, 'We are here, we are here, until Mandela is free. On this non-stop picket of the em-ba-ssy' a few times before resuming our seats, when they would return to the urgent task of instilling revolutionary consciousness into the bourgeois comrade who had come among them.

• • •

Although I still had a few weeks left of the Easter holidays, I decided to head home to the school before setting out on further adventures, not least because I had contrived to pack a huge backpack full of books and every other item that I thought I might conceivably need when I embarked on my travels at the beginning of the holiday, which had become a complete pain in the arse to carry.

I got back home around lunchtime on a Tuesday and, after a quick bite to eat, set about washing my clothes in the large plastic pink tub we had purchased for the purpose. However, when I paused halfway through my washing to reward myself with a cup of tea, I discovered we were out of Calor gas, so I abandoned my clothes in the washtub and left rapidly to try to reach Mutare before the gas store closed. When I returned in the evening, the tub was gone from the veranda and, with it, my clothes, sending me into a momentary panic because the tub had contained the bulk of my wardrobe. However, when I opened the door to the house, I found the clothes inside, washed, dried and ironed and neatly stacked on the table.

I went in search of the pupil who kept a spare house key for us and asked him who was responsible for this kindness. He smiled proudly and said, 'I know you're a busy person, sir, so I did it for you.'

I felt both touched by this thoughtful gesture and also a little guilty, as it was hard to claim I was busy in the middle of the holidays. I told him that he must let me pay him for his efforts, but he resisted every entreaty, insisting that he had just wanted to do something to help.

Throughout my time at Zongoro, I was constantly in receipt of these sorts of acts of kindness and friendship, which sealed my love for the place.

I stayed just two days at the school before setting out again, back on the bus to Masvingo to see Great Zimbabwe. I stayed one night at the Great Zimbabwe Hotel, where I had a tentative arrangement to meet up with Alan, giving me the chance to visit the magnificent remains of the city state, which had flourished here between 1200 and 1500, the centre of a great empire.

I woke early and walked the mile or so from the hotel up to the Great Enclosure as the sun rose. It was a magical morning in which I had the majestic ruins almost entirely to myself. I let my imagination populate the site with the ancestors of the Shona people, going about their business, when the city was the heart of a great empire which held sway across the region. It may have been the effect of the early morning light, but I felt a great sense of calm and spirituality around me, and it remains one of my favourite places in the country.

I waited until lunchtime at the hotel to see if Alan might show up, and then set off for Harare, where I was to catch a train back to Bulawayo before transferring to an ancient steam train to Victoria Falls.

Short of cash as usual, at Bulawayo I bought myself a third-class ticket and settled down on the wooden benches of the third-class carriage as the engine shuddered and strained into motion. An hour or two into the journey, one of my fellow passengers returned from the bar and got chatting to me; he told me he had met a second-class passenger who was also from the UK and teaching near Mutare. His name was Joe. I went to investigate and, sure enough, there he was in the second-class bar. It was great to see him after having been on my own for so long, and we settled down to a few beers and a catch-up, until I was sent packing by an over-attentive ticket inspector.

The train arrived at Victoria Falls Station at about 6 a.m. We walked into town and found a campsite with a range of accommodation from dormitories to small chalets, and then we went in search of the Mosi-oa-Tunya – The Smoke That Thunders – the rather more poetic Zimbabwean name for the breath-taking falls, which David Livingstone named for Queen Victoria, declaring, 'Scenes so lovely must have been gazed upon by angels in their flight.'

Back then, there was no regulation of how you viewed the falls, no walkways or entry fees, just a walk along a path by the side of the gorge. First you heard the thunderous noise, followed by the plumes of spray, and then, turning a bend, you came across this jaw-dropping wonder of thundering, smoking water, a mile wide, hurling itself off the plunging precipice and into the gorge below. Rainbows thrown up by sunshine refracting through the spray criss-crossed the sky as the spray rained down, soaking you to the skin.

I had heard the falls raved about so often that I was sure I would be disappointed by the reality. Instead I was amazed, dumbstruck by the power and the beauty.

I stayed a couple of nights in Victoria Falls with Joe and two other teachers from the SPW scheme, Dave and Alex, both former schoolmates of mine, whom we had met up with at the campsite. Then I took the train back to Bulawayo and, from there, home to Zongoro via Harare to prepare for the new term.

20

FEELING AT HOME

It felt good to be back in Zongoro. By now Morgan and Alice had returned from visiting their families and most of the Zimbabwean teachers had also arrived in advance of the new term.

Life was much easier at the house, too. As time had progressed, our living conditions had improved. Now we had the Calor gas rings, which replaced our rickety old paraffin heater, we could cook food in less than a lifetime. On top of this, and our table and benches, Joe had bought a 'tsotso' or 'small-stick' stove on his weekend travels, a chimney-like structure which concentrated the energy from burning small sticks into a powerful source of heat, capable of heating a large metal pail of water. This was critical for Joe's next invention: a hot shower.

At the side of our house there was a small outbuilding, about two metres high, with an open entrance, rather like a wide sentry box. At the back of this, Joe attached a semi-circular shower rail to the roof and ran a shower curtain – procured from Lord knows where – around it. A wooden pallet was placed on the ground on which to stand when showering.

To take a shower was not the simplest of operations. First, one had to heat the water on the tsotso stove and then heft the heavy pail onto the roof of the outhouse. Once ensconced behind the shower curtain, you reached for a piece of hosepipe which Joe had strapped to the inside of

the bucket and sucked at the pipe to start the syphon effect. This usually involved getting a mouthful of hot, dirty river water in your mouth
which had to be hastily spat out. But then you had hot water showering
down on you from the pipe. It was bliss when it was cascading down
your body, but the experience was sadly short-lived and the effort required to achieve it was such that I kept it as a weekend luxury and most
of the time washed in the freezing water of the river.

There were separate places on the river for washing, one for women
and one for men. The river was down the track from our house, past the
primary school, at the bottom of a steep incline. The men's section was
below a slight fall in the river, hiding it from general view. There was a
big pool at the top and then a further pool below. It was cold at the best
of times – icy when the winter months came – but it was always fresh
and invigorating, a wake-up tonic in the morning which I never regret-
ted afterwards, although, when lying warm in my bed, the prospect of
the freezing river water often seemed less than compelling. If I didn't go
to the river and didn't have time for the rigamarole of the shower, then
I would have to wash with a hand flannel, standing in the startling-pink
plastic bath, a procedure which never left me feeling fully clean and certainly didn't have the invigorating effect that the river provided.

Following Tim West's visit, Joe's mother, Prunella Scales, came out
to see us as well. Like his dad, she was kind and generous with all of us,
procuring a mattress for each of us, so that at last we had something
more than the cold concrete floor to sleep on. That was luxury indeed.
Alan had also secured a subscription to the *Guardian Weekly*, whose
arrival in our post office box in Mutare, printed on airmail paper, was
eagerly anticipated by all of us, giving us a feeling of connection to the
wider world.

As a result of all these improvements, life became more comfortable
and I am struck by how my diary and my letters home reflect a real

sense of happiness and contentment at that time. My weekends, when Alan and Joe were away, were spent reading on our veranda, visiting Mandi and Alice, or playing chess with Eric, a moustachioed Zambian who almost without exception beat me. The chess game out of the way, Eric would turn to his other favourite subject, literature, and share his thoughts on Vonnegut, Miller and Shakespeare, leaving me feeling as lacking in literary knowledge as I was in chess ability – shamefully, I didn't even know who Kurt Vonnegut was until I was schooled by Eric. And then of course there was the bottle store.

Friday night was the big night at the bottle store. The week over, teachers and other locals made a beeline for it. As the sun set, the beers would start to flow, the table football games became ever more intense, and once darkness had fallen, deafening blasts of Zimbabwean music would resound across the bush – the Bhundu Boys, Thomas Mapfumo, Oliver Mtukudzi and often in that year the No. 1 hit 'Ishe Komborera President Mugabe', or 'God Bless Mugabe', which had been sung by Peter Muparutsa and his local band, the RUNN Family, at Mugabe's inauguration as President – not a tune you will hear often now.

In the main bar there would be dancing and shouting, and in the saloon bar store room Mr Manyumwa would hold court, sitting on an upturned Castle beer crate, surrounded attentively and respectfully by the three of us, Mandi, and a middle-aged primary school teacher called Cornelius who Manyumwa had determined was distinguished enough to be invited into the inner sanctum.

Simon Manyumwa's main focus for discussion was what he regarded as the absurd decisions of the Education Minister, Comrade Fay Chung. Fay Chung was an unlikely Zanu-PF minister, a member of what was then a tiny Chinese-Zimbabwean community who, having qualified as a teacher, found she was only able to teach in township schools. Radicalised by what she witnessed in those schools, she ended up in exile teaching in the military camps of the Zimbabwe African National Liberation Army across the border in Mozambique before returning with the triumphant ZANLA forces in 1980.

None of this counts for much with Simon Manyumwa, however, when set against the decrees that are issued from her department. The latest determines that corporal punishment is to be banned from schools, a proposal that Mr Manyumwa at first finds laughable – a person 300km away in Harare is going to dictate what happens in his school? – but as the beers flow, so does the indignation.

He leans forward conspiratorially; we all lean in respectfully. 'Fay Chung, she speaks nonsense!' He hisses and looks to us for a reaction.

Mandi responds first: 'Ah, you are not wrong,' he says gravely. 'Definitely she speaks nonsense.' Mandi leans back, satisfied that his affirmation of the headmaster's point has been sufficiently emphatic. But the headmaster does not share his complacency. 'I would tell her myself. In her ministry. I would tell her to her face. Has anyone ever heard such nonsense?!' Cornelius shakes his head, doubtful that this is even possible.

We remain silent. Alan, Joe and I have had a run-in with Simon over this very issue, refusing to use corporal punishment in our classrooms or to allow anyone else to do so – Simon's proposed compromise. But there is no point arguing with him now. Instead, I mumble excuses and go and join a table football game.

The decree on corporal punishment is not the only thing emanating from the Ministry of Education that is troubling Simon Manyumwa. He is also worried by their decision that there will be no paid headteacher until 1990, when the school will have enrolled pupils in three academic years. As we are due to leave the school at the end of term in August, Simon will have to replace three fifths of the staff and will be lacking a head and deputy head for over a year. Somehow, during a discussion about this predicament, the idea emerges – I am not sure whether from him or from me – that perhaps I would be willing to stay on for an additional year and take on the role of headteacher.

It's a big deal because it would involve deferring my university entrance for a further year, which I am pretty sure won't go down well with my parents. I also worry that I would be lonely with Joe and Alan gone. But as I think it through, I realise that much of my free time is spent with Mandi and Alice and other friends in any case, especially when Joe and Alan are away, so while I know I would miss them a lot, I am confident that I will have plenty of company. In fact, in many ways, the prospect of being in Zongoro on my own is enticing. It will give me an even greater opportunity to feel like a real part of the community and hopefully to learn some more Shona. I ask Mr Manyumwa to let me think about it, and I decide that I will visit Ken and Polly at Peterhouse and seek their advice before sharing the idea with my parents.

That Friday, I finish school at lunchtime and head to the tarmac road and the bus stop. I sit myself under the shade tree, get out my book, currently *Catch-22*, and settle down for what may be a considerable wait for the bus.

I remember that on one of our first nights in the saloon bar of the bottle store, one of us asked Mr Manyumwa and his assembled acolytes if there was somewhere we could get hold of a bus timetable. This was the cause of some of the greatest hilarity ever witnessed in the village. Mr Manyumwa almost fell off his beer crate, such was his comedic delight at the preposterous idea that had been advanced. Eventually, he and his colleagues pulled themselves together and he told us gravely, 'No, there is no such thing as a timetable. They come when they come, and they don't when they don't.'

Today, though, I am lucky. I wait less than half an hour before I hear the rumble of the bus heading down the road towards us. I get off at the junction of the Nyanga road with the main Mutare–Harare road and cross to the stop on the other side of the main road to wait for the Harare bus. When it comes, it is packed with weekend travellers. I squeeze myself into a seat next to an elderly lady and give the afternoon greeting in Shona. She looks surprised and studies me openly, but she responds politely with a slight smile. There is the usual craning of necks among other passengers – a white man on a bus? – as we set off down the road, but before long everyone settles down for the journey. Eventually, we reach the stop for Peterhouse School and I alight from the bus and walk the half-kilometre or so down the road to Ken and Polly's house.

Ken and Polly's home is a sanctuary of good food and wise counsel. Ken is a scholarly, thoughtful man with a massive enthusiasm for the new Zimbabwe, and his wife, Polly, is vivacious, warm and always welcoming. But this weekend she is away. I am disappointed by her absence, but it gives me a chance to speak to Ken at length about the proposition that I should stay on for another year. Ken is encouraging. 'It must be your decision,' he says, 'but if you decide to stay, I don't think you will ever regret it.'

After I have spoken with Ken, I call my parents. They listen to me, but they are not convinced. They would like me home, and they are also concerned about my university place – will Exeter really be prepared to defer my entry? They may also be worried that after two years in Zongoro, I won't want to come home at all. Nevertheless, despite their concerns, they also tell me that ultimately it is my decision.

I follow up my call to my parents with a number of letters over the next few days, setting out the pros and cons of my decision, seeking to convince them – and myself, if I am honest – that this is the right thing to do. In the end, having ascertained that Exeter University is willing to defer my entry for another year, I make the decision to stay. I inform a delighted Mr Manyumwa and then I start gathering the various letters and endorsements required to accompany my application for a work permit extension.

Over the next few weeks, I settle into the idea that I am staying, and the decision grows on me. Relationships seem to develop further and become deeper because the local people know that I am committing myself to their community. I start planning how we will organise the school when I am in charge, how we will raise funds and get the building work done. I even develop plans to construct a wind turbine – though happily, given my almost non-existent technical knowledge, this plan is never put into action. The months pass, my parents make plans to come out and visit me in the August holidays, and I feel myself become ever more settled. Happier than I think I have ever been.

And then Zimbabwe Air Force Group Captain Gary Kane goes and screws everything up.

For me and a lot of other people besides.

21

GROUP CAPTAIN GARY KANE

I am listening to Radio 3, ZBC's pop music channel, when the news comes through on Monday 4 July 1988.

The State Security Minister, Sydney Sekeramayi, announces that Zimbabwe security forces have foiled a plot to spring six South African spies from detention. The men are awaiting trial for their involvement in a car bomb attack on a homestead used by the ANC on the outskirts of Bulawayo. The car bomb had killed two people.

The minister accuses South Africa of attempting a commando raid to spring the detainees as they were transported from Chikurubi Maximum Security Prison to a Harare court.

Zimbabwe Air Force Group Captain Gary Kane, the minister informs the public, stole a Zimbabwe Air Force helicopter for use in the raid, later abandoning and destroying it when the raid was aborted. An eleven-year-old Zimbabwean girl was shot and wounded when Kane opened fire to destroy the helicopter. He subsequently fled on a plane which had been sent to pick him up and take him to South Africa.

Not unreasonably, Minister Sekeramayi concludes by saying, 'Naturally, with an incident of this kind, government confidence in white members of the security forces has been shaken.'

I am not sure whether I grasped immediately the significance this news report would have for me. But I do remember a sense of real anger at the damage that Kane had obviously done to trust in the white community. This was not the first incident involving white officers in the armed forces. In 1982, nearly a third of Zimbabwe's air force had been destroyed on the ground at the behest of South Africa, and a whole series of attacks had taken place in the country, led by white serving or former members of the security forces. These attacks had massively undermined confidence, and this was just one more nail in the coffin of harmonious relations between communities.

If I do not appreciate immediately the impact this is going to have on me, it becomes increasingly apparent over the next few days. It appears that at least one of the leading members of the South African commando team is a British national, and a number have entered the country using British passports. The British government, which had warned Zimbabwe of the impending raid, protests strongly to the South African government, but suspicion of British nationals is now widespread and is clearly being encouraged by government sources.

My work permit has still not been granted. Until now this has not been a major cause for concern – Zimbabwe's bureaucracy moves slowly at the best of times – but now I am worried that in light of recent events and faced with an application from a British national, it will grind to a complete halt.

At the end of the week, I take the bus back to Peterhouse to consult with Ken and Polly. He shares my alarm. The atmosphere is getting pretty difficult and he is not at all convinced that my application will be granted. I stay the weekend at Peterhouse and on Monday take the bus into Harare to speak to the Ministry of Education and get their advice. I have a recollection of meeting the minister, Fay Chung, but I am not sure that can be right. In any event, the message I get from her department is that while they remain fully supportive of my application, ultimately the decision lies with the Home Affairs Ministry, not with them. They are not encouraging about my prospects with their colleagues. They are happy to put in another letter of support, but they have to be candid: in these times it is unlikely I will be successful. Most likely my application will never be explicitly refused; it will probably just never be determined.

I return to Ken and Polly's that afternoon deeply despondent. If I don't act soon, I face the prospect of having neither a university place nor a job. A-level results will be out before long and once they are, places will be allocated, and I will have to wait out another year before taking up mine. I am massively torn. I have my heart set on staying in Zimbabwe, but the thought of having to return to the UK and work at some dead-end job for a year before being able to take up my university place is not attractive.

Ken agrees that it is now too big a risk to wait on the possibility of a successful work permit application and that, in the circumstances, the only sensible thing to do is to see if Exeter will restore my university place. I daren't ring my parents, as they have never been convinced that I should stay on, so I turn to my former housemaster at Marlborough, Terry Rogers, to make my case to Exeter. It is a task that he kindly accepts and very soon accomplishes. It is only then that I call my parents and let them know of my changed plans.

• • •

The last month of that final term is very different from what I have envisaged. Instead of preparing for new responsibilities, I am readying to return home, with the future of the school unclear. Mr Manyumwa and the school committee will doubtless find new teachers, but it means the majority of the staff will be new to the school, two thirds of the way through the academic year.

I feel depressed and angry. Not only by the fact that this opportunity has been taken away from me, but also by the cause of it. The actions of Gary Kane have spread further distrust through Zimbabwe, and many Zimbabweans now wonder if any whites can be relied upon. It's just one more incident in the steady chipping away of faith in a multiracial future for the country.

As so often, it is whites, refusing to embrace the message of reconciliation, who have undermined confidence that such a future is possible, but when that future finally evaporates completely in the 1990s, it is on the government that the blame is almost exclusively focused. Certainly, they bear much of the blame for what has gone wrong in Zimbabwe, but it is one part of the story. It is by no means all of it.

One piece of good news does arrive during that otherwise dispiriting month. One evening in July, Mandi knocks on my door, a beaming smile on his face. 'Jonny, I want you to come to my house.'

He offers no further explanation but instead holds open my front door, ushering me out. We walk together the few yards to his house. Leslie is asleep on the armchair and Bridget is snuggled on the sofa next to Alice, who holds in her arms a small bundle of snuffling life. 'Jonny, this is Gerald Routendo,' Mandi happily announces, 'the newest addition to our family.'

Alice looks up and smiles, indicating that I should sit down beside her. Once I am seated, she proffers the little bundle to me. I take Gerald in my arms nervously, rocking him inexpertly, monitoring his face intently for any sign that he might be about to break into tears. He looks back at me with a slight hint of irritation and seems to consider the option of tears, eventually discounting it in favour of continuing his snuffles.

I sit there between Bridget and Alice, with Gerald Routendo in my arms, Leslie dozing in the armchair and Mandi beaming with his immense fatherly pride, and I feel so at home and loved that the thought of going back to the UK is unbearable.

22

COMING TO TERMS

I was not well prepared for Exeter University. In fact, I was not really prepared for university at all. All my focus had been on readying myself to take on new responsibilities as a headteacher in the life-affirming community of Zongoro, which I had come to love so much.

So I arrived feeling bleak as a result of my premature return and nervous at the prospect of having to introduce myself to a whole new set of people. On the second day, I was in the university bookshop, searching out a particular text on one of the lower shelves, when one of my fellow students interrupted my endeavours.

'Hi, I'm Dom. I think we're both studying politics, aren't we?'

I looked up, to see a handsome, sandy-haired student grinning down at me.

Such natural friendliness and ease of manner being entirely alien to me, I was immediately suspicious of his motives. It didn't occur to me that he might just be a friendly guy who wasn't as horrifically socially awkward as I was.

Nevertheless, once I had managed to get over my suspicion, we became good friends. It was an important friendship for me as I struggled through that first term at Exeter, and I always appreciated his easy friendship and willingness to tolerate my never-ending desire to drone on about Zimbabwe.

South Africans used to mockingly describe white 'Rhodesians', as 'Whenwes', a reference to their grating habit of starting every other sentence with the phrase 'When we ran Rhodesia'. Sometimes I fear I was my own version of a 'Whenwe', constantly regaling friends with unsolicited information that began 'When I was in Zimbabwe'. But I couldn't shake it out of my system. I mourned the loss of my place there and I found it hard to adapt to being a student myself again.

Apart from Dom, I made other friends in those early weeks. My bedsit was in Hope Hall, just off the main campus, and one day in the bar I got talking to an art and literature student who seemed almost as intense as me. His passion, apart from art and literature, was music, and he had a band back in his hometown near Oxford, in which he was both a singer and a songwriter. We immediately clicked and an unlikely friendship began.

A few evenings after we met in the bar, Thom knocked on my door with a bottle of spirits of some description in his hand. He'd broken up with his girlfriend and wanted to drown his sorrows with someone. So we sat up late into the night drinking and sharing life experiences – I even shared some bad poetry I had written in Zimbabwe, which he at least pretended to like and even put to music. By the time we had finished the Scotch, we had firmly bonded.

When I stood unsuccessfully for president of the student union, I think I am safe in asserting that I was the only candidate who boasted an artistic manager, a role that Thom created when I asked him if he would help my campaign. Among other things, he took charge of a photoshoot; designed my stickers and posters – a large image of a moody-looking me, which would not have looked out of place on an album cover – and also provided musical accompaniment to my campaign, strumming his guitar as I was interviewed for a student union video. The interviewer, another friend, Jonathan Dearth, is memorably heard on the video pleading with the future lead singer of Radiohead: 'Thom, Thom, just a bit quieter, can't hear Jon's dulcet tones.'

I attended Thom's gigs in the early days after university, when Radiohead were playing support at venues like the Powerhouse and the Shepherd's Bush Empire, but we gradually lost touch, which was largely my fault. To this day when I go to speak in schools about politics, the first question I am invariably asked by students is: 'Is it true you were friends with Thom Yorke?'

Another important friendship for me was with a fellow politics student called Sonia. She was slightly older and had a maturity that made her stand out from other students. I clicked with her and we developed a strong friendship. Sonia was the first person who asked me directly whether I was gay. I was still struggling to come to terms with my sexuality and, shamefully, I lied and said no.

During the early months at Exeter, I also received the bittersweet tonic of letters from my former pupils. I was hugely touched by them, knowing what a sacrifice it was for these children of families, mostly dependent on subsistence farming, to find the money for paper, envelopes and stamps to England. Mandi also wrote fairly regularly, although I was a less good correspondent, something that Alice was to firmly berate me for when I next saw her, seven years later.

The first letter I received from one of our pupils was from a star student, Patrick Zengeni, which finished with the salutation, 'My greetings to all those with whom you share your smile.' I sat in my room in Hope Hall reading those words over and again, moved by their poetry, thinking of how much my life had been enriched by those I had met in Zongoro, and cursing the name of Group Captain Gary Kane.

23

'THE WALLS ARE TUMBLING AND FREEDOM IS COMING'

also made friends through student politics. I joined the Student Democrats, the student wing of the newly merged Social and Liberal Democrats. The merger had not gone well, the party was almost bankrupt and its membership had slumped. Consequently, we were a very small student group, I think only five or six in that first year.

Our leader was Sam Green, a politics student in the year above me. Sam didn't have much time for the student union politics that I got embroiled in, but we did share a passionate interest in world politics which was being reshaped around us. In my first year I had persuaded an initially sceptical Sam that the Student Democrats should challenge the Conservatives to a debate on mandatory economic sanctions against the apartheid regime, which Margaret Thatcher was resolutely refusing to impose.

To our surprise, the Conservatives took up the challenge. The debate was reasonably well attended and gave a spotlight to the group on an issue that interested students. I am not sure we changed anyone's minds, but we did not disgrace ourselves. It was my first real experience of public speaking, and I still treasure the memory of it and of Sam's willingness to take part in it despite his scepticism.

A large part of my politics degree course in that first year was a comparative study of western political systems against those of the Soviet Union and its Eastern Europe satellite states. As the academic year unfolded, our textbooks became increasingly irrelevant. Glasnost and perestroika – openness and economic reform – had been gaining momentum in the Soviet Union since Mikhail Gorbachev had come to power in 1985. Now the reform movement was shaking societies in the other eastern bloc countries too.

I was in a politics tutorial when a student entered the room to breathlessly announce to the professor and the class that the East German government had announced it was opening its borders. This later turned out to be a miscommunication by an East German government spokesperson, but by then it was too late: crowds gathered at the Berlin Wall and other border points and on the night of 9 November 1989, the gates were opened and East and West German citizens came together and started destroying the wall.

A few weeks later, I was involved in a protest of my own. I was sitting on the floor of the NatWest bank on the campus, protesting the proposed introduction of student loans (the irony will not be lost), which the banks were originally intended to administer. It was Tuesday 21 November 1989, the first day that the House of Commons was televised, and the manager of the bank solicitously provided a portable TV so we protesters could view proceedings.

In the midst of this, Sam appeared. He gave a dismissive look at our self-indulgent student protest and beckoned me outside.

'Do you want to go to a real student demonstration?'

I looked at him blankly.

'Prague, that's a real student protest, not this petty stuff. Let's go and be part of what they are doing in Prague, it's going to change the world.'

I was immediately sold on the idea. Demonstrations had broken out across Czechoslovakia following a student protest in Prague which had been brutally broken up by riot police and, in the aftermath of the fall of the Berlin Wall, it seemed that change was coming. This was history in the making, which would have made me keen to go anyway, but I also had a personal interest in the country, ever since I had watched a BBC documentary on the crushing of the Prague Spring at the age of twelve or thirteen. The closing minutes of the documentary had had a particular impact on me. Images of Warsaw Pact troops surrounding the headquarters of Radio Czechoslovakia were accompanied by the sound of gunfire and the increasingly desperate broadcasts of the courageous journalists inside.

So the idea of being there and part of this history was too enticing to resist, but I had one problem. And it was a big one. My student overdraft was already maxed out and there was no way I had the money to buy a flight to Prague. Sam had anticipated this and was quick with his response. 'That's not a problem, I have the money, I want to go, I don't want to go on my own and you are the only person I know mad enough to want to go with me. You can pay the money back to charity one day when you are rich and famous.'

And with that, the decision was made.

We drove up to London on Friday, left the car at Sam's house in north London and headed to the Czechoslovak Embassy in Kensington to secure our visas. This proved much easier than I had anticipated, although I received a sharp kick from Sam when I replied unthinkingly to the consular official's question about my status with the word 'student'.

Sam was right to administer the kick: it wasn't the most sensible answer, given that students were, at that very moment, demonstrating with the explicit objective of bringing down the government that the official represented. I suspect he must have been a sympathiser because he showed no reaction to my answer and rapidly stamped Czechoslovak visas into both our passports.

We left the embassy and headed to a travel shop on Kensington High Street, where Sam booked a hotel in central Prague and two flights on Czechoslovak Airlines for the next morning, and then we headed to the Tube. It was here that I had my first misgivings. At the entrance to the Underground station, the headlines screamed out at us from the *Evening Standard* billboards, reporting from Prague that 'the army stands ready to defend socialism'.

This did not appear to me to be an idle threat. Only four months previously, student protests in Tiananmen Square in Beijing had ended in a massacre, and less than a week ago, the Prague riot police had demonstrated a level of brutality in breaking up a peaceful protest that suggested that squeamishness was not the security forces' foremost characteristic.

'Sam, umm, do you think this is a good idea?' I asked him cautiously.

Sam looked both nervous and irritated, but he didn't hesitate in his response or his resolution. 'We've paid for the tickets. We're going. We'll just have to stay out of trouble.'

And so we arrive in Prague on Saturday 25 November 1989, the snow swirling around the streets, as demonstrators head home from Letná Plain. After booking into our hotel near Wenceslas Square, we set out to get the lie of the land. Student demonstrators are evident in most of the squares around central Prague. We walk to the top of Wenceslas Square and stop at the place where, twenty years earlier, a young student, Jan Palach, had set himself on fire in protest at the Soviet crushing of the Prague Spring.

We walk on through the old town and get chatting to a student group holding vigil in one of the smaller squares. They are a disciplined and determined group who sweep the streets clean of rubbish after the protests and avoid any action that the Communist government could exploit as 'anti-social' behaviour, declining a drink from the half-bottle of Scotch that Sam has in his pocket to ward off the cold.

That night, we head to the Magic Lantern Theatre, where the Civic Forum, the opposition movement loosely led by Václav Havel, has set up its headquarters and is holding a press conference. When we get to the front of the line, where a student is checking credentials, Sam asserts firmly, 'Studentsky journalist.' The student looks at us, unsure for a moment, because although Sam has correctly gathered the Czech word for 'student', he is nowhere close for 'journalist'.

At that moment, a prominent British TV journalist tries to push past us, waving his credentials at the student. But the student-credential-checker will have none of it. 'Studensky novinar,' he asserts on our behalf and lets us in, in front of the frustrated journalist and his camera crew.

Inside the theatre we take up our seats to the rear of the auditorium. The press conference is addressed by Václav Havel and Alexander Dubček, while Václav Klaus, an economist and later a right-wing Prime Minister and President of the Czech Republic, is also there. Klaus speaks excellent English and is prone to interrupt and correct the translators, who are there for the benefit of the world media. He is urbane and witty, and it is obvious he has a high opinion of himself.

Following the resignation of the General Secretary of the Czechoslovak Communist Party, Miloš Jakeš, and the entire presidium of the party on Friday night, today it is the turn of the hardline Secretary of the Prague Communist Party, Miroslav Štěpán, to bow to the inevitable and step down. By now, the Communist Party is in complete disarray. The Federal Prime Minister, Ladislav Adamec, announces his intention to form a reconstituted government and invites the Civic Forum leaders to meet him the following day at Prague City Hall.

On Sunday, there is again a mass rally on Letná Plain, just across the Vltava River. It is another freezing cold day and the hotel porter halts me at the door, point-blank refusing to let me out of the hotel until he has found me a hat. After rummaging through a box, he comes up with a flat cap and hands it to me with a smile. Now, both suitably behatted – Sam has had more forethought than me – we walk through the old town, following the crowds of people streaming across the Čechův Bridge to Letná Plain. The scale of the demonstrations is now so vast that they have outgrown Wenceslas Square.

At Letná Plain, we are met with the sight of hundreds of thousands of people as far as the eye can see, spread out across the snow-covered park. We stand and watch for a while, not able to understand the words that are spoken but in no doubt of the momentous nature of what we are witnessing. The first speaker takes the rostrum, but after speaking for a moment or two he falls silent. For a second, I think he has got stage fright as he stands stiffly and silently before the banks of microphones, but then the crowd falls silent too and it is clear that the silence is in memory of all who have suffered under the regime.

Being part of a crowd of nearly a million people as it stands utterly silent is a unique and almost overwhelming experience. In front of me, all across the plain, I can see Czech flags fluttering silently above people's heads, and fingers held up in V for victory signs. After the minute is up, the man at the rostrum breaks the silence and the immense crowd erupts in chants.

The Civic Forum has invited Prime Minister Adamec to address the crowd following their meeting with him earlier in the day. They want to bolster him against the hardliners, who might, even at this late stage, be tempted to try to reverse the momentum for reform. However, when Adamec takes the rostrum, he seriously misjudges his audience. He has only been speaking a minute or two before the boos and whistles start to ring out across the park.

An English-speaking Czech TV producer whom Sam and I have befriended helpfully explains that the Prime Minister, instead of talking about plans for reform, which the crowd wants to hear, is speaking in the language of the party about the need for discipline and an end to strikes, which they most definitely do not want to hear. The TV producer keeps us abreast of what is going on as the boos and whistles echo off three quarters of a million lips, rising to a deafening crescendo which drowns out Adamec's words and leaves him with no choice but to bring his speech to a rapid close. If he was in any doubt before about the degree of change that is coming, he surely can't be now.

Later, we push our way to the front of the crowd and at the side of the stage manage to locate one of the student leaders. We suggest – with staggering self-regard – that we would like to address the crowd, to bring fraternal greetings from students in the UK. Astonishingly, the student leader doesn't simply tell us to piss off. Instead he takes us behind the stage and disappears for what seem to be extensive discussions with his colleagues.

In the end, he returns to politely and apologetically explain that this will regrettably not be possible. There is already a packed schedule – amazingly, the crowd are apparently keener to hear from Czechoslovak heroes Alexander Dubček and Václav Havel than they are from Sam Green and Jonny Oates – oh well, their loss.

On Monday, the general strike takes place for two hours between 12 p.m. and 2 p.m. It is estimated that more than 75 per cent of workers take part. Later in the afternoon, a huge demonstration takes place in Wenceslas Square. Sam and I get there early and find ourselves somewhere to eat, opposite the balcony of the Melantrich building, where, just a few days before, Alexander Dubček, leader of the Prague Spring of 1968, and Václav Havel, the playwright, dissident and leader of the opposition Civic Forum, appeared for the first time together. It was Dubček's first public appearance in Prague since he was forced out of office following the 1968 Soviet invasion.

After the speeches are over, Sam and I walk through the streets of protesters and strikers. Older people, who until now have been wary, looking – sometimes literally – over their shoulders for the Warsaw Pact tanks that surely must come, as they came twenty-one years before, now suddenly believe. It is over. Now, it is definitely over. The Communists are done for and already it is far too late for Soviet tanks to rescue them, even were they inclined to.

We push through crowds at the bottom of Wenceslas Square, and a plump elderly lady grabs me and hugs and kisses me and pins a piece of ribbon to my coat in the colours of the Czechoslovak flag, then does the same to Sam. We smile warmly but say nothing. She clearly believes us to be from that band of valiant student protesters who lit the spark that has freed this country from five decades of communist dictatorship. We choose not to disabuse her.

We leave Prague the following day, the same day the Communist Party accepts the abolition of its 'leading role' in Czechoslovak politics. The next day, Wednesday 29 November, Communist domination of the country formally comes to an end when the Federal Assembly deletes the reference to the party's 'leading role' from the Czechoslovak constitution.

President Gustáv Husák swears in a new government on Sunday 10 December, the first in forty-one years that is not dominated by the Communist Party. He resigns his office the same day and eighteen days later, on 28 December 1989, my twentieth birthday, Alexander Dubček is elected chairman of the Czechoslovak Federal Assembly, twenty-one years after being stripped of power following the Soviet invasion. The following day, the Federal Assembly elects Václav Havel as President of Czechoslovakia.

•   •   •

It's not only in the Communist bloc that dramatic change is happening. In August 1989, three months before the fall of the Berlin Wall, comes the fall of P. W. Botha, the unbending State President of apartheid South Africa. Despite his attempts to cling to office, 'Die Groot Krokodil' finally succumbs to the inevitable and gracelessly resigns the presidency. F. W. de Klerk, who succeeds him, is from the hardline, *verkramp* wing of the National Party, but he has the intelligence to realise that the game is up.

Events in South Africa are moving at a pace. On Friday 2 February 1990, F. W. de Klerk is trailed to make a major speech in Parliament. But there is scepticism. The country has been here before with Botha's 'crossing the Rubicon' speech, which was supposed to herald dramatic change but from which, at the last minute, he held back.

A group of us are gathered around the TV screen at university as de Klerk takes the podium in the South African Parliament in Cape Town, which not so far in the future will be my place of work. From the outset it is clear: this will no repeat of the Rubicon speech. Nonetheless, I listen in astonishment as de Klerk announces the unbanning of the African National Congress, the Pan African Congress, the South African Communist Party and a host of other proscribed organisations and declares his intention to free Nelson Mandela and enter into negotiations for a democratic multiracial constitution.

I think back to that bus journey in April 1988. My sense of relief as the bus crossed the border at Beitbridge out of apartheid South Africa. I vowed then that I wouldn't return to the country until apartheid had ended. In April 1988, that looked like a lifetime away; something that would most probably only be achieved at the end of a blood-soaked race war. Now, less than two years later, de Klerk has signalled the beginning of its end.

On 2 May 1990, for the first time in South Africa's history, the ANC and the apartheid government sit down together for formal talks. On the same day, Archbishop Tutu, the courageous South African cleric who has campaigned for an end to apartheid, comes to speak at the university as hopes grow that reform is now unstoppable. It is quite a coup for the vice-chancellor, David Harrison, and his team, but I sniff the scent of hypocrisy.

I am commissioned to write an article about the visit for the student magazine, *The Third Degree*, but the university won't give me access to the press conference with the archbishop. Undaunted, I find someone who is to be allowed to attend and they agree to raise the question that I want to ask: isn't it hypocritical of the university to seek the prestige and publicity that comes with Archbishop Tutu's visit while still maintaining its investments in apartheid South Africa? The vice-chancellor does not much like this question.

Tutu is diplomatic but clear. He tells the press conference that institutions such as Exeter University have a critical moral role to play and they must consider whether they are compromising it. 'What we are saying', he tells the audience, 'is: "Are you on the side of oppression or freedom?"' The vice-chancellor is grim faced; his answer, slippery and ambiguous. 'I can tell the speaker that that is what we do,' he says, and unfortunately no one presses him further.

When Tutu makes his speech later to nearly 2,000 students and faculty, he is even more emphatic. He tells his assembled audience that he has no time for those who 'cry crocodile tears' over the suffering that they allege sanctions will cause to black South Africans, 'for your massive profits have been gained on the basis of black suffering and misery'. I might be imagining it, but the vice-chancellor seems to shift in his seat.

At the reception after the speech, orange juice is being served to the assembled guests. I glimpse one of the cartons and note with a jaded, unsurprised cynicism that, notwithstanding Tutu's exhortations on sanctions just a few minutes earlier, the orange juice that the archbishop has been given to drink is South African.

Tutu's speech, however, is about much more than sanctions or even South Africa. It is about freedom. Repression, he says, is in the end condemned to failure because people are ultimately created free and wherever that freedom is removed, they will strive to regain it.

> There is something in the make-up of this man or woman that refuses to be manipulated, to knuckle under, however horrendous the pressures and however inhumane the methods used to try to dehumanise them … God's mills grind slowly, but they grind very fine all the same. We have waited for vindication since 1652, when Jan van Riebeeck landed at the Cape. It now seems that our deliverance may be at hand.

The last racial dictatorship in Africa is disintegrating, the communist dictatorships of Europe are collapsing and the shadow of nuclear confrontation, which has hovered over us all our lives, is lifting. There is a sense of euphoria in the air. Dictatorship is out of fashion and freedom is coming. It feels, in that moment, like the world can only get better.

● ● ●

Student politics becomes a big feature of my time at university. My first act at the freshers' fair has been to join the anti-apartheid movement; my second, to join the Student Democrats, then headed up by Sam.

When Sam graduates the following year, I become the chair of what has by then been renamed as Exeter University Liberal Democrats. We have just a few members at the time, so there is an urgent recruiting job to do. I had got to know the liberal-minded student entertainment officer, Jon Dearth, and I decide he is exactly the sort of person I need in the group. He is well known and liked and will help us attract others into the fold.

He is initially sceptical and, despite my best efforts, at first, I can't shift him. In the end, I tell him that if he will join, I will step down to deputy chair and he can be the chair of the group. This seems to do the trick and I somehow persuade my fellow group members to accept the new leadership arrangements. Jon takes to his new role with enthusiasm and immediately helps me to breathe life into the student group.

On a Thursday morning in late November, I am lounging in bed in the house I share with Jon and two other friends, Sarah Gilchrist, a student at the education faculty whom I have got to know in her time as deputy president of the student union, and Steve Tervit, a mutual friend who has left the university but stayed on in Exeter. Suddenly Radio 1 interrupts its schedule to bring some dramatic news from Downing Street: Margaret Thatcher is to resign as Prime Minister. The news cuts through my student lethargy and I immediately leap out of bed and dance a jig around my room. Thatcher has been Prime Minister since I was nine years old, and now, finally, she is going. She has been a huge figure, dominating the political landscape; my political beliefs have been shaped in opposition to her stern, unbending politics and her inability – to my mind – to walk in another person's shoes.

At the university, there is much glee among the left-leaning students who tend to be my friends. I locate Jon Dearth, who has already seized the initiative and booked the Lemon Grove, the student entertainment space, for a 'Thank God She's Gone' party that evening and is designing a flyer to rally people to the event.

There's a sense of huge optimism at the event. A feeling that after eleven years of Conservative government under Margaret Thatcher, Britain is going to be able to move on from the battles of the 1980s and that along with all the change that is happening around the world, things are going to be different at home too. Little do we imagine that we have another seven years of Conservative government ahead of us yet.

24

BACK TO AFRICA

I graduated from Exeter in the summer of 1991 with a lower second-class degree and a sense of missed opportunities, having spent my university career overly embroiled in the minutiae of student politics, drinking too much and as personally troubled as ever. But I had a job, which was more than many in recession-stricken Britain.

My job was as political assistant to the Liberal Democrat Group on Kingston Council. It mainly consisted of photocopying, babysitting for a gorgeous toddler called Katelin, whose mum, Louise, worked afternoons for the council group, and desperately trying to impress the group leader with answers to crossword questions that he was struggling with.

On my first day in post, I was scheduled to call him at work to get instructions.

'Ah, Jonny,' he said, 'good to have you here. You wouldn't by any chance know who shot Archduke Franz Ferdinand, would you?'

It was a novel start to a conversation with my first ever boss, and I was determined not to flunk it. 'Um, err. I know this.'

And I did, that was the worst thing. I did. I had studied this period of history intently at school, but now, at this precise moment, probably the only time, ever, in my whole life when it would be practically useful for me to be able to access this information, shy and embarrassed, it had fled and buried itself in the recesses of my mind. So I wittered on:

'Umm. It was... No, sorry, yes. It's on the tip of my tongue. Umm, no I've lost it.'

John was a patient man, but eventually he interrupted. 'Never mind.'

An hour or so later, it appeared in my brain out of nowhere: Gavrilo Princip! I called John excitedly at the Department of Health, probably interrupting a meeting, for he took a while to come to the phone. 'It's Gavrilo Princip,' I exclaimed triumphantly.

'Gavrilo Princip? Ah yes.' And then, 'Actually, it's probably best if you stick to calls at the times we have arranged unless it's an emergency. Otherwise it can be a bit difficult here.'

I was crushed.

Sensing my despondency, he said kindly, 'Gavrilo Princip, of course, very good. Thank you.'

My job with the council was on a one-year fixed-term contract, the idea being to get a series of young graduates into the borough in the hope that they would remain involved with the party after their contract ended. Despite this practice – and notwithstanding the Gavrilo Princip debacle – John and his fellow councillors generously offered me an extension of another year.

I was torn. The early 1990s recession was still in full swing, meaning it wouldn't be easy to find another job, and the people I worked with had almost come to feel like another family, so it would be a wrench to leave. Nevertheless, I knew by then that politics was going to be an important part of my life and I thought I should get some wider career experience, so I decided to move on.

I stayed living in Kingston and before long I had been arm-twisted into standing for election to the council. I was elected in 1994, the year the Liberal Democrats gained a majority on the council for the first time, and I was soon heavily embroiled in the administration as chair of a committee and later deputy leader of the council.

One evening after attending a party meeting in the Bull and Bush pub on the Norbiton estate, Dan, my predecessor as political assistant, introduced me to a party member who had just joined, called Vijay Solanki.

The three of us got chatting over a few beers. Vijay was both engaging and direct, and we found we got on. Over the next few weeks, we got to know each other better and as we were both looking for accommodation at the time, we ended up sharing a house.

In 1995, I had saved up enough money to go on a three-week holiday to Zimbabwe, my first return visit since 1988. Vijay was also intending to spend the summer in southern Africa, visiting a friend who was teaching in Botswana, but when his trip was cancelled because his friend had to return home due to his mother's illness, Vijay decided to join me in Zimbabwe instead.

• • •

The *Sunday Times* carries a special feature on the 'growing backlash against whites and Asians' in Zimbabwe on the weekend before we leave for Harare. I note that Vijay and I are the perfect combination of these two racial characteristics, and I wonder nervously how much the place will have changed during my seven-year absence. Nevertheless, my excitement at the prospect of returning to Zongoro overcomes any anxieties as I prepare for the trip.

The day we are due to leave, I come down with an agonising throat infection. There is no time to see a doctor, so I board the plane feeling like I am swallowing broken glass. Our flight to Zimbabwe is via Addis Ababa and Kilimanjaro, and the first leg is eight hours of unmitigated agony.

By the time we arrive at Addis, I am worried that I am going to have to call the trip off. Vijay, however, who has a rudimentary knowledge of medicine from a year at medical college, and an even greater knowledge of alcohol, produces a half-bottle of Johnnie Walker and suggests I gargle it. So I find myself at six o'clock in the morning, sat on a heavily worn seat in the transit lounge at Addis Ababa Airport gargling Scotch. Happily, it proves to be a miracle cure, and by the time our flight to Kilimanjaro is ready to depart, I am fully restored and perhaps a little animated by the Scotch, much of which I have swallowed after gargling.

As we proceed through the security checks before boarding the flight, I greet the security man in one of the twelve words of Amharic that I know from my visit to Ethiopia a decade before. He responds warmly and at length and I have to interrupt in English to explain that it is one of only a very few words that I know, before for some reason adding that I can also count to ten.

The security man seems delighted with this information. 'Then I will teach you to count to twenty and you will have doubled your knowledge of Amharic,' he says.

'OK,' I reply, a little unsure, as Vijay has already gone through security and will now be wondering where I am.

The security man, it turns out, is a stickler for pronunciation and by the time he is finally satisfied that I have sufficiently grasped the Amharic for the numbers eleven to twenty, Vijay is in a state of high anxiety, assuming I must have been detained. I, on the other hand, am simply amazed at the difference between this friendly, if eccentric, security official who has just schooled me in numbers and those cold-eyed officials who so terrified me ten years before.

We spend a day and a night in Harare, staying at a backpackers' lodge and drinking in a club where the Congolese band the Lubumbashi Boys are playing and demonstrating a novel, knee-raising dance routine which captures our imaginations. The next day we meet with Sebastian, a student at the University of Zimbabwe in Harare, whose attendance is

Photo taken at Heathrow Airport aged fifteen and sent with the letter to my parents informing them that I had left for Ethiopia

Addis Ababa: arch celebrating eleven years of revolution from 1967 to 1978 (1974–85 in Western calendar)

Our house at St James School, Zongoro

With my wonderful friends Morgan and Alice and their children Bridget and Leslie, Zongoro, 1988

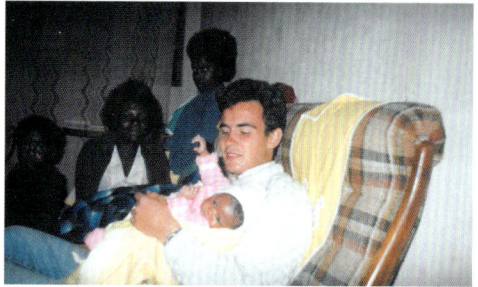

With newly born baby
Gerald Routendo, 1988

At the mass demonstrations of the Czechoslovak Velvet Revolution on Letná Plain, Prague, in November 1989, shortly before the resignation of the Communist government

Left to right: Gerald, Leslie, Morgan, Alice, Yolande and Bridget at their home in Chikanga following Morgan's graduation with a Bachelor of Education degree from the University of Zimbabwe, 1997

The late Inka Mars, who looked after me so well in South Africa

With my sister in Africa, Nicky Lucas, on the balcony of the IFP HQ in Durban in January 1999

With Sabhuku Ndorikanda, my dad and the headmistress of St James Secondary School, 2000

Pupils at St James Secondary School, Zongoro

Speaking at my leaving party at IFP HQ in Durban; to my left is Joshua Mazibuko and to my right, Velaphi Ndlovu MP

With Minister of Home Affairs Prince Mangosuthu Buthelezi at Ulundi, January 2001

The best day of my life: our civil partnership ceremony, June 2006

Prince Mangosuthu Buthelezi and Reverend Musa Zondi MP campaigning in KwaZulu-Natal during the 2009 South African general election

With Nick in No. 10 on the first day of the coalition

On the steps of 10 Downing Street

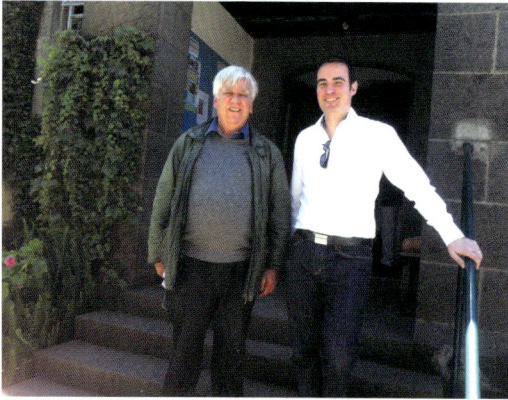

With Father Charles Sherlock outside St Matthew's Anglican Church, Addis Ababa, in 2013, twenty-eight years after my first visit

At the stadium in Umtata, where huge screens had been set up to show the funeral of Nelson Mandela, which was taking place a few miles away at his ancestral home in Qunu in the Eastern Cape

The DPM's diary Star Chamber meeting in the Cabinet Room: *(clockwise from left)* Lucy Smith, me, Sam O'Callaghan, James Sorene, Stephen Jones, Hollie Voyce, Lena Pietsch, James McGrory, Emma Gilpin Jacobs and Jonathan Crisp

Liberal Democrat and Conservative advisers with the Deputy Prime Minister and Prime Minister in the last week of the coalition

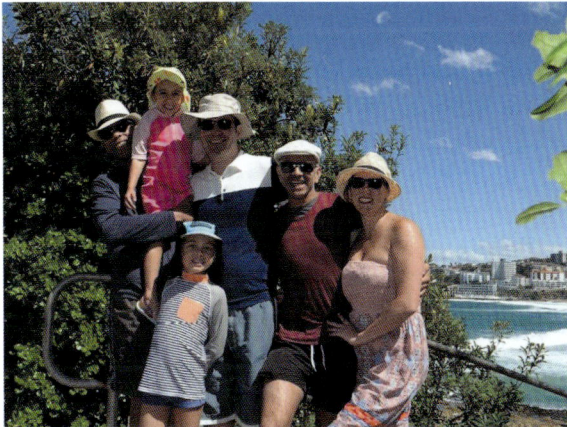

With David, Kira, Darcy, Vijay and Devina in Sydney, 2016

With my amazing eighty-year-old mum after we had completed our 2.5km swim for Macmillan Cancer Care, 2017

A wonderful last Christmas with Mum and all the family

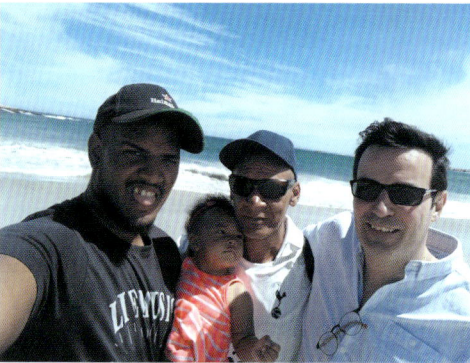

With Zakeer, his daughter Zia and Ebrahim on Camps Bay Beach, March 2017

With David in San Francisco, with the Golden Gate Bridge in the background

made possible in part by the support of the congregation of St Bride's. He is the first pupil of St James School to attend university and, although I didn't teach him, it is great to see how the school is succeeding and how St Bride's Church is continuing to support its pupils.

That evening, we get the overnight train to Mutare. The train leaves Harare around 9 p.m. and is scheduled to arrive at Mutare at around six in the morning. We finally limp in at ten, having averaged around 20km an hour, and I recall why, when I lived here, I always took the bus.

After lunch in Mutare, we board a bus to take us the 30km or so to the school. At the Old Mutare stop, an elderly lady rises from her seat to disembark. She has a large blue sack of maize which she is trying to manoeuvre off the bus. Vijay is closest to her and offers to help her. She looks astonished by his offer but accepts it and thanks him warmly. It is discomfiting, this level of surprise whenever an Asian or white person offers a simple courtesy to an African.

As the bus rattles its way up the Nyanga road towards the school, I have an overload of nostalgia at the familiar sights and sounds and smells. The bus judders to a halt at Zongoro, just opposite the late Baba Mwashita's shop, and I immediately feel that I am home.

We cross the stepping stones and walk up the bank of the river. To the right, at the top of the incline, St James Secondary School now stands proudly, where once was just open bush. I pause for a moment, taking in the transformation that has occurred.

Despite all my excitement at returning to the school, I have not planned well for the visit. Most notably, I have failed to write to Morgan and Alice to let them know that I am coming until it is too late. As a result, I find that Morgan is away on school business and will not be back until the following day. Alice rightly scolds me for this and more generally for my poor communications over recent years. 'Jonny, Morgan is sad when you don't respond to his letters. He thinks you have forgotten him.'

I feel ashamed that I have been too caught up in my own world to keep in touch properly with these friends who have shown me so much love and care.

One of the secondary school teachers, James Maimbo, who with two other teachers now occupies the house that Alan, Joe and I once lived in, offers to put us up for the night so that we can see Mandi when he returns the next day. It will also give me the chance to attend the secondary school assembly in the morning.

Inevitably, we spend the evening in the bottle store. The music is still blaring out as usual and the table football is as frenetic as ever, although the table looks considerably more battered. A number of my former pupils, now in their twenties, join us and we pass an enjoyable evening, chatting and drinking and, as the beers flow, even dancing, Vijay and I introducing the Lubumbashi Boys' knee-lifting moves to the local populace.

When we return to the house, James and one of his colleagues insist on giving up their beds for us. Despite our protestations that we will happily use our sleeping bags, they will not allow it. We are touched by this gesture and insist that if James or his colleague are ever in London, they will always have a place to stay with us.

Our pledge is genuine, but given the very poor salary of a Zimbabwean teacher, it seems unlikely that we will ever be called on to honour it. We are somewhat surprised, therefore, to receive a telephone call from James just before Christmas in the same year to tell us that he is at Victoria Station and is it OK for him to stay a few weeks. It turns out that his brother works on the freight airline and he has somehow been able to hitch a ride on a flight to Gatwick.

The morning after the night at the bottle store, I have to rise early in order to attend the school assembly, where, a little hungover, I am called on to address the pupils. I look out from the podium across a sea of students' faces, assembled in the central square of the school, around which the classrooms are arranged. Despite my hangover, I feel invigorated to be here with the students in their new school, and I wonder how things might have turned out differently for me if the antics of a Zimbabwe Air Force pilot hadn't brought my time here to such an abrupt end.

By early afternoon, Morgan has still not arrived and I am afraid we are going to miss him, as we need to get to Juliasdale, the next stop on our itinerary, before it gets dark. Eventually and very reluctantly, I tell Alice that we will have to go but that we will pass back to see Morgan on our return from Juliasdale.

Then we walk over to the bus stop to wait for a bus or a lift, whichever comes first. After about half an hour waiting, a car pulls up, and to my delight Mandi steps out. He is naturally astonished to see me here so unexpectedly after seven years of absence. He beams a huge smile and embraces me and then we sit down together under the shade tree to chat. Like Alice, he rightly berates me for my poor communications over the past couple of years, and again I apologise and vow to myself that we will not be out of contact again.

After about half an hour, Morgan recognises the driver of a car as it passes us and he rushes out into the road after it, waving his arms and shouting. It pulls up a few hundred metres further up and Morgan gestures us to hurry and follow him. When we get to the car, he is speaking to the driver in Shona – it turns out he is giving him instructions to check that the backpackers' place we are intending to stay at in Juliasdale is of a decent standard and that we get a good price.

●　●　●

Over the three weeks that we are in Zimbabwe, Vijay and I get to know each other much better. We share stories about our respective families, and I find it liberating to discover that there is no such thing as a 'normal' family. By the end of the trip, I sense that I have found a kindred spirit. We share the same capacity for both silliness and seriousness, and Vijay has an enthusiasm for life which is infectious. That's not to say that our relationship during the trip is all plain sailing.

While staying in a backpackers' lodge in Chimanimani, a small town in Zimbabwe's eastern highlands, Vijay decides mid-afternoon that it is time for us to be a little more adventurous. He proposes that we should head out to a national park site in the mountains themselves. I am rather enjoying relaxing here with the other backpackers, but Vijay is insistent, so, sceptical and reluctant, I grumpily agree and we set out, walking down the road and trying to hitch a lift as we go. As time passes and we still have not managed to get a lift, my scepticism reasserts itself: 'Are you absolutely sure there is accommodation for us at the site?' I grumpily demand. 'Because I don't remember reading that anywhere.'

Vijay, by now exasperated by my negativity towards his plan, responds sharply. 'Yes, how many times do you want me to tell you? Do you want to read the guide book yourself?!'

And he starts to take his backpack off to retrieve the book, in an ostentatious display of irritation. Feeling contrite, I tell him that is not necessary. If he is sure, then I am OK with that.

Eventually, we do get a lift, but it is dusk by the time the pick-up truck drops us at the dirt track that leads to the national park site, and we still have over a mile to walk. We arrive just as darkness is setting in and the park ranger is locking up his office for the day.

It turns out, as I had suspected, that there is no accommodation here, just a campsite. We have no tent, it is winter and we are in the mountains where the temperature is already dropping rapidly and Lord knows what dangerous animals lurk out there in the darkness.

Vijay asks the ranger if we can get a lift back with him, but his mode of transport is a moped, so this is not feasible. Vijay then asks him if we can stay the night in his office. The answer is no. Vijay suggests we could pay a fee. The answer is still no. Vijay starts to specify ever-increasing amounts that the fee might consist of. But the answer is still an implacable no. When Vijay gets to Z$1,000, the ranger simply climbs on his moped, wishes us good luck and drives off into the night.

By now I have stormed off in high fury to the campsite. This, at least, is lit. I put my backpack down and slump against a wall. Vijay comes after me. He is worried by our situation but also amused by my cold, unspeaking fury.

He decides, therefore, that this is an opportune moment to take a photo of me. I stare out of it sullen and unyielding, further incensed that his photo-taking antics just demonstrate that he doesn't appreciate the predicament we are in. All we have with us is our sleeping bags but nothing else to ward off the cold or the animals.

As it's winter, the campsite is largely deserted. The only exception is an Austrian couple who have arrived in a battered VW Beetle, hoping presumably for some romantic solitude. Vijay approaches them – I am still sat silent with fury – and explains the situation we are in. Reluctantly, they offer to share their tent with us. It is a two-person tent. Ideal for an intimate night together for a couple. Less than ideal to have to share with two random Brits you have only just met.

That night is one of the most uncomfortable and socially awkward of my life. As soon as the dawn comes, I crawl out of the tent with my sleeping bag and Vijay follows. As the sun starts to light up the sky, we decide that we will set off on a walk into the mountains. We climb for about half an hour until we find a large slab of slanting rock which has a breath-taking view of the valley below, and we stop here and sit down. We have still hardly spoken since the evening debacle. After a few moments, Vijay risks a comment: 'I can't believe we have just spent a night in a two-man tent with a random Austrian couple. You have to admit that was quite an experience.'

I look over, willing myself to maintain my irritation with him. But I can't. The situation is too absurd, so I laugh and say, 'And what about the park ranger? You had to find the most incorruptible official in the whole of Zimbabwe.'

We lean back against the rock, restored to good humour, and watch as the sun lifts itself above the spectacular Chimanimani Mountains and sparkles and shines off the stunning landscape below us.

• • •

Zimbabwe was really where we became close friends, learning each other's stories and coming to know each other's strengths and flaws. In December 1995, just before Vijay was heading back to his family in York for Christmas, I told him I was gay.

I don't think he expected it, but I don't think he was surprised by it either. He was concerned for me, that I was OK and that I was going to be able to handle the stigma that still existed at that time, but it never seemed like it fazed him. At least, if it did, he didn't show it.

By that time, I had met someone. Our relationship didn't last long – I don't think either of us really knew what we wanted then – but it spurred me to come out to my family and friends, who were universally loving and supportive. I expected that this would lift a huge burden off my shoulders, but I found that it didn't.

I had spent so many years worrying about what other people would think about me being gay that I had never really given any thought to how I felt about it. I wasn't sure I liked it. I wrote bad poetry, dripping with self-pity, and sank back into depression.

In 1996, Vijay got a job at Rank Hovis McDougall and moved up to Manchester. His then girlfriend, Sandy, had moved into our shared house by then, so she stayed on in the house with me, and Vijay came down regularly to stay.

On one of his visits, the two of us repair to the Lamb, the pub just opposite the house. I am at rock-bottom. The few relationships I have had have all failed, and I feel weighed down with sadness in a way I haven't since my Ethiopian misadventure. Vijay is worried about me and he tries to get me to open up, but I find it almost impossible to communicate with this crushing weight on top of me.

In the morning, I wake feeling dreadful, my depression accentuated by the after-effects of the beer from the night before. I don't want to go on. It isn't that I am suicidal; I have no plan nor desire to take my life. I just want it to be over.

I set off on my commute up to Westminster, laden with the sadness of another day in a world where I don't seem to be able to locate my place. On the train, I open my briefcase to retrieve the book I am reading at the time and inside I find a card that Vijay has placed there the night before. I turn it over and read it. In large, clear handwriting, he has written:

I will avoid all the Doris Lessing quotes and just say: I love you lots.
Please lift your head up and be happy.
    Vijay x

•   •   •

The love and care embodied in those few sentences had an immense impact on my life. Of course, I wasn't transformed overnight – or indeed at all – into a happy-go-lucky bundle of joy. But it did make me realise two things: firstly, how lucky I was to have a friend who knew how to show such care and such love, and to show it in exactly the right way and exactly at that right time; and secondly, that things weren't going to get right on their own – I needed to play my part.

I was recently listening to a podcast when I heard an actor who had lost his brother to suicide say, with an urgency and sincerity that stopped me in my tracks: 'All I can say is, if you are suffering, you matter. There's loads of people who want to help you, but they aren't going to be able to do it without you.'

It took me immediately back to Vijay's card, written over twenty years ago, which had shown me that I mattered, at just the point when I needed to know it.

25

GETTING THE ELECTION BUG

In 1995, Ed Davey, who had become the Liberal Democrat candidate for Kingston and Surbiton, asked me to be his election agent. I had first met Ed in the Sports and Social Bar in the House of Commons when he was the party's economics adviser (and a bit full of himself) and I was a lowly political assistant in Kingston (and very full of myself). We had had an absurd and heated argument about the Maastricht Treaty in which we both accused each other of clearly not having read the full text of the treaty, which, of course, neither of us had done.

When Ed approached me about being his agent, I was reluctant. The nominal Conservative majority for the newly created seat of Kingston and Surbiton was 15,000; we had very limited resources as a party and it was going to be a shedload of work on top of being a councillor and holding down a full-time job.

In the end, however, Ed convinced me. His plan for the 1997 election campaign was compelling and his dedication and determination inspiring, so over lunch on the beachfront in Brighton, with Ed and one of his key local backers, Bob Steed, with a cool September wind blowing our papers about, I agreed.

The campaign was a fantastic experience. We had an amazing and eclectic team of talented campaigners, Belinda and Dan and John and Vicki and Ash and Mark and Adam and Rob and Wyn and a whole host of other incredible characters who became like family for me, all of them working entirely voluntarily.

On polling day, we feel we have done well, but it is not credible to believe we can overturn such a substantial majority at the first attempt. When the verification process is completed, our box count tallies suggest we are 2,000 or 3,000 votes behind the Conservatives – an impressive result, but not good enough.

Belinda, the campaign organiser, and I go downstairs to the office where Ed is waiting, to let him know. He looks disappointed – all candidates think they are going to win, however unlikely the prospect – but he is sanguine. We all hug and he thanks us both for all our work and then he says he should go and call his grandmother and tell her not to stay up for the result.

As I walk back to the count, I pass John Harris, who runs our computerised polling operation. He calls out to me: 'Why the glum face, Jon?'

I explain that it looks like we have lost by about 2,000 to 3,000 votes.

'Nah,' he says, peering at the figures on his laptop screen, 'I got it we win by about 100.'

I am used to John winding me up, so I respond with a friendly 'Oh fuck off, John' and walk back into the count.

In the council chamber, however, things seem to have changed significantly while I have been away. The piles of Liberal Democrat and Conservative votes look practically even and the strained looks on the faces of the Tory counting agents suggest things are a lot closer than Belinda and I have thought. I approach one of the counting staff, the committee secretary for the council committee that I chair, and I say tentatively, 'Ann, it looks like we are neck and neck with the Conservatives. Can that be right?'

She looks back at me and, trying to hide her excitement, says, 'Oh, Councillor Oates, I think you are ahead.'

I put my hand to my mouth, unable to take it in. The returning officer summons the party agents together and informs us of the result: Ed Davey is fifty-eight votes ahead of his Conservative opponent. Unsurprisingly, the Conservative agent demands a recount, which, equally unsurprisingly, is granted.

The recount results in an increased lead for Ed: now he is 258 votes ahead. The Labour agent urges the Tories to concede; presumably he is eager to go and celebrate the landslide victory his party has won across the country.

'A recount will just give them a bigger majority,' he warns the Tory agent.

The Tory agent looks for a moment like he might heed Labour's advice, but I am desperately worried. If the majority can change by 200 votes one way, surely it could go the other way too.

Just as the Tory agent looks like he is going to throw the towel in, the Conservative candidate, Richard Tracey, sensibly intervenes – conceding in these circumstances would be insane. The returning officer agrees that there are grounds for another recount. However, he stipulates that if the next count is within two votes either way of the original count, he will declare the result.

Another nail-biting period follows as the count is started again. The reason for the 200-vote discrepancy is rapidly established: four bundles of fifty votes each, due to the Referendum Party, have wrongly been placed in Ed's pile. The count is rapidly completed and the result is a Liberal Democrat majority of fifty-six – within the two-vote margin the Returning Officer has stipulated. By now it is about four o'clock in the morning.

At this point, the Conservative Party agent, a short man, chastened by his earlier near concession, pulls himself up to his full height and instructs the returning officer in an imperious tone: 'As the official agent for the Conservative and Unionist Party, I demand that this count is now suspended and sealed by the police until another recount can take place later today.'

The acting returning officer, at over six feet tall, towers over him. His response is calm but with an authority which brooks no dissent: 'And I, as the official returning officer for the Royal Borough of Kingston, am informing you that I am declaring this as the result.'

With that, he hands a slip of paper to the Mayor, who takes it to the rostrum and announces the result. It is official. We have won by fifty-six votes in a seat that is not even on the party's target list, and for the first time in its history, Kingston is represented by a Liberal Democrat MP.

As the room erupts in Liberal Democrat euphoria, I slip out and sit myself down on an out-of-the-way staircase and breathe deeply. I want a moment or two on my own to savour what we have achieved.

Before I go back into the count, I switch on my phone and it beeps furiously with messages, a number of them from my dad, who is watching the election on TV at the rectory in Fleet Street. His final message reads: 'The BBC says that Kingston and Surbiton has gone to a second recount. I am going into my church to pray.'

His prayers have worked.

26

CHASING A RAINBOW

Early in 1998, Simon Hughes, the Liberal Democrat MP for South-wark and Bermondsey, who had been a mentor to me since I first worked as an intern for him in 1987, approached me to ask if I would be interested in putting my name forward for a role working for the Westminster Foundation for Democracy, supporting MPs in South Africa's first democratic parliament. It was a two-year posting which would let me play a part, however small, in the early days of South Africa's multiracial democracy. I leapt at the opportunity and, after some back and forth, I was happily successful in securing the role.

The process of actually getting to South Africa was long and drawn-out. I was the last of four advisers sent out to assist the Parliament, the previous three having been assigned to work with the ANC. Recently, the South African media had taken an interest in the fact that the project was only providing assistance to the ANC, which had access to the full resources of government, and that all the advisers had come from the UK Labour Party, the ANC's sister party. The Speaker of the South African Parliament, who it turned out had not been informed of the project, and the other parties which had been previously excluded from the system were extremely unhappy.

Richard Caborn, the inspiration behind the project and by then a government minister, called me over to the Commons. We went for a drink in the Strangers' Bar and he explained the situation: 'Look, lad, I'm sorry for the delay but there have been some complications in South Africa. The long and short of it is that we are going to assign you to work with the Inkatha Freedom Party.'

I was stunned by this bombshell. Up to this point, I had assumed – although I am not sure I had actually been told – that, like the advisers who were already in place, I would also be working with the ANC. Inkatha was a whole different matter. I had been a member of the anti-apartheid movement since university and this had given me a very polarised view of South African politics in which Inkatha was one of the chief bogeymen.

Dick Caborn recognised and understood my disquiet. 'I know how you feel about this,' he said, 'but you need to approach this role as if you're a civil servant. You are there to advise Inkatha in an impartial way. They are part of the government with the ANC so it's important they also have the resources and support that they need in Parliament.'

I was very unhappy with this development and not convinced by Dick's attempt to mollify me. But as I had already resigned my job and given up the lease on my house, I wasn't in much of a position to object. Accordingly, I reluctantly accepted the assignment and began to make preparations for my move to South Africa. My work permit came through in December 1998, and I arranged with the IFP to take up my post in January 1999.

• • •

In time I was to discover that the history of Inkatha was more nuanced than my monochrome anti-apartheid lens allowed.

Mangosuthu Buthelezi was a complex man navigating a set of conflicting pressures as both a trenchant opponent of apartheid and a traditional Zulu leader who had to engage with the system he opposed. His hagiographers cast him as a saint, the polemicists as an ogre. Neither do justice to a nuanced and thoughtful character who throughout the apartheid years remained committed to the ideal of a multiracial democracy in South Africa and consistently demanded the release of Nelson Mandela and his fellow prisoners.

Opinion polls in the early 1970s record him as one of the most popular leaders in South Africa, but as the ANC turned on him in the late 1970s, he found his KwaZulu administration and Inkatha movement increasingly embroiled with – and at times compromised by – the apartheid state. Nonetheless, his consistent refusal to accept independent status for the KwaZulu homeland of which he was Chief Minister – in marked contrast to other traditional rulers – played a major role in undermining apartheid. Later in life, he was to bravely take on the taboo of HIV and Aids, openly talking about the loss of his son and daughter to the disease at a time when few were willing to speak publicly about it and when President Thabo Mbeki was pursuing his catastrophic policy of Aids denial.

The Inkatha movement had been formed in 1975, with the backing of the ANC, as a national movement against apartheid, but in time it became synonymous with Mangosuthu Buthelezi and the KwaZulu administration (KZA) over which he presided as Chief Minister.

As popular unrest grew against the impacts of apartheid, the KZA increasingly clashed with radical youth elements and the wider public as they boycotted buses and schools under the control of the KZA. The KwaZulu Police, who reported directly to Buthelezi, were not shy about using force to quell protests, and as a result the movement became increasingly associated with the actions of the apartheid state, whose own police force was crushing similar dissent.

Radical youth anger with Buthelezi culminated in 1978 at the funeral of the Pan Africanist Congress leader Robert Sobukwe. When Buthelezi rose to give a eulogy, an element of the crowd shouted him down and demanded he leave. When he refused to do so, they rushed the stage, throwing stones and shouting, 'Kill the pig' and 'Sell out', forcing his bodyguards to fire shots in the air before assisting Buthelezi to make a rapid exit from the funeral.

For a man with Mangosuthu Buthelezi's acute sense of dignity, that public humiliation must have been very hard to bear. Only the previous month he had addressed 15,000 supporters in Soweto without incident. But this was really the turning point, and ever after, the radicals shunned him. The breach with the ANC leadership, however, did not take place until a year later, following a meeting in London between Buthelezi and the ANC leadership in exile. The ANC believed that Buthelezi had leaked confidential information about the meeting to the press, and after that they joined the radicals in shunning and criticising him. Despite this hostility, Nelson Mandela remained in contact and on friendly terms. Over a decade later, after the journalist involved had revealed the facts, the ANC conceded that it had been one of their own members who had leaked the information.

During the 1980s, as unrest against the white government increased, the hostility spilled over from the confrontations between migrant workers in the townships around Johannesburg into KwaZulu and Natal itself. By the late 1980s, a low-level civil war was under way between ANC-aligned organisations and Buthelezi's Inkatha. Thousands of people were tragically killed in this conflict, which only found resolution in the years after the end of apartheid. There was blame on all sides, but principally it must be placed on the white government, which relentlessly fuelled the confrontations as it sought to cling to power.

The level of violence reached a crescendo in the lead-up to the first democratic elections in 1994. Buthelezi had rejected the semi-federal model arrived at in the negotiations between the parties for an interim constitution, which he believed would not provide sufficient autonomy and devolution to the provinces of South Africa, nor appropriately recognise the Zulu identity. Consequently, Inkatha quit the all-party talks, and Buthelezi declared Inkatha's intention to boycott the election. As the date of the elections approached, there was huge trepidation that the situation would explode if elections went ahead without IFP participation.

Just a week before polling day, on 19 April 1994, Buthelezi dramatically agreed to abandon the boycott, signing an agreement with the ANC president, Nelson Mandela, and National Party leader and State President, F. W. de Klerk, which guaranteed the status of the Zulu King and made various commitments about the actions that each of the parties would take to bring an end to the violence. It also provided for international mediation on any outstanding issues in respect of the 1993 interim constitution.

A month before the agreement, the ANC and the National Party, along with the other parties in the Multi-Party Negotiating Process, had agreed unilaterally to amend the interim constitution to try to satisfy the demands of the IFP and other parties which were refusing to participate, by strengthening the powers of the provinces, particularly with regard to fiscal powers. The Constitution of the Republic of South Africa Amendment Act 1994, which gave effect to these changes and also renamed the province of Natal as KwaZulu-Natal, may have had a significant bearing on Buthelezi's ultimate decision to participate in the elections. The final constitution of South Africa, which was promulgated in 1996, retained significant powers for the provinces in a quasi-federal state.

Arranging the IFP participation at such short notice was no easy task: stickers had to be stuck on millions of ballot papers which had already been printed and further polling stations provided to meet the increased turnout that was expected. Nevertheless, the elections went ahead successfully, with millions queuing to vote across the country as South Africa entered a new era in its history. Despite the IFP's late involvement in the election campaign, the party managed to secure over 10 per cent of the vote and forty-three seats in the National Assembly. In the KwaZulu-Natal Provincial Legislature, it took over half the votes, gaining a narrow overall majority.

The 1994 settlement made provision for a government of national unity to include all parties, which Buthelezi agreed to join, taking the post of Minister of Home Affairs in the government led by Nelson Mandela. This was the position he held, alongside fellow IFP Cabinet ministers heading up the Departments of Correctional Services and Arts and Culture, when I arrived in South Africa in January 1999.

27

GETTING TO KNOW INKATHA

Early in January 1999, I flew to Durban, where the then chairperson of the IFP parliamentary caucus, Inka Mars, had kindly offered to put me up until the parliamentary session began a week or so later in Cape Town.

Despite her name, I assumed that Inka would be a Zulu, so I was a little surprised to be greeted by a striking blonde woman, who welcomed me enthusiastically as she ushered me into her home.

Inka's story is worth a book in its own right. Born in Hamburg, she split her formative years between her father's home there – I think her mother had died when she was young – and a boarding school in southern Germany, growing up through the years of the Nazi dictatorship and the Second World War.

When Germany finally collapsed in the face of the Allied advance, her teachers fled, leaving Inka and her schoolmates abandoned to whatever fate awaited them. Inka, however, was not one to wait on fate – she preferred to make her own – so she set out alone across the ruined country, navigating around the advancing armies and eventually arriving home in Hamburg to an astonished and highly relieved father.

After the war, her father sent her to au pair with Jewish friends who had escaped to Britain in the 1930s, and while there she met her future husband, Paul, a South African who was training to be a doctor. After they were married, they returned to South Africa and settled in Durban. Paul's family were well connected and Inka knew some of the leading politicians of the time, including the former South African Prime Minister, Jan Smuts.

Inka had been the chair of the Red Cross in what was then Natal Province. She had travelled widely in rural KwaZulu in that role and had got to know Buthelezi well through the Red Cross's work with the KwaZulu administration. Over time, Buthelezi had become close with Inka and Paul, and Paul subsequently became Buthelezi's personal doctor. Inka, who had always seen disturbing parallels between the National Party's ideology of racial supremacy and those that had brought such disaster on her native country, increasingly got involved in the politics of opposition, which in Natal was primarily centred around Inkatha.

When change came to South Africa, Buthelezi asked Inka to serve on the Inkatha team at the CODESA negotiations (Convention for a Democratic South Africa), and in 1994 she was elected to the National Assembly from the IFP list. Tragically, shortly after she had been elected as an MP, her husband died very suddenly of cancer.

I learnt a little of this that evening, sipping off-dry wine with Inka in her sitting room, but most of it later, over breakfasts and dinners and long evenings chatting over a bottle of wine. That night, however, after an hour or so of getting to know each other, Inka told me we should get to bed as we would have to be up at 5 a.m. to drive the three hours to Ulundi, where the National Council of the IFP was due to meet the next day. I asked Inka what I should wear and she advised a suit, although she provided no further suggestions as to what I might need to take on our trip.

Inka's house was up on the Berea, the ridge above downtown Durban, where many of the well-to-do houses were located. The huge bedroom that Inka now showed me into looked out across the Durban racetrack and the North Beach onto the vast expanse of the Indian Ocean beyond. It was a fantastic room, with its large windows through which I observed the most dramatic lightning storms I had seen in my life. Sheet lightning, lighting up the whole sky, exposing the huge container ships at anchor out to sea, waiting in line to enter Durban Harbour as the torrential rain hammered down.

Inka's house became my home from home whenever I was in Durban, and I spent many fascinating hours listening to the stories of her life. After I had returned to the UK, it was always my intention to take a month off and come to Durban in order to sit with Inka and record her fascinating life experiences. Like many of the things I have put off in life, I found, one day, that I had left it too late.

●　●　●

The next day, we set off just after sunrise, stopping to pick up Suzanne Vos, another of Inkatha's eclectic bunch of MPs. An Australian by birth, Suzanne got to know Inkatha as a journalist, eventually taking a job heading up the party's media relations and subsequently being elected as a Member of Parliament from Inkatha's party list.

A few years before, Suzanne was a passenger in a terrible car accident and now she cannot be in a car unless she is driving it herself, so she takes the wheel from Inka and I sit in the back, leaning forward uncomfortably to respond to their questions and try to join in their conversation. This is easier said than done: both women are of strong and often varying opinions, which they forthrightly express, interrupting one another frequently, so that it is hard to follow the conversation, let alone take part.

After we turn off the main highway on to the road to Ulundi, I sit back and leave Inka and Suzanne to their disputes, which largely seem to centre on internal party politics. Instead, I focus on the world outside the car as we wind our way through a landscape of undulating hills and sugar cane fields, past settlements of thatched huts and ever deeper into the rural heartland of South Africa. It is impossible not to be mesmerised by the verdant beauty all around.

Eventually, we arrive at Ulundi. It is a modest-sized town of 20,000 or so people, but as the traditional capital of Zululand, administrative centre of the erstwhile KwaZulu government and now seat of the Kwa-Zulu-Natal legislature, it has a status well beyond its size.

We pull up at what was, at the time, the world's smallest Holiday Inn; that it no longer holds this title is not, to my knowledge, due to the construction of a yet smaller Holiday Inn but rather because our Ulundi hotel ceased to bear the Holiday Inn brand.

As we get out of the car, Suzanne tells me I should get my bag as we will check in now before departing for the meeting. At this point, I realise that Inka's instructions the night before have left out the rather crucial piece of information that we are to stay the night in Ulundi. Consequently, I have neither toiletries nor change of clothes, which is not an ideal situation in the sweltering humidity of Ulundi at the height of summer.

After checking in, we drive to the KwaZulu Parliament building, where the meeting is to take place. Inka has warned me that she will have to negotiate my admission to the meeting and it may be that she won't be successful, but in the end there seems to be no problem and I am greeted in friendly fashion by all those I meet.

Before the meeting starts formally, I am briefly introduced to Mangosuthu Buthelezi. He offers a greeting and smiles but doesn't appear to take much interest. He takes his place on the dais with his fellow Cabinet ministers and the Premier of the province and then the meeting is ready to begin. It starts with prayers and Bible readings. An IFP

Member of the Provincial Parliament has been selected by Buthelezi to read a particular passage from the Bible which is largely focused on the retribution that will be visited on those who speak with forked tongues – there is much nudging and whispering in the assembled audience as he reads the passage, and I later discover he is suspected of being behind recent leaks to the media.

The formalities over, we move to a PowerPoint presentation on the forthcoming general election campaign, which is led by a Taiwanese-South African businessman. From what I can gather, the main element of the election strategy involves distributing huge volumes of T-shirts which the said businessman will manufacture in his factories in Taiwan. The presentation is hilariously unsubtle, complete with glaringly absurd spelling mistakes in the slogans he has chosen to emblazon on the shirts.

Buthelezi has come off the stage so that he can see the presentation which is being projected on to a backdrop at the back of the stage, and now he is sitting just in front of me. Halfway through the presentation, he leans back and turns his head to me. 'Mr Oates,' he whispers, 'when this man has finished speaking, I would like you to comment on this presentation.'

I gulp and whisper to the back of his head that as I have been in South Africa a very short time, I feel it would be presumptuous of me to comment on something I know so little about. Buthelezi's head revolves once more, and he says in the firm, but slightly bewildered tone of someone unused to dissent, 'As I have said, Mr Oates, I would like you to comment on the presentation.'

There is no choice but to do as I am bid, so I start furiously to scribble down a few notes to refer to when I am called on to speak. I make the instant judgement that Buthelezi has not been impressed with the presentation and wants me to be the independent voice that kills it.

Eventually, the businessman winds up his presentation. Buthelezi returns to his place on the stage and calls on me to speak.

Less than twenty-four hours after arriving in South Africa, I rise to speak to the National Council of the Inkatha Freedom Party in the Kwa-Zulu Parliament, damp with sweat and seized with a terrible fear that if I get this wrong, I will blow my South African career before I have even started it.

I damn the presentation with faint praise. It is interesting. The slogans are fascinating. T-shirts no doubt have a role to play. But they are just collateral, a vehicle for a message, sure, but they cannot be THE strategy. First, the party must decide on the story it wants to tell and who it wants to tell it to. Once they are clear on that, then they can turn to how they will deliver their message. It can't be the other way around.

I sit down sweating profusely; the air conditioning has decided this is the moment to pack up. Inka whispers, 'Well done,' but I can't read Buthelezi, who sits impassive on the stage. The T-shirt man is not so unreadable. He has on an unambiguous face of fury.

I needn't have worried about Buthelezi's response. At lunchtime, I am invited to sit at his table, an unmistakable signal of favour. I have received the mark of approval and, more importantly, everyone can see that I have. This is to make my time in South Africa much easier than it might have been, particularly when things later get ugly between myself and the IFP Chief Whip, Koos van der Merwe.

In the evening, Inka and I are invited to dinner at the house of Daphne and Eric Lucas, a 'coloured' couple, in South Africa's crazy racial parlance, who identify as black and who have made their home in Ulundi. It is a beautiful home, with a stunning living area, a double-height space, with a landing all around that leads to the upstairs bedroom. Outside is a walled garden with a pool and a *rondavel* (a large, round thatched hut). But the most beautiful thing about the house is the family who live in it.

Eric and Daphne's daughter, Nicky, who is a few years older than me, welcomes me with huge, sisterly warmth. She has a smile, edged with dimples, which couldn't fail to light up even the most curmudgeonly soul – which is lucky as she is dealing with me – and, combined with her twinkling eyes and forthright spirit, makes her impossible to resist. She becomes a friend in an instant and my main partner in crime over the next two years.

Eric, Nicky's dad, is a member of the National Assembly. Although on occasion he can be quick to anger when he senses an injustice, it is really just the flip side of the emotional warmth that is his dominant gene. Nicky's mischievous nature has clearly been inherited from Eric, who loves to tease and play practical jokes. He instantly christens me 'Jungle', after the South African brand of porridge oats. It's only my second evening in the country, but the warmth of the welcome I have received from both Inka and the Lucas family has already made me feel at home.

28

CAPE TOWN

In early February 1999, I fly to Cape Town ahead of the parliamentary session which is due to start later in the month. I am met at the airport by two Afrikaans women who work for the Chief Whip in Parliament. Elize and Elsje greet me warmly at arrivals and tell me they have been instructed by Koos to take me on a tour of Cape Town and the surrounding area and to stand me lunch. First, we will go to the flat that Inka has helped organise for me in the Garden Centre so that I can drop my bags.

I groan inwardly. I had hoped to be able to arrive discreetly and get my bearings before meeting new people, and the last thing I feel like right now is a guided tour by two women I have never met. Given my experiences in South Africa a decade before, I also have a highly prejudiced suspicion of Afrikaners.

Despite these reservations, the time I spend with Elize and Elsje is a revelation, in which the seeds of friendship are sown with both of them and I gain a rather more nuanced view of Afrikaners than I had formed on my first visit to South Africa.

Elize has worked for Koos for some years and is in her forties, slim, tall and elegant, but in a constant state of stress as a result of trying to juggle her demanding boss and her demanding family. The bubbly and vivacious Elsje, by contrast, who is in her late twenties, refuses to take anything too seriously.

They give me a wonderful tour of the key sights around Cape Town, but I remember in particular the vast empty beach of white sand at Noordhoek and then the drive up and along Chapman's Peak, a spectacular road clinging to the cliffs as it winds its way high above the Atlantic Ocean before descending into the fishing village of Hout Bay. Here, we stop for lunch, looking out over the water and chatting, at first tentatively and awkwardly as we try to work each other out, but increasingly easily, finishing our lunch amiably, laughing and smoking over coffee.

Despite their conservative Afrikaans background, they are genuinely working out how to play their constructive part amidst the new and alien dynamic in which they find themselves. There is an honesty about their efforts to adjust that is largely absent from the English-speaking white community, who hide behind their fiction that apartheid was an exclusively Afrikaans product.

•   •   •

Parliament reassembles in mid-February for a short session ahead of the general election, which is scheduled for June 1999. The IFP are housed in the Good Hope building, a beautiful whitewashed Cape Dutch construction within the parliamentary compound, adjacent to the Tuynhuys, the President's Cape Town office.

I am given a spacious room overlooking the Tuynhuys gardens, the first office I have had of my own and in a setting that is yet to be matched. There is a little school just a few yards away, which serves children of around five or six. In the early days that I am in the office, if the teacher pops out of the classroom for a moment, they will all run to the window and call out 'Hello' to me an interminable number of times until she returns and admonishes them.

Once I am settled in, I turn my attention to the task I have been assigned. The IFP caucus lacks an organised media and research capacity, and it is my task to help establish this. When I arrive, there is one media officer, Joyce Moretlwe, who must serve the conflicting demands of forty-three MPs. Joyce is smart, enthusiastic and accomplished in managing relations with the media, but the parliamentary leadership has no strategy for its communications, so whatever individual media successes she achieves fail to make a wider impact.

The burden of the research function is also borne by one person, a kindly and effective English-speaking white woman in her fifties called Patricia. She is also pulled in every direction by the IFP's eclectic group of MPs, who demand more of her time than there are hours in the day, each of them insisting that they are the absolute priority.

Although the parliamentary caucus accepts my argument that we must establish a better-resourced and -focused research and media function, they are not in a position to commit to employing additional staff ahead of the general election. I understand the constraint, but it is frustrating nonetheless.

In the interim, I set about working with Joyce and Patricia to ensure we can be as effective as possible for the remaining period of the parliament. The first major parliamentary event is the Budget, and I decide this is a good opportunity to demonstrate to the IFP caucus how effective its existing staff resource can be if it is focused effectively. I am aided in this by Inkatha's finance spokesperson, Dr Gavin Woods, former head of the Inkatha Institute, Inkatha's think tank, who is a joy to work with and immediately buys into my argument that we must have a clear media plan to ensure we are first off the blocks with our Budget response. We work over the weekend ahead of the Budget to analyse and anticipate the approach that Finance Minister Trevor Manuel is likely to take and to agree the proactive message that the IFP should convey.

On Budget Day we are well prepared. At 1.55 p.m., just before the

Finance Minister gets to his feet in the National Assembly, Gavin emerges from the room in which he and the other party spokesmen have been provided with an advance copy of the Budget and hands me a floppy disk containing a detailed five-page response.

I return to the office and tweak the draft press statement we have already prepared, while Joyce positions herself on the steps of the National Assembly to marshal reporters and ensure that Gavin is in front of the TV cameras as soon as the Budget is over. As the Finance Minister sits down, I start to fax the major news outlets and each of the parliamentary journalists with our toplines and detailed response.

Thanks to our preparations and Joyce's sharp elbows, Gavin duly appears on every major TV and radio bulletin, and our 'Budget of missed opportunities' topline headlines the half-page splash on *Business Day*, the main financial daily. It's an effective first outing for the media and research unit, for which we receive much praise. I can't help noticing, however, that there is a fair amount of jealous carping directed at Gavin Woods as a result. The IFP don't seem to be happy when a poppy grows taller.

●　●　●

At Inka's suggestion, I rent a small studio flat in an apartment block above the Garden Centre shopping mall, where she also stays while in the Cape. From the outside, it is a nondescript grey concrete tower rising out of a nondescript grey concrete shopping centre; the apartments are small and confining and regularly harassed by the Cape Doctor, the powerful south-easterly wind, which whips and wails its way around the building whenever it comes to town. Nevertheless, despite these drawbacks, it is conveniently close to Parliament, has fantastic views over the city and offers easy access to the shops. It is also where I meet Ebrahim, who is to become a close friend.

Ebrahim is a Tottenham-supporting security guard who works in the building. I meet him through Hugh, a friend of mine who is working for the Democratic Party in Parliament and also stays at the Garden Centre. Ebrahim and I bond immediately over football – in my limited experience, there are not so many ardent Tottenham fans in Africa as to let the opportunity go wanting. Over time, I get to know him and his family – Shirley, Ashraf and Zakeer – well, often visiting them out in Eersterivier, just beyond Khayelitsha on the Cape Flats.

Ebrahim is a tall, slim man with a hearty laugh, a sing-song Cape accent and a strong sense of the absurd. His life symbolises the injustices of the apartheid system: intelligent and knowledgeable, his opportunities were stunted by apartheid's grotesque system of racial classification, which condemned him to substandard education and a lifetime of discrimination.

Although the poverty that afflicts Ebrahim's family is far less acute than that of many who live out on the Cape Flats, my friendship with Ebrahim at least gives me some understanding that the gilded white life I live in Cape Town is the exception and that the vast majority of South Africans, even those fortunate enough to be in work, live very tough lives indeed.

● ● ●

It was also Hugh who introduced me to what became another important feature of my life in Cape Town, the Savoy Cabbage. My first meal there was with Hugh and Ben – who was also working on the Westminster Foundation project and was based in the National Council of the Provinces, South Africa's upper house of Parliament – and Ben's then partner, Samantha. I don't remember that much about the meal, but it must have been good because when Vijay came out to visit me in Cape Town, it was the first place I took him.

We got chatting with the waiter and Vijay asked him if there were any good places to go out in Cape Town. In the end we stayed until the restaurant closed and then all went out together. Gavin was fun and irreverent and handsome, and I immediately took a shine to him. We had a good night out and subsequently Gavin and I became an item for a while. Although our relationship didn't last that long, we remained friends, and through Gavin I got to know Caroline, the owner of the restaurant, and many of the staff.

The Savoy Cabbage became one of my favourite haunts and Caroline one of my closest friends. She was funny and sharp-tongued and shared a love of books even more intense than my own. I had my thirtieth birthday at the Cabbage, and it was the first place I visited whenever I returned to Cape Town, usually staying with Caroline at her beautiful Victorian home in Newlands. When Caroline finally closed the restaurant after twenty-one years, it felt like a personal loss.

My other haunt was the Fireman's Arms, where I would watch football or rugby matches with Richard Calland, Lawson Naidoo and others. Lawson was a former ANC activist and special adviser to the first Speaker of the National Assembly who had lived in exile in London during the apartheid years. Richard was an English barrister turned democracy activist and journalist who became an important mentor to me. Together with Lawson and Gaye Davis, a leading political journalist then married to Richard, he helped guide me through the world of South African politics and media. When things became difficult for me with the IFP Chief Whip, both Richard and Lawson proved great sources of wisdom and support.

• • •

The final session of South Africa's first democratic parliament takes place on Friday 26 March 1999. President Mandela is to give his last speech to Parliament after five momentous years. A seat in the gallery is the hottest ticket in town but, as so often, Inka comes through for me, generously giving me her one guest ticket.

I can't quite believe that I am here in the public gallery of the South African Parliament, looking down as Nelson Mandela bows out as President. I think back to the upturned milk crates of the non-stop picket outside South Africa House in London; the ache that came to your bum after an hour or so of sitting, and the relief of standing to chant our slogans demanding Mandela's release. It had seemed an impossible dream then, but now the dream is nearly ten years old and for five of those years Mandela has been President. An inspiration not just to South Africa but to the world.

I feel immensely privileged to be witnessing this moment in history as the opposition leaders, followed by the Deputy President, Thabo Mbeki, and the Speaker of the National Assembly, Frene Ginwala, take to the rostrum in praise of Mandela, before he speaks himself. It is the last time he will speak as President in this, the first democratic parliament in South Africa's history, come into being because of his struggle and sacrifice and the struggle and sacrifice of thousands of others like him.

The uptight, wiry Democratic Party leader, Tony Leon, who is usually more at home pouring opprobrium down on the ANC, gives a surprisingly generous and powerful address. Buthelezi strikes a slightly discordant note, unable to resist attacking the ANC, even while praising Madiba himself. Patricia de Lille, speaking for the Pan Africanist Congress, is funny and warm. The Reverend Kenneth Meshoe, the African Christian Democratic Party leader, raises Mandela's proximity to meeting with his maker, which seems a bit close to the line and causes his audience to wince.

Deputy President Mbeki's speech is a flowery, literary effort, full of poetry but lacking an essential real warmth. It leaves me speculating, in a letter home, that it might be better if Mbeki dedicated his life to literature rather than politics. Given the catastrophe that his bizarre denial of the Aids crisis sweeping South Africa was to cause when he became President, that would have been much the better call.

It is the speech of Marthinus van Schalkwyk, the leader of the opposition New National Party, however, that strikes me most powerfully. Van Schalkwyk is almost universally regarded as a hapless figure and disastrous leader of the opposition. A mousy, schoolboy-faced man, more often than not referred to by his nickname 'Kortbroek' – literally, 'Short trousers' – he seems a small figure beside his predecessor, F. W. de Klerk. But that day, it is what he and Mandela have to say that most interests me.

For sure, it is not the power of his words that strike me: Leon is far more articulate and Mbeki more poetic. But the simple fact that the leader of the National Party is speaking in praise of a black President in the Parliament that until just a few years ago was the preserve of the racial dictatorship that his party created is astonishing. He concludes in English, halting Zulu, Xhosa and then his native Afrikaans:

'Mr President, you are leaving the world richer for having been here.'

'Hamba Kahle, Madiba.' ('Go well, Madiba.')

'iSouth Africa Ikujongile Halala.' ('South Africa salutes you.')

'Mooi loop!' ('Walk carefully!')

Perhaps even more astonishing is that when he finishes, the ANC benches rise as one to applaud.

To someone with even the very passing involvement in the anti-apartheid movement that I had, it is an electrifying moment. The leader of the National Party praising a black President, applauded by ANC MPs, who now make up a majority in the South African Parliament. It is thrilling and moving, and you can tell that Marthinus 'Kortbroek' van Schalkwyk means every word.

History will afford van Schalkwyk the most minor of footnotes, if it remembers him at all, and I suspect the footnote is likely to be unkind. It shouldn't be. For all the derision that is poured on his head, for all that the result of the 1999 election is a devastating rejection of his approach – the NNP slumping from 20 per cent of the vote in 1994 to less than 7 per cent in 1999 – and despite the farcical merger and then split with the Democratic Party, followed by the NNP's ultimate merger with the ANC, van Schalkwyk is to my mind a bigger figure than his principal political rival, Tony Leon.

Where Leon sees that by ruthlessly exploiting and stoking the fears of minority ethnic groups, predominantly the white, coloured and Indian populations, he can seize the political initiative, van Schalkwyk can see that, while this may be the best route to short-term advantage, it will sow further seeds of discord for the future.

The session ends with Mandela's closing speech. It is a short speech that takes pride in South Africa's achievement in establishing a multiracial democracy and yet is full of humility about where the government and the country have fallen short.

As he concludes his remarks, the whole of Parliament comes to its feet and the ANC benches erupt in a praise song to Madiba. Looking down on the chamber, full of colour and hope and joy, the future of the rainbow nation seems bright.

29

KWAZULU-NATAL

The farewell tributes to Mandela mark the end of the first democratic parliament, and after a party at the President's residence at Groote Schuur, MPs disperse across the country to begin the election campaign. I remain in Parliament for the first few weeks, working with the parliamentary authorities to plan the induction of new MPs after the election. Then, with that work largely completed, I head up to KwaZulu-Natal.

I am now the owner of a ten-year-old white BMW 318i, my pride and joy, purchased from Wayne Motors, proprietor Mr John Wayne – obviously. The white BMW isn't my first choice; standing next to it in the showroom is a beautiful red convertible 320i of similar age. Unfortunately, it is some way above my price range. I try to bargain the price down, but Eugene, son of the above, is having none of it.

He fairly points out that the car is ill suited to me. Firstly, because it is crazy to own a convertible in South Africa: convertibles, he says, are suitable for England, perhaps, but definitely not South Africa, where the heat and the crime rate mean that you will only be able to have the hood down on the rarest of occasions – mostly when the car is secured in your garage.

Secondly and most saliently, the car is unsuitable for me, Eugene explains, because I don't have the money to pay for it. I am forced to accept

Eugene's brutal logic and purchase the white BMW instead. I leave the showroom the proud, if slightly disappointed, owner of my first car.

It is in this car that I set out before sunrise one Saturday morning in April, heading through the quiet streets of Cape Town and onto the N1, the main highway to Johannesburg, which snakes its way through the winelands and up into the mountain passes before descending to the arid semi-desert of the Karoo.

The air is cool in the April dawn, and I drive at first with the windows open, the sounds of nature coming through the car windows. But as I get towards Paarl, smoke is in the air from wildfires burning uncomfortably close to the road. I put my foot to the floor and drive on through the smoke, anxious in case the fires close in around me.

Just before I begin the climb up the Hex River Pass, a red light appears on the dashboard. I pull in and call Faiez, the mechanic at Wayne Motors. He asks me a few questions before reassuring me it is nothing to worry about. So I set off again up the steep mountain highway. As I begin the descent down the other side of the pass, my mobile begins to ring. I can see it is Faiez calling, but it is too dangerous to answer the phone, so I wait until I am at the bottom of the pass before pulling over and calling him back.

'Sorry, Jonny, man,' Faiez starts, 'I got that wrong, it's the brake disc light! That's a problem. You need to replace them.'

'FAIEZ! I have just driven up and down the mountain and you know that I am on my way to Durban. I thought this was all checked in the service.'

'Ya, we don't check that except in the full service, which you didn't want, no?' he says pointedly. 'But don't worry, it'll be OK for a couple of thousand ks. But you know when you're in Durban, you should definitely get that fixed.'

Slightly reassured, I resume my journey. The spectacular mountain valleys now give way to the Great Karoo, a vast expanse of flat, arid scrubland, largely empty except for sheep, ostriches and isolated farmsteads.

As I drive through the Karoo, it starts to take a hold on me. I have heard it dismissed as 'flat and empty, mile after boring mile', but I love the desolate beauty of the boundless emptiness, the one-horse towns that pepper the highway, the sense of freedom that is engendered by space.

The Karoo is punctuated by small but majestic towns built with the wealth generated by the ostrich feather mania that gripped the world in the mid- to late nineteenth century. During this period, the feathers, used in women's fashion, most notably hats, were worth more than their weight in gold, and this part of South Africa had cornered the market. Now, the ostriches that still stride the Great Karoo are farmed mostly for their meat rather than their feathers and today are worth somewhat less than their weight in gold.

I arrive in Hanover in the Northern Cape in the late afternoon. A pretty Afrikaans town that claims to be at the centre of the country, the midpoint on a journey between Cape Town and Johannesburg and Durban, it feels like the centre of nowhere. It's a Saturday afternoon and the streets have been abandoned by the inhabitants – disciples of the Afrikaans true religion of rugby – in favour of the Springboks game. It feels like a gold rush town after the rush.

At its height, Hanover was a key stopping-off point for adventurers on their way up from the Cape to seek their fortune in the Kimberley diamond mines or the gold fields of the Witwatersrand, but the railway brought an end to most of that trade. Today, it just feels like a lost place to me, a town that time has washed over, leaving a dispiriting residue of Sunday afternoon sadness.

Lacking anything else to do, I watch the end of the Springboks match before going in search of dinner. Afterwards, I retire to the bar of the small hotel I am staying in to enjoy a beer and scribble down some notes about the spectacular beauty I have seen on my journey so far. The only other occupants of this drinking spot are a couple – like me, in their twenties – who are constantly switching between English and Afrikaans in a way that intrigues me, not least because they appear to be talking about Winston Churchill.

On one trip from my seat to the bar to collect another Castle lager, they say hello and ask me if I am writing a book, to which I answer yes, which in a way is true, and they invite me to join them. It turns out they are colleagues who work on the long-distance tourist buses.

Piet has just finished his shift and is keeping Klara, his colleague, company before dropping her off to meet the night bus, which is due in Laingsburg later in the evening. We sit and chat for a few hours and it becomes clear there is an attraction between Piet and me. He gives me the address of the motel where he stays, 30km up the road in Laingsburg, and I promise to drop in for a coffee on my way through later in the morning.

I wake early and slightly hungover and get on the road, stopping at the Engen petrol station in Laingsburg and grabbing two coffees before heading to Piet's motel. I am unsure whether he really wants me to call on him at this time of morning, but he had been insistent that I should, so I don't feel I can pass through Laingsburg without doing so. He is, not surprisingly, still asleep when I knock on his door, but he rallies and makes a good effort at insisting that he really had wanted me to call on him at this ungodly hour.

Our conversation is amiable but stilted and brief. So, after we have both drunk our coffee, we say slightly awkward farewells, exchanging cell numbers and making commitments to keep in touch that probably neither of us really intend to keep.

I drive fast along the straight clear road towards KwaZulu-Natal, and as the kilometres begin to disintegrate under my determined assault, the Karoo gradually gives way to the flat farming land of the Free State. I stop every few hours to load up on caffeine and petrol and keep pushing on, determined to get to Durban that day. The sun is setting as the road turns towards the coast, winding its way down through KwaZulu-Natal, the spectacular peaks of the Drakensberg Mountains to its right. The last two hours through the darkness are a strain, and I arrive in Durban a little stressed and not in the best frame of mind to navigate the streets, which are still unfamiliar to me. Eventually, however, I pull up at Inka's house and I am immediately restored by the warmth of her greeting and the wine and food she has ready for me.

• • •

In the morning, we head into town to the IFP headquarters. I drive and Inka navigates, issuing my instructions only just before they must be carried out, which makes for a stressful journey, particularly once we emerge on the other side of the racecourse into the downtown traffic, with the minibus taxis swerving and hooting around me. At the office, Nicky and Walter Ntsele, the office manager, welcome me with a warmth that immediately makes me feel at home. When I am issued with my IFP pass, it reads 'Jonathan Nkosinathi Oates'. 'Nkosinathi', Walter and Nicky tell me, is now my Zulu name. Apparently, it means 'God is with us', and at that moment I feel he is.

The IFP election campaign is being advised by two consultants from the UK, Andrew Smith and his colleague James Prior. They are both on the political right: Andrew is a Conservative whose favourite phrase during the campaign – 'Well that's us completely fucked then, matey' – is always cheerfully delivered; James is a former adviser to the Conservative Party who jumped ship to James Goldsmith's Referendum Party for the 1997 general election. I have reason to be grateful to James and the Referendum Party, their 1,470 votes in Kingston and Surbiton having allowed Ed Davey to beat the Conservatives by a whisker in Ed's first outing as a candidate and mine as an election agent. James Prior is later dubbed one of the 'bad boys of Brexit' as the result of his work with the Brexit campaigners.

Despite the very stark differences in political outlook between the three of us, we all manage to get on well most of the time. Jimmy is in charge of organising the rallies that are a staple of a South African election campaign, and I am invited to attend one that is due to take place in Phuthaditjhaba, a mountain town nestling amidst the Drakensberg peaks in the Free State, bordering both KZN and Lesotho.

The town is nondescript, but the setting is magnificent. Phuthaditjhaba means 'the meeting of the tribes' and it was once the capital of the apartheid 'independent state' of QwaQwa, now absorbed into the Free State. For the purposes of the rally, the town is once again a meeting place of the tribes, this time of the Zulu and the Basotho, and Mangosuthu Buthelezi is coming to town to be part of it.

In the apartheid-era stadium, James Prior, Nicky and a team of assistants are constructing a stage with a huge IFP backdrop. James knows what he is about and organises things quickly and efficiently. I offer to help, and soon I am part of the gang, carrying poles and canopies and organising T-shirts and flags for distribution.

As we work, the stadium starts to fill up with people in vibrant local dress, at first a trickle and then an ever-increasing flow until there are perhaps a thousand people in the stadium. The stage complete, there are lots of other things to attend to. The media have to be managed, the dignitaries attended to and the issue of the cows and sheep addressed.

The traditional leaders of the area feel duty-bound to provide a gift of sheep and cows to their fellow traditional leaders, but this is a poor area and they want somehow to be recompensed, and they are asking Jimmy for the money. He asks me to get on to the national election coordinator and discover if we are allowed to pay for this. I call him on my cell phone and to my surprise manage to locate him. 'Jonny,' he says, 'you can pay for cows or sheep or goats or lizards for all I care. Just do not pay for people. That is not allowed.'

I impart this news to Jimmy, who is frustrated that he doesn't have a reason to refuse to pay. He discreetly pulls out a wad of cash and peels off the amount that has been demanded. As I suspect he feared, this payment encourages other demands. Next in line are the horses. The Basotho tribesmen of this area are renowned horsemen; they will be greeting Buthelezi's arrival with a demonstration of these skills, but there is, ahem, the question of who will pay for the horse feed, which is very expensive, many days riding to get here, you understand, of course, that they must be recompensed...

Eventually, around midday, the Minister of Home Affairs and Inkatha President, His Excellency Mangosuthu Buthelezi, along with the Premier of KwaZulu-Natal, Lionel Mtshali, arrive in gleaming bullet-proof Mercedes-Benzes with accompanying security vehicles. As soon as they are in their places in the stadium, the tribesmen on horseback, dressed in their colourful traditional blankets and conical hats, thunder into the stadium to greet them.

A clergyman now takes to the rostrum. He is determined to spin out his time in the limelight and drones on interminably with his prayers. Eventually, he is finished and Jimmy, who is standing to the right of the stage, is now approached by an emissary of the clergyman. The clergyman has come a long way, he has been generous with his prayers, you will understand he must, ahem, be compensated for his troubles.

At this stage, Jimmy has had enough: 'I've paid for the sodding cows. I've paid for the sodding horses. I've paid for the sodding sheep. I am NOT paying for the fucking clergyman.' He turns to me: 'Didn't you say we were allowed to pay for anything except people?'

I confirm that this is what the national election coordinator has told me.

Cue an angry glare and the furious exit of the clergyman, who will presumably be saying prayers for the ANC in future.

• • •

We stay the night in guest cabins up a steep mountain pass above Phuthaditjhaba. In the early morning light, the views down into the valley are stunning. Jimmy comes to my cabin while I am smoking outside and admiring the view. He asks if we can go inside, as he has something to ask me. He explains that after the rally he is flying to Johannesburg with Nicky and he doesn't want to worry her that he carries a gun, which will become apparent if he has to check it in at the firearms desk. He wonders, therefore, given I am driving back in the minibus to Durban with Andrew, whether I would be willing to carry his gun back and give it to his wife.

I say no, without hesitation. In the first place, I explain, I am not licensed to carry a weapon.

'That's not a problem,' Jimmy tells me. 'Under South African law, if I write a letter authorising you to carry my gun, you can do so for seven days.'

This sounds like bullshit to me, although later I discover that, absurdly, this actually is the law.

In any case, whether it is lawful or not, I have no wish to carry a gun, ever. So, despite Jimmy's entreaties, I remain adamant and when he realises he is not going to convince me, he departs good-naturedly.

Andrew and I leave in the minibus later that morning and head back to Durban. We arrive at the house that Jimmy is renting in Kloof to drop off some gear from the rally, and as he gets out, Andrew reaches under the driver's seat and pulls out Jimmy's gun. It seems he has been more amenable than me.

•   •   •

The election is not only for members of the National Assembly but also for the legislatures of the nine provinces that make up the semi-federal structure of South Africa.

In KwaZulu-Natal, for the first time, there will be a televised debate between the candidates for Premier of the province. In 1994, no one would have dreamt of holding such an event; it would have begun and ended in violence and bloodshed. It may do yet in this campaign, but the organisers believe the situation has changed significantly enough to be worth the risk, and the police are prepared to facilitate it.

It's my first experience of taking part in negotiations for a TV debate – albeit that they are really just a dictation of terms by the news organisations that are running it – but it isn't going to be my last.

On Monday 26 April, supporters and candidates assemble at the International Convention Centre in Durban. The first instruction on our tickets is that no firearms or other weapons are allowed. We are segregated like football fans: the IFP on the left, the ANC on the right, with the Democratic Party and New National Party forming a buffer zone in between. At the back of the hall are twenty or thirty heavily armed police officers in their light-blue South African Police Service fatigues. Their unmissable presence does the opposite of instilling confidence in me. I sit down nervously in my place next to Nicky.

The debate starts relatively good humouredly, but when the hardline IFP Premier, Lionel Mtshali, begins to speak there is a palpable increase in tension, which he decides to ramp up much further. He starts out on a routine attacking the ANC – 'When we were building schools, you were burning them. When we were creating jobs, you were destroying them…' – and then the heckling and catcalls start from the ANC side of the audience and increase in volume with every one of Mtshali's refrains.

Then a member of the IFP section stands, looks imperiously over at the ANC ranks and shouts out a short staccato sentence in Zulu, in a voice that cuts through all the noise.

For a nanosecond no one moves and then suddenly everyone seems to be on their feet shouting. The SAPS start to finger their weapons nervously. I turn to Nicky to ask what has been shouted.

Nicky says, 'He shouted, "Silence in the squatter camps." It's a big insult to the ANC.'

Then, as the hostility in the room continues to build, Nicky says, her voice tight with tension, 'Jonny, we may need to move very rapidly.' Adrenalin is already flowing through my veins and I am sprung and ready to run.

But suddenly another shout cuts through the hubbub and is met with laughter and then the cacophony of noise starts to subside and, as rapidly as it had begun, the tension dissipates, and calm is restored.

Notwithstanding the brief hiatus, the rest of the debate passes off peacefully, and the fact that it has done so is seen as a major step forward for the normalisation of politics in the province. But there is still some way to go, as we are about to find out.

There are other firsts during the campaign as well. A first for me is seeing an elected representative – in this case a Member of the Provincial Parliament – unveil a huge arms cache in the middle of the election campaign.

A fortnight before polling day, IFP strongman Philip Powell, a Member of the KwaZulu-Natal Provincial Parliament, leads investigators to a huge cache of arms that have been hidden near Nquthu in the heart of Zululand. The cache includes rocket launchers, mortars, hand grenades, small arms ammunition and other ordnance. 'Enough weaponry', the Attorney General declares, 'to start a war.'

Walter Felgate, a former IFP member who has defected to the ANC – and is the ex-husband of Buthelezi's secretary – claims that Powell, who was in charge of training Inkatha Self-Protection Units, reported directly to Buthelezi. Buthelezi denies all knowledge of the arms, and Powell is an ex-apartheid security policeman, with who knows what agenda besides saving his own skin. Nevertheless, it is hard to think this latest news will help the public to conclude positively as they prepare to cast their ballots.

On Monday 31 May, the last campaigning day before polling day on 2 June, Mangosuthu Buthelezi and Lionel Mtshali are campaigning around Durban. I decide to go along for the ride and join James, Nicky and Gladys, a volunteer from the UK, in the minibus. The first stop is the vast Pavilion shopping centre, north of Durban, where Buthelezi and his entourage tour the shops and walkways, to the initial bemusement of the shoppers, who gradually warm to the novelty of the event.

It is then on to Mariannridge, a township and alleged ANC stronghold on the outskirts of Durban. A good supportive crowd awaits Buthelezi, however, and as I alight from the minibus I find myself mobbed by supporters desperate for one of the fistful of Inkatha paper flags that Nicky has handed me. I dispense them quickly, making myself an instant hero with those who receive one and an instant enemy of those who don't. The boss waves and shakes hands, and a clickety-clack chant starts up from the crowd – 'YaWin Inkatha, YaWin. YaWin Inkatha, YaWin.' Then Mandla, a former radio jockey on Zulu-language Radio Ukhozi, using Buthelezi's praise name, Shenge, starts the crowd singing 'Thuma mina we Shenge' ('Send me Shenge, I am ready'). Flags wave, T-shirts are handed out and then the convoy is off again, this time to Chatsworth, an Indian township just down the road. This turns into a debacle. The Minority Front leader, Amichand Rajbansi, is lying in wait for the convoy, and a bizarre stand-off takes place between Rajbansi and an IFP MP from the Indian community. Accusations of affairs are made and denied and insults fly. It turns out that in denying an allegation of an affair with a fellow IFP candidate, the IFP MP has suggested in his defence that the person in question is not exactly attractive so why would he? This remark understandably ignites the indignation of his fellow candidate, who hurries off to the police station declaring that she intends to lodge a complaint of malicious defamation. The entourage makes a rapid retreat. It seems unlikely that many votes have been won here.

The last stop is Umlazi, the fourth biggest township in the country and also a traditional area of ANC strength. The reception is once again positive, and the convoy makes many more stops throughout the township than had been planned. At each there is chanting and signing and the call and response of 'Amandla' ('Power') and the crowd roaring in response 'Awethu' ('To the people'), along with much Viva Shenge-ing. At one stop on the route, there are a number of ANC youth milling about on the other side of the road sporting Mbeki T-shirts, but if they look a little sullen at this showing of IFP support, there is no sense of threat.

At the final stop in Umlazi, I leave the minibus and join Andrew on Dr Buthelezi's campaign bus, emblazoned in IFP colours. Buthelezi is sitting towards the back of the bus conducting a radio interview with the BBC World Service. The interviewer has offended him and now he is berating her on tape. Andrew comes forward looking harassed and asks the bus driver to start the engine in the hope that the engine noise will make the recording unusable. Buthelezi looks up sharply and reprimands the driver and orders the engine off – 'Doesn't he realise a radio interview is taking place!' Andrew shrugs despairingly, apologises to the driver and returns to his seat.

The radio interview finished, we set off. I am right at the front, by the well of the steps that lead to the door. This is where Des, Buthelezi's head of security, has taken up position. His head is constantly moving, searching out any source of potential danger, constantly alert. But today he is relaxed enough to talk as he keeps up his vigil.

'You know, Jon,' he says, 'in 1994 I wouldn't have let him go near some of the places we have been today. He wouldn't have come out alive. None of us would.'

He pauses, and then he says reflectively, almost to himself, 'Ya, you know, it's different today; it's a different country now.'

● ● ●

Election Day does not have quite the spine-tingling, history-making feel of five years before; nonetheless, it is an awesome and humbling sight to see the lines of voters that stretch around the polling stations across the length and breadth of the country. Many of them, in the rural areas, have walked for miles to take part in this amazing exercise of freely choosing their own government.

The results flow into the Independent Electoral Commission Operations Centre in Pretoria over the next few days, where Reverend Zondi, the party's national spokesperson, and Koos van der Merwe, the Chief Whip and a lawyer by trade, are positioned. It is clear from the outset that the ANC will probably get the two-thirds majority in Parliament denied to them in 1994, that the New National Party is in big trouble, having been overtaken by their Democratic Party rivals, and that the IFP vote share has not collapsed as widely predicted ahead of elections.

On Friday 4 June, I am with Inka and Nicky on my way to a farewell party for Andrew Smith and Jimmy Prior, which is being held on the pool deck of the Holiday Inn Crowne Plaza on Durban's North Beach.

Just as we step out of the lift, my phone rings. It is Andrew, and he can't hide his excitement. The latest figures from the IEC have put the IFP in front of the Democratic Party, which will make the IFP the official opposition. I am a little sceptical, as the IFP was 200,000 votes behind when I left the office, but Andrew is adamant and as we arrive on the pool deck, the euphoria becomes infectious. Another IFP MP arrives and tells us that SABC radio and TV has confirmed the news. The sense of euphoria grows.

I am standing in a group, chatting with Buthelezi, who is exuding good humour, his face awash with smiles, when his aide approaches with a cell phone. President Mandela is on the line. Buthelezi retires from the group and returns a few minutes later, beaming even more than before. The President has rung to congratulate him on his success in taking the second spot. The excitement among the gathered party supporters is intense.

And then, on the edge of the crowd, I sense a problem. Andrew is on his cell phone and his face is tense and unhappy. As I walk over to join him, he concludes his call. 'There's a problem with the IEC results,' he says dejectedly. 'I am not sure what it is. It's not good.'

I reach for my cell phone and call Hugh Simpson. Hugh is working for the Democratic Party in Johannesburg and will know what is happening. As soon as Hugh answers, he tells me; there is no need to ask him anything. The IEC has made a huge, monumental mistake. They have credited the IFP with hundreds of thousands of votes, when they should have credited the party with just a few hundred. When the details are later revealed, the mistake becomes explicable. But here, now, with hopes raised so dramatically and dashed so brutally, it is not explicable at all.

Fortunately, throughout the evening, Buthelezi has resisted the entreaties of journalists to make a statement. 'No,' he has repeatedly stated, 'the only result that counts is the final result that the IEC declares. That is when I will make any statement.'

Back in Pretoria, the IFP Chief Whip, Koos van der Merwe, is, perhaps understandably, unable to contain his anger, bellowing across the election centre at the IEC officials, 'You've made us all look like bloody fools, and I hope it sticks in your throat!'

Buthelezi's caution has proved well judged. A tight smile remains on his face, but he must feel crushed. He and Premier Mtshali make their exit shortly afterwards, and the party fizzles out in a desultory fashion.

It's a shame, really: by any standard the IFP has defied the odds. The last opinion poll before Election Day had condemned it to 3 per cent of the vote nationally and just 17 per cent in its traditional stronghold of KwaZulu-Natal. Instead, when the final results are declared it has secured 8.6 per cent nationally and has beaten the ANC in KZN by 42 per cent to 39 per cent.

In any other circumstances, it would have been quite something to celebrate.

30

TROUBLE

I return to Cape Town in early June for the opening of Parliament and set about planning for the new session.

Through Hugh and some of the friends he has made in the British High Commission, I am invited on a trip to the winelands that they are organising. It's a nice bunch of people who I later get to know well, mostly watching football and rugby at Cape Town's Fireman's Arms. But there is one person on this trip to the wine farms with whom I feel a particular and immediate connection.

Julia is the director of the British Council in Cape Town and despite being on this winelands tour with me, it is clear as we talk that she is wary, like me, of falling into an expat lifestyle. Her interest is in the South Africa that lies beyond the natural beauty of the place or the pleasures we can enjoy on our expat salaries, in the part that will allow her to understand more of the reality of the place.

I like that about her. I also like her because she is forthright and direct, often challengingly so. And though she is often serious, even intense, she is also funny and sometimes silly – as I am to find out when she visits me in Durban and, after a dinner on the beachfront, chases me over giant toadstool stepping stones across the shallow pools of the Durban pleasure beach, trying to push me in, or when I end up fully clothed in a swimming pool at a Christmas Day lunch, because Julia simply cannot resist the huge opportunity as I walk obliviously along the pool edge, my indignation simply adding to her hilarity.

Over the next two years, we get to know each other well. We argue heatedly over life and politics and people, and we fall out badly on occasions, most often because of my thoughtlessness. But when we are not fallen out, Julia introduces me to a world of different experiences and makes me see things through different lenses, wrestling me out of my conventional views.

We travel together and argue together and see new things together. She takes me to ballet in Khayelitsha, introduces me to the music of Salif Keita and Ismaël Lô at concerts I would otherwise never have attended, invites me to an unforgettable evening with Benjamin Zephaniah, who performs his poetry from a balcony in Cape Town's Long Street to a crowd that has gathered in the street below.

It's with Julia, sat side by side on a rocky outcrop at Hermanus, that I witness for the first time the spine-tingling sight of a southern right whale breaching the surface of the Atlantic Ocean, flinging its immense body into the air before crashing below the surface again. It's an experience of such intense, almost spiritual impact that without thinking I reach out and grab hold of her arm, needing to give physical expression to the sense of awe that overwhelms me.

Together in Grahamstown, we watch the satirist Pieter-Dirk Uys hauntingly playing out 'Nkosi Sikelel i'Afrika' ('God Bless Africa') in single chords on a grand piano in a pitch-black auditorium, save for one spotlight lighting up the piano stool, where he is sat dressed as the former apartheid President P. W. Botha, the target of his most devastating satire.

Afterwards we dance (me under duress) in a local nightclub and I start an argument with Julia over a handsome red-T-shirted man who may not be interested in either of us but most certainly isn't interested in me. And we don't talk until breakfast the next day.

Despite our arguments and despite the gulf of understanding that sometimes gapes between us, Julia teaches me, probably without being aware of it, to gain confidence in my life. My sexuality, which I am struggling so hard to come to terms with, is nothing to come to terms with, to her. It's not something she ignores; it's something she confronts, and because to her it is so self-evidently not a problem or issue, she helps me to guide me partially, although not wholly yet, to that understanding myself.

One December weekend, Julia flies up to Durban and we drive north up the KwaZulu-Natal coast to the HluHluwe-iMfolozi Game Reserve. We arrive in the late afternoon and after a swim and supper we return to our *rondavel*, which serves as bedroom, living room and kitchen, where we drink red wine and play cards. Julia normally beats me, but tonight she doesn't. The best of three becomes the best of five and then seven before, about midnight, I say, 'Sorry, Julia, you have to concede, I am going to go to bed.' Needless to say, she doesn't, and my decision to go to bed is declared instead to be my concession that I have lost.

In the morning we have agreed to wake early and go for a game drive. I duly set my alarm clock and as arranged wake Julia.

'You go. I'm not,' she snaps through grumpy semi-sleep.

'Come on, you'll regret it if you don't. It's the most stunning morning.'

'I need my sleep. Leave me alone.'

'You need your sleep no more than me. Come on, get up.'

'You got more sleep than me!' A note of some bitterness enters her voice, followed by a muttered comment about snoring, which I choose to ignore.

So I leave alone and drive at a snail's pace through the bush in the beautiful early morning light, the windows of the car open, taking in the stillness of the air and the sounds of the bush as some of its inhabitants slouch home to sleep and others begin to stir.

I pause as elephants pass just a few yards in front of my car, moving majestically, even delicately, despite their huge bulk, and I smile at Julia's grumpiness and think of all our rows and fallings-out, and I realise just how much she means to me. Because she is true. Because there is nothing superficial about her. And because, without knowing it, she has helped guide me to a much brighter place.

● ● ●

Back in Parliament, I have a job to do. When MPs assemble after the election, I present a paper to the IFP parliamentary caucus proposing the establishment of a media and research unit made up of four people. The caucus endorses this unanimously, and I am charged with setting in motion the recruitment process. But there is a problem: the Chief Whip.

Although Koos van der Merwe was initially hostile to my appointment, he has recently been trying to co-opt me. He has been very friendly to me and even invited me to stay with him on his game farm somewhere in Gauteng, an invitation I have politely declined.

However, Koos doesn't seem to like the idea that I have set out an open recruitment process, which undercuts his powers of patronage, nor that I have organised the presentation at the caucus through Inka Mars, rather than through him, although it is he who has told me I must look to Inka for instruction.

His obvious displeasure at having his authority challenged in this way is probably something that can be overcome, but then one day, in a meeting with Koos and another white adviser, he makes a disparaging racial remark, which is supposed to be funny but isn't. The other guy awkwardly tries to move the conversation on, but I sit coldly silent and Koos seems to realise he has made a foolish and potentially dangerous miscalculation.

From then on, it seems, I become his enemy. If he assumes that I will report him to Buthelezi or anyone else, his concern is misplaced. Koos has quite a history: it includes serving as a Member of Parliament for the National Party until quitting to form, with others, the even more racially extreme Conservative Party – reportedly storming out of a National Party meeting shouting, 'I'm finished with that bloody progressive P. W. Botha.' The IFP have chosen to take him on despite all this. They can hardly have missed his racist past, and if they have, I don't feel it's my job to point out such a glaring oversight.

At first Koos is just obstructive; he delays everything. The media and research unit takes months to set up because of this. The various requests I make for resources for the media unit go unanswered. After months of delay, we finally manage to recruit a media and research team on a reasonably transparent basis, and I set about working with them to ensure they can deliver effectively for the IFP in Parliament.

The recruitment process has generated hundreds of applications, many of them entirely unsuited but painful in the desperation that they convey. There is one in particular that strikes me in my heart: 'My name is Brightness. I am nineteen-year-old female and unemployed … You can offer me any job you like, I will take it. Please help me, I've done so many applications and they regret me, I don't know what to do any more.'

Shortly after the media unit is established, Koos summons the head of the unit, Joshua Mazibuko, his deputy, Joyce Moretlwe, and me to his office. With him is the Deputy Chief Whip, Mrs Seaton. He starts the meeting by saying that he has rung his colleague, the Democratic Party Chief Whip, and asked him how many press statements the party puts out each day. The response, he says, is eight to ten. He wants the media unit to do the same.

He gives instruction that from now on the unit will go through the newspapers every day and will write press releases on all the key stories.

His tone is overbearing and dismissive throughout the meeting. For obvious reasons, I object to this approach. I point out that the IFP needs to make the news, not follow it. That no one will be interested in publishing comments on day-old stories and that consequently the process will be entirely counter-productive, undermining the credibility of the IFP with the media and ensuring that when there are important stories, they will most likely be ignored.

Koos's big, wide face is by now glowing red. He is a large man, with a rugby player's build gone slightly to fat, a physically intimidating figure, quick to anger, who is not used to being challenged in this way. But I feel I have no choice. We have to gain credibility for the unit with the media, and this approach will destroy it.

I ask Koos why this meeting is taking place without the presence of the national spokesperson of the party, who is responsible for the party's media relations, and I suggest that in view of his absence we should resume at a later date when he can be present. With that, Joshua, Joyce and I get up to leave.

Koos sits at his desk as if he is trying physically to control himself, and then he picks up his coffee cup from the table and says, 'Jonathan, let me teach you the Zulu word for "cheers".'

He raises the cup and spits out a word. It is Afrikaans, not Zulu. '*Voetsek.*'

It's a derogatory word that means 'get lost' and is most commonly applied to a dog.

I turn back and meet his gaze, now full of fury myself, and then I close the door behind me.

I go back to my office, which I now share with Craig, a parliamentary researcher funded by the Dutch equivalent of the Westminster Foundation, who is from KwaZulu-Natal. I bash out a letter to Koos that is angry and intemperate and which Craig wisely persuades me not to send. 'Ignore the man, don't get in a fight with him. It's not worth the effort.'

Luckily, I have some important allies in Inka, who is now deputy chairperson of the parliamentary caucus, and the party's national spokesperson, Reverend Musa Zondi.

Musa is a soft-spoken Lutheran minister with a sharp mind and an infectious smile. He is a peacemaker and a social democrat, often at odds with the militant conservatives in the IFP who want confrontation with the ANC and revenge for what they see as ANC-inspired violence. Musa is a key figure in the peace talks between the ANC and IFP in KwaZulu-Natal which eventually bring the bulk of the violence to an end.

The day after my contretemps with Koos, Musa searches me out. Mrs Seaton has been to see him to complain about Koos's behaviour towards me, and indeed towards her. Musa apologises to me for Koos but tells me not to let it bother me and says the Chief Whip has no business giving any instructions on how the media unit should operate.

I agree with his advice, but I explain that the media unit is missing a number of basic resources, which despite my repeated requests in writing and verbally over the past six months, Koos has failed to provide. As Koos is in charge of the resources of the parliamentary caucus, this is a problem. Musa asks me to provide a memo to him setting out our requirements and he will get it sorted, which I duly do.

In response, I receive a terse letter from the Chief Whip instructing me not to bother Musa on these matters and telling me that I report to him, not Musa – something that is a matter of dispute as Koos himself has told me to report to Inka. I respond the next day.

I bash out another intemperate letter, which Craig once again sensibly persuades me to moderate. I share it with Inka and Musa, to check they agree it is the right response and because I intend to copy them in. They both endorse it strongly. So I take it to Koos's office and hand it to Elize. The blue touchpaper is now alight and it's time to stand back for the explosion.

It's not long in coming, although Koos does not have the guts to confront me directly. The first I know of his reaction is when a staff member comes to my office to tell me that on receipt of my letter Koos has been ranting and raving and shouting that he will crush me like a fly. He calls Richard Caborn, now Minister for Trade in the UK government, to complain about me. He hauls in Joshua and one of the other researchers and tries to get them to badmouth me. They refuse to do so, which is kind and brave, because Koos is going to be around and affecting their careers much longer than me.

Musa and Inka, however, are running interference of their own. They have spoken to Buthelezi about Koos's behaviour and a day or two after Koos has embarked on his campaign to undermine me, there is a knock on my door. It is one of Buthelezi's staff, holding a letter for me. After he is gone, I open it and read it with relief. It is a direct rejection of Koos:

I am so grateful that we have someone like you helping us in our party. I was delighted to read how well you get on with our colleagues. I have only heard praise from all sides about the assistance you are giving us and your friendship to our members…

My warm regards.

Yours sincerely,

Mangosuthu Buthelezi

After this, I know that Koos will have to get back in his box, although our relationship remains hostile and unpleasant for my remaining nine months in South Africa. Musa has already proposed that I move up to Durban for the remaining part of my contract in order to provide support to members of the KwaZulu-Natal government and Parliament, and this now seems very attractive. So, in June, I pack up my belongings and head to KwaZulu-Natal.

31

'A COUNTRY THAT YOU DON'T KNOW AND THAT YOU WILL NEVER UNDERSTAND'

It is late morning by the time I set off from Julia's house, where I have been staying in the time between giving up my flat and departing for Durban. Consequently, I am unable to make as much progress as I intend, and I end up staying overnight at Beaufort West, the largest town in the Great Karoo, a truckers' stop with a railway marshalling yard, a few handsome buildings and not much else. I stay at a cheap hotel, chosen because of its secure parking, which hopefully will keep safe all my belongings, boxed up in the car.

After I check in, I decide to stretch my legs. My stroll takes me past the elegant Dutch Reformed Church, past the police station and into the residential neighbourhoods where teenagers sit in twos and threes on the stoops of their houses, looking bored and sullen.

Steep hills loom over the town, immediately to the north, giving a suffocating, oppressive sense of being watched over; the great flat lands of the Karoo extend desolately, hundreds of kilometres to the south, east and west. It's a minimum of 400km to the nearest city in any direction. I try to think myself into the shoes of these young people, living their teenage years in this isolated town, with so little to do and nowhere at all to go. I managed to be sullen enough growing up in one of the world's major cities; imagine how much more of a miserable pain in the arse I would have been if I had grown up here.

I try but give up the effort; it is beyond calculation.

Those who have graduated from adolescence to adulthood have swapped the stoop for the dismal hotel bars that punctuate the town. They range themselves disconsolately on tall stools around the bar, drinking heavily. This may be the new South Africa, but you wouldn't say much for the chances of a black man who stepped foot over these thresholds.

My hotel is one such establishment, as I discover when I settle down with a beer in the bar. I am reading a book, *Country of My Skull* by Antjie Krog, an Afrikaans journalist and poet. Krog first broke with her white tribe when, aged eighteen, she penned a poem for her school magazine with these opening lines: '*Gee vir my 'n land waar swart en wit hand aan hand / vrede en liefde kan bring in my mooi land*' ('Give me a land where black and white hand in hand / Can bring peace and love to my beautiful land').

The book I am reading is about her experience following the hearings of the Truth and Reconciliation Commission for the SABC, South Africa's public broadcaster. I find the book chilling. It twists at my insides. I want to put it down. To run away from the horror of humanity that is so excruciatingly and painfully catalogued in the personal accounts of those who suffered so cruelly, both black and white. But I can't. It is impossible to escape the nightmare.

While I poured water on the tea bags, I heard this devastating noise. Six men stormed into our study and blew his head off. My five-year-old girl was present ... That Christmas I found a letter on his desk: 'Dear Father Christmas, please bring me a soft teddy bear with friendly eyes

... My daddy is dead. If he was here I would not have bothered you' ...
She is now a teenager and has tried twice to commit suicide.[*]

• • •

Do you know, you Truth Commissioners, how a temperature feels of
between six and eight thousand degrees? Do you know how it feels
to look for survivors and only find the dead and the maimed ... Do
you know how it feels to look for your three-year-old child and never,
Mr Chairman, never to find him again and to keep wondering for the
rest of your life where he is ... I sit for days ... I simply sit ... I lost my
business. I am reduced to a poor white.[†]

Archbishop Tutu says after the first day of hearings of the Truth and
Reconciliation Commission, 'We should all be deeply humbled by what
we have heard, but we've got to finish quickly and really turn our backs
on this awful past and say: life is for living.'
  But it is not finished quickly. It goes on as if it will never cease.

This inside me ... fights my tongue. It is ... unshareable. It destroys
... Before he was blown up, they cut off his hands so he could not
be fingerprinted ... So how do I say this? – this terrible ... I want his
hands back.[‡]

Antjie Krog comments on the effects on her and her fellow journalists
of those weeks and months of testimony: 'Every week we are stretched
thinner and thinner over different pitches of grief ... How many

---

[*] Antjie Krog, *Country of My Skull* (London: Vintage, 1999), p. 43.

[†] Ibid., pp. 72–3.

[‡] Ibid., p. 41.

people can one see crying, how much sorrow wrenched loose can one accommodate?"

I turn a page to another person's painful testimony and start to read:

Let me start by giving my story ... I had a three-year-old on my lap. The police entered with heavy coats and asked for the owner. My wife gave me my overalls and a coat. I put on my socks in a disorderly manner ... I saw they were very severe ... They pushed me into the van ... They told us to keep quiet. They divided us into groups and drove us to Beaufort West...[†]

My eyes freeze on the words 'Beaufort West' and I know I cannot go on reading this. That I cannot bear to discover whatever horrors may have been perpetrated in this lifeless town. Not now, not here, in this bar, in this town, with the police station just down the street.

I put down the book and order another beer. I find myself looking around the room through glazed eyes and wondering what involvement these men ranged around the bar may have had in the unspeakable horrors of the past. I feel completely numb. After a few moments I get up and go to my room. I sit on the bed for perhaps an hour or two staring unfocused at a blank page in my notebook, trying but failing to write what I feel. Eventually, I get into bed and try to sleep. Waking early, I slip out of the hotel and drive as fast as I can away from the place.

Antjie Krog comments, 'When the Truth Commission started last year, I realised instinctively: if you cut yourself off from this process, you will wake up in a foreign country – a country that you don't know and that you will never understand.'[‡]

---

* Ibid., p. 73.

† Ibid., p. 269.

‡ Ibid., p. 199.

I give myself a week's grace and then I return to the book. 'They made me stand like an aeroplane on my toes. They beat me all over, I fell. They kicked me severely. They tortured me for three days … They said I should die as I cannot live with white people."

Antjie Krog's harrowing account of South Africa's Truth and Reconciliation Commission is a hard read but a necessary one for anyone trying to understand where South Africa has come from. Sadly, few of the people who really needed to hear the testimony actually did.

I am not a fan of the Truth and Reconciliation Commission. Though I admire the amazing work that Archbishop Tutu and his fellow commissioners undertook to try to bring about reconciliation, I think it was doomed to failure.

The commission was established correctly on the principle that the truth had to be told before there could be reconciliation. Yet its essential premise – that the actions of the liberation movements and the apartheid regime had moral equivalence – was a lie. That was like saying that there was a moral equivalence between the actions of the Allies and those of Germany during the Second World War.

I wasn't under any illusion that agents of the apartheid regime were the only perpetrators of appalling brutality, and I agreed that the truth about both sides had to be told. I just didn't believe that the actions of both sides were equivalent. As even the Freedom Front leader and former apartheid military commander General Constand Viljoen conceded, 'The terror of the tyrant invited the terror of the revolutionary.'[†] The one came before the other.

The second problem I saw with the Truth Commission was that the people who most needed to understand what had been done in their name tuned out of the hearings, turned away from a reality that was too

---

* Ibid., p. 5.
† Ibid., p. 5.

grim and too enormous to bear. This problem was related to the first. By asserting moral equivalence, the commissioners had allowed whites off the hook.

'Agh, man, they were all as bad as each other,' white South Africans could now claim, as they reached for the off switch on their TV or radio.

This was as damaging for the white community as it was for the black, because without a real understanding of what had happened, genuine reconciliation was impossible.

As a consequence, to borrow from Antjie Krog, many South Africans now live in a country that they don't know and, tragically, that they will never understand.

32

CAMPAIGNING IN
KWAZULU-NATAL

My final six months in South Africa are among the best times. I feel embraced with friendship in Durban; the office is buzzing and vibrant, a stark contrast to Parliament, where Koos's heavy presence hangs over everything. I love the chance to work more directly with Musa and to feel truly part of the team working alongside Nicky and Sipho and Arnold, two members of the party's media unit in Durban whom I have come to know well over the past two years. Inka is just up the road, when she is not in Cape Town, and together with Alex Hamilton, another friend who is a Member of the Provincial Parliament, we form a triumvirate, meeting for dinner regularly to argue good-naturedly over politics and history and whatever else we can think of to disagree on.

The work in Durban is more interesting too. With the help of Nicki Hoosen, another member of the IFP team, we manage to get funding from the Dutch government for a programme to help train party activists in how to campaign effectively in democratic elections. It gives me the opportunity to travel throughout KZN and to meet people from a huge range of backgrounds, as well as to work with a UK trainer called Jim Bewsher, whom I gel with immediately and whose experience helps ensure that the programme is engaging and practical. It is inspiring to see how much people want to learn; how important it is to them to have the tools to engage effectively in their new democracy. So much of what we take for granted is entirely novel to them.

The training programme is timely because South Africa is heading for municipal elections in December. Nicky asks me if I will work with her on this, as there is much bureaucratic indecision about employing Andrew and James, and time is ticking on. I am in somewhat of a dilemma. Technically I am supposed to be assisting only on parliamentary matters. I am not supposed to be a partisan advocate. However, I see it as vital that the IFP is equipped to compete effectively with the ANC in democratic elections, as this is likely to do more than anything to encourage them to look to the democratic process as the way to compete for power. The more effective they are in competing in that arena, the more the nascent peace process in KZN is likely to become embedded. So, after a short period of indecision, I say yes, and Nicky and I set about designing the campaign.

We base the campaign on two pillars. The first, which Nicky conceives and champions, is a Charter for Development – a pledge of what IFP councillors will do to bring development to their communities and to improve the lives of the people. Through the charter we will seek to contrast the IFP's record of action with the broken promises and service delivery failures of the ANC. Buthelezi buys into the charter and declares that those who fail to uphold the principles of the charter in office will be dismissed by the party.

We also decide, again at Nicky's behest, that wherever possible, we must use local resources and employ local people for the campaign, so that we live the ideals of the Charter for Development. Consequently, when we come to appoint a creative agency to support the campaign, we pick a local start-up agency, set up by a group of unemployed creatives who have decided to take control of their own destiny.

On the surface, they are the most laid-back people I have ever encountered in the business world. How much of their creativity is inspired by weed is debatable, but judging by our meetings, it is not an insignificant portion. Nevertheless, despite their languid demeanour, they have sharp creative minds and help deliver the content we are looking for.

Our second focus is turnout. Given the experience of municipal elections throughout the democratic world, where turnout drops dramatically compared with a general election, it is clear to us that if the IFP can generate a significant enough turnout differential, it can win big in KZN. Our vision for the campaign is to drive turnout through a concise, consistently repeated message based around the charter. This, however, is complicated, because Mangosuthu Buthelezi is not known for concise speeches; indeed, the Guinness World Records credit him for making the world's longest legislative speech.

Nevertheless, Buthelezi has not survived in South African politics for this long without having considerable political savvy. He understands the strategy and commits to it. I push to be allowed to write the speech for the opening campaign stop and, with a little assistance, I am successful.

I sit down in my apartment in Umhlanga Rocks with my computer and a copy of the King James Bible and I write a tight stump speech, hammering the messages of development, turnout and ANC broken promises. The King James Bible has been my speech-writing companion in South Africa ever since my early days in Parliament when I was invited to the office of Inkosi Hlengwa, a distinguished MP and traditional leader from Mfume, a rural area on the KwaZulu-Natal south coast.

'Mr Oates,' he began, 'you speak the language of King James, so I would like you to help me with a speech I am to make.'

Ever after, I have tried to keep the cadences and idiom of the King James Bible in my head whenever I am helping draft a speech for an Inkatha Member of Parliament.

Buthelezi's stump speech has its first outing at Ladysmith on 25 November 2000. I drive up there from Durban in my beloved ten-year-old BMW with Andrew Smith, who has by now arrived with Jimmy Prior for the campaign. We meet Buthelezi's plane at Ladysmith Airport. Des, Buthelezi's head of security, decides to travel with us in my car. But, he says, you will have to keep up with the convoy and do exactly as I say. This makes me nervous and I persuade Andrew to take the wheel instead.

I squeeze myself into the back, while Des takes the front passenger seat next to Andrew, and then we are off, hurtling down the airport road towards Ladysmith, slotted into the convoy directly behind Buthelezi's armoured Mercedes, sirens wailing. As we enter the town, we rendezvous with Nicky and Jimmy and a flatbed truck decked out with Inkatha colours, a sound system and enthusiastic party workers who will distribute T-shirts.

Once again, the now enlarged convoy sets off down Cemetery Street, this time at much slower speed. As we get towards the stadium, the streets start narrowing and people are crowding in on the truck, desperate to receive a T-shirt. Des is nervous: his view of his principal is getting blocked as they start to surround the boss's car. He is barking orders at Andrew to get closer and then he opens the door of the car and stands up on the doorsill, scanning intently ahead. People continue to converge on the truck and the convoy is now just crawling. Suddenly Des drops from the doorsill onto the road, slamming the door closed as he goes, and as he is running towards the vehicles he is reaching for his pistol.

The convoy is completely surrounded by people; if the crowd turns hostile, there is little anybody will be able to do. The image of the street sign 'Cemetery Street' flashes back into my mind and it doesn't help my mood. Des is now alongside Buthelezi's car, constantly scanning to left and right for threats, and he is shouting at the SAPS officers to clear the crowd off the road and shouting at the activists on the truck to stop throwing T-shirts and shouting at the driver of the truck to get moving, and Andrew and I are holding our breath.

Then, as suddenly as the threat arose, it starts to dissipate. The crowds start to back off the truck and the car as the SAPS officers respond to Des's commands, and now the convoy is picking up speed again and Des is dropping back. Andrew slows the car and Des jumps on board, urging Andrew on – 'Faster, man, you must keep right on the boss's car, you understand?' – so we stay close to Buthelezi's vehicle and although the immediate threat has gone, Des's face is taut with tension. He is not happy that he has allowed this situation to arise. The convoy is now navigating the narrow streets that cling to the stadium, and Des does not relax in any way until, a few minutes later, we sweep to a halt inside the stadium and a sense of calm is finally restored.

After the usual formalities and greetings and prayers and warm-up speeches, Dr Buthelezi takes the rostrum and delivers the speech. He has adjusted it very slightly to make it his own, but the key messages continue clear and strong. Above all, it remains short, which means the messages have a chance of being reported. The crowd responds well, and I begin to think we have hit on something. The South African Press Association reports the uncharacteristically short speech, highlighting the key messages exactly as we want them and, critically, delivering our turnout message.

The campaign is not all plain sailing, however. A low point is when Nicky rushes into my office in an agitated state and says, 'Jonny, we have spelled something wrong on the flags!'

This is a not insignificant problem. We have just had 1 million of them printed. I feel sick.

'What? How could we? We both checked them God knows how many times.'

'I know, we just missed it somehow.'

I am confused when she highlights the word that has been misspelled – surely that is how you spell it? 'Are you sure it's only with one "s", not with two?' My voice is plaintive, because I realise it is me who wrote the copy for the flag and that is how I spelled it.

Nicky is adamant. 'I checked the dictionary. It's one. But hey, maybe people won't notice.'

She departs the office forlornly.

I feel even sicker. Can we really hand out a million flags wrongly spelled and hope no one notices? We will look like complete idiots. But can we really pulp a million flags, and at what cost? How will we explain it? I drop my head into my hands and sit staring blankly at the map over my desk. It was all going so well.

Ten minutes later, Nicky enters my office again to find me in the same position, elbows on my desk, head in hands. She is in an equally animated state as on her last visit, but this time she is all smiles and dimples. 'Hey, Mfowethu, we're in the clear! Nicki Hoosen looked it up online – apparently that's how you Brits spell it, so it's OK.'

The word that I have British-spelled is 'focussed'. I have used a double 's' where South Africa takes the US spelling and uses only one. Luckily, both are apparently acceptable in South Africa. I feel a wave of relief, and that night Nicky and I go and celebrate with too many beers.

Notwithstanding these and a number of other little local difficulties, the municipal campaign is a stunning success. The IFP wins forty-six out of fifty-three municipalities in KwaZulu-Natal, 'trouncing the ANC in their historical strongholds', in the words of South Africa's main business newspaper, *Business Day*.

It is a nice way to conclude my final month in South Africa.

• • •

While I am living in KwaZulu-Natal, I receive an invitation from Ve-laphi 'VB' Ndlovu, an Inkatha Member of the National Assembly, to attend his daughter's coming-of-age party at his home in a township close to Pietermaritzburg. VB and I have formed an unlikely friend-ship; unlikely because he is a fiercely proud Zulu who is understandably quite sceptical of the motives of white people after decades struggling against apartheid. His scepticism is reinforced by many of the current white politicians who, often with the best of intentions, come across as patronising or arrogant, and quite often both. VB and I bonded over a mutual distrust of Koos, and the work we did together on legislation to reform South Africa's firearms laws when he was the party's safety and security spokesperson.

VB stipulates that I get myself to the Imperial Hotel in Maritzburg, where I will be met by a friend of his who will take me to VB's house. His friend duly shows up at the appointed hour and we drive in convoy the short distance to the township where VB lives. The party is already in full swing at VB's home, which is at the top of a street, commanding a view over the township. There are a lot of people congregated on the lawn in front of the house enjoying the sunshine and the company.

VB greets me and introduces me to his daughter and her friends, who are warm and welcoming, but it's impossible not to be unnerved by the two armed young men, VB's sons, I think, who are patrolling the perimeter of the property. VB seems to sense my anxiety, because after a while he invites me inside the house and explains the need for security. The township is apparently a strong ANC area and his home has been attacked in the past, so he isn't going to take any risks with his daughter's safety on this important day.

Many MPs have abandoned the townships for more genteel suburbs, but VB won't think of it. 'This is my home,' he says. 'I refused to be driven out of it during the worst days of the conflict and I am not going to leave it now.' He takes me into the kitchen, where he shows me his refrigerator, still damaged from ricocheting bullets during an attack some years before. He fixes me another drink and we retire to his study, where he talks to me about the years of the struggle against apartheid, the fighting between ANC and IFP and the challenges that the country still faces.

Despite the armed young men and the tension they generate in me, I feel immensely privileged to have been invited to be here with VB and his daughter and their friends and neighbours, sharing this important event in their lives.

Back in Cape Town, shortly before I leave for England, VB invites me for a farewell dinner at the Long Street Café, where, after finishing our meal, we sit over whisky late into the evening, putting the world to rights. We are as different as two people can be in our background and our experiences, but despite that we have forged a friendship and shared moments that I will always treasure.

Nicky's family invite me to spend the Christmas holiday at their family home in Ulundi, the home where they showed me such welcoming warmth and kindness on my first full day in South Africa. As my time in the country comes to a close, it seems fitting that my final Christmas should be spent there with them.

On Christmas Day itself, Nicky's family are invited to a Christmas meal hosted by Prince Buthelezi at the Holiday Inn in Ulundi, and the invitation is also extended to me. Sue Felgate, Buthelezi's personal secretary, has called me a day or so before to explain that while Buthelezi is not averse to alcohol, it will not be served at the event. She has therefore come to an arrangement with the hotel that whenever she orders a tonic water, they will instead bring her vodka and tonic. She asks if I want to be in on the deal and I readily accept the invitation.

Sue is a fascinating character, an eccentric English woman in her fifties or early sixties who has somehow ended up living her life in the Zulu capital Ulundi, a councillor on the Ulundi municipality and personal secretary to the Zulu leader, with whom I think she may be slightly in love. If a film were to be made of her life, Maggie Smith would be perfectly cast to play her.

Her husband Walter has left her for someone else and left the IFP for the ANC, spilling many secrets on the way.

Although we tussled on a number of occasions, I felt a great affection for her and I can see her now in her small bungalow in Ulundi, where we would smoke cigarettes and drink spirits together and put the world to rights. Tragically, and not unconnected to the cigarettes, she died of cancer not long after I left South Africa.

On Christmas morning, Nicky, Eric, Daphne, their two grandchildren, Kim and Megan, and I set off for the Christmas service at the Anglican church in Melmoth. Megan is around two years old, a sparkling and determined kid who has already commanded my involvement in one of her tea parties. Today she is sat demurely on the wooden pew next to her grandmother. At a moment of silence in the proceedings, she lets out a rip-roaring fart, so powerful it sends reverberations shooting down the pew. Nicky, Daphne and I look to Megan, incredulous that such a small person could generate such a loud sound, and then to each other. For the rest of the service we are violently suppressing our giggles, desperate to contain the hysterical laughter that is fighting for supremacy within us.

Christmas lunch at the Holiday Inn is a big affair. We are arranged on a series of round tables, with the top table occupied by Buthelezi and his family. Seated alongside the Prince is the Bishop of Zululand.

I assume that Sue has organised the table plan, as I am on a table with her, but I am surprised to find myself between two Nigerian doctors who are working at the government hospital; surprised because they are both from the Muslim north of Nigeria and presumably do not approve of alcohol, so it is unclear why Sue has sat me between them. I decide that I'd better keep off the vodka given the circumstances, so despite the waiter regularly and sometimes quite insistently offering me tonic water, I decline and say I will stick to plain water. 'But it is tonic water, sir, I was told you like tonic water!'

A local band arrives after lunch and starts to play. Buthelezi urges everyone to dance but no one is ready to make the first move, so he gets to his feet and says, 'You young people, what's wrong with you? Can't you dance? The bishop and I will have to show you.'

With that, the Minister of Home Affairs and IFP leader and the Bishop of Zululand in his full ecclesiastical purple take to the dance floor together and start to dance. If only smartphones had been invented then, it would have made the most wonderful video. Soon everyone is joining them and I, stone-cold sober for the first Christmas in as many years as I can remember, look on with a broad grin on my face, taking in another unique experience that life has handed me.

The following day, on the drive back from Ulundi to Durban, some-where beyond Eshowe, I stop to pick up an elderly woman who is sat by a tree seeking a lift. I have been warned that under no circumstances must I pick up hitchhikers; it is far too dangerous. But I struggle with this, given that when I worked in Zimbabwe it was only thanks to the kindness of people stopping to give me lifts that I managed to get around the country at all. Anyway, this elderly lady does not seem to pose any threat, so I slow to a halt.

As soon as I have stopped, a large man appears from behind the tree and a large lump of fear appears in my stomach. This, exactly this, is what I have been warned about. It doesn't occur to me to drive off. I am paralysed, convinced I am about to learn the consequences of my arrogant failure to heed good advice.

The man approaches the car, but he is not pointing a gun or holding a knife, just a battered shoulder bag. 'Thanks for stopping,' he says.

He is clearly surprised that I have. And he is presumably aware of the fear his sudden emergence from behind the tree will have caused. But I guess it is the only way to get a lift. The truth is I wouldn't have stopped had I seen him first, worried about being carjacked or falling victim to the horrific violence you hear reported so often. By sitting unthreateningly by the roadside flagging down cars, the old lady is obviously providing a service to those who otherwise would not get a lift, as she makes no move to come to the car and waves a dismissive hand when I call out to her.

'Are you going to Durban?' the man asks.

'Yes,' I say, reassured by his matter-of-fact manner and his friendly voice. 'Please hop in.'

And so we drive together to Durban. His name is Peter and it turns out he is a trade union official who has been helping organise the ANC vote in the province for the municipal elections. I am ambiguous with him about what I am doing in South Africa, posing as a Brit who is just interested in the politics of the place and asking him to tell me more about the recent elections.

He does so readily, explaining how the ANC were taken completely by surprise by the IFP campaign, about the fact that for once they seemed to have a clear message and a concerted drive to turn out the IFP vote. I smile inwardly as he says, 'You know, they just came out of nowhere. We were not expecting that at all.'

When we arrive in Durban, I drop him off in Smith (now Anton Lembede) Street. He offers me money for the petrol, but I decline. His company and his description of the IFP campaign have been reward enough for me.

● ● ●

I am making the final preparations for my departure back to the UK at the end of an amazing two years in South Africa when I receive a hand-delivered letter from Mangosuthu Buthelezi.

Dear Mr Oates,

It is sad to know that you will be leaving our shores soon.

We just cannot quantify how much you have done for us and our cause. You have spoiled us, and your departure will leave a void in our community. You will be sorely missed.

I look forward to bidding you farewell at the National Council meeting on 20 January at Emandleni-Matleng.

With my warmest regards,

Yours sincerely,

Mangosuthu Buthelezi

The letter is dated 19 January. The meeting is the 20th – tomorrow – when I am supposed to be starting the drive back to Cape Town, before my departure to London. I ring Sue.

'Sue, I really don't think I can make it. I have to drive back to Cape Town and—'

Sue cuts me off. Her response is firm and concise.

'Jonny, you can't miss it. The boss wants you here. You must come. You just can't say no.'

And that's it. So I go.

The meeting of the National Council is the first such gathering since the success of the municipal elections the previous month. Councillors from all over the province have also been invited to celebrate the victory. It is held in a large marquee at the Emandleni Youth training centre, once allegedly a training centre for the Inkatha Self-Defence Units.

It is baking hot in Ulundi in January, and the speeches drone on in the stifling tent. I had understood that Buthelezi wanted to do his farewell in the morning, but it is now midday and there is still no sign it will happen. I sit with a large wrapped picture frame leaning against my legs.

Inside the wrapping is the present I have bought for Buthelezi, which I had anticipated giving to him in Cape Town. I have been thinking for some months of what present to get him, knowing he is a great present-giver and that to be able to give him anything in return that will mean anything, will require thought. Then suddenly, sat on Um-hlanga Beach reading Roy Jenkins's biography of Gladstone, I come across some words and I instantly know the answer. The next day, I hurry to Buthelezi's picture-framer in Durban and explain what I want to do.

It is getting more stifling by the hour in this tent and I am beginning to wonder whether anything will even happen today. I had hoped to be able to leave Ulundi before dark so I could get back to Durban tonight and on the road to Cape Town the following day. I explain to Nicky that I think I will have to leave, and I ask her to give Dr Buthelezi my profuse apologies and also hand him my present. But Nicky, like Sue, insists I can't go. Whatever other arrangements I might have, I will just have to rearrange them. She will try to find out when Buthelezi will arrive.

I am hot and bothered and frustrated. My departure date from Cape Town is now fixed with the airline and I had planned a leisurely journey, driving the coastal route for the first time, stopping off on the way and enjoying the beauty of new experiences. Instead, I am stuck in this stifling tent. One day is already lost and now it looks like I will lose two.

Then, suddenly, Nicky is back. He is on his way; I must be ready.

As Prince Buthelezi takes to the stage, copies of his remarks are handed out:

A Farewell Tribute

To Jonathan Oates

By

Mangosuthu Buthelezi MP,

Minister of Home Affairs and

President of the Inkatha Freedom Party

Ulundi, 20 January 2001

He begins to speak, and my previous grumpiness vanishes. It is a warm and almost overwhelming speech. As I listen to it, I think of all the friendships I have formed over the past two years, all the kindness that has been shown to me and all the amazing experiences that I have shared.

He talks of my work for the party in Parliament and in the province and of my role in the recent election campaign that returned the councillors assembled, with the National Council, at this conference.

Throughout my time in South Africa and Zimbabwe, I have seen countless examples of unthinking white arrogance towards black people, so I particularly treasure one sentence of his remarks: 'In spite of his great skills, he has never shown any arrogance, and we will always remember him for his gentle and elegant personality.' He concludes by saying:

We wish him well for all that which he will undertake during the rest of his life and pray God Almighty that He may see fit to bestow upon him all life's blessings. May Jonathan Oates go well on his journey back to his home and may our friendship and gratitude accompany him for ever.

I sit in my seat overwhelmed as the audience applauds him, but I manage somehow to haul myself to my feet to join him on stage as I am commanded. When I reach the rostrum, Buthelezi presents me with a large, heavy, wrapped box. I already have in my hands my large framed present, so this is an awkward exchange. I try to hold the heavy box under my arm as he attempts to embrace me with the large picture frame under his, but I fear I will let the box slip and I have visions of whatever precious present is inside smashing in front of the hundreds of delegates assembled in front of us. So I disengage and put the box down before trying the embrace again. Inside the box, as I will later discover, is a beautiful carved elephant.

Buthelezi invites me to speak at the rostrum. I thank him and the party for all their friendship over the past two years and for all they have taught me, finishing with a salutation in halting Zulu.

As I have been speaking, Buthelezi has been unwrapping the present that I have given him, and I can see it has been a hit; he is beaming from cheek to cheek. He gives me another hug and I stand aside as he takes back the rostrum and holds the frame up for the conference to see, and then he explains what it is.

There are two cut-outs in the mounting inside the frame. In one is a line drawing of William Gladstone, Liberal Party leader and four times British Prime Minister, and in the other is a short extract from one of his speeches denouncing the imperialist policies of his arch-rival Prime Minister Benjamin Disraeli: 'He adopts a showy imperialism, as cruel to its overseas victims as it is corrupting to its home supporters. Ten thousand Zulus have been slaughtered for no other offence than their attempt to defend against your artillery with their naked bodies, their hearth and their home, their wives and family.'

Buthelezi reads the quotation first in English and then in Zulu. It is something, this, to hear the Zulu leader speak Gladstone's words condemning the Anglo-Zulu war, in Zulu, here in Ulundi, site of the final battle that defeated and subjugated the Zulu people and condemned them to a century of white tyranny.

33

THE THINGS THAT MATTER

The plane that brought me back to England from that idyllic South African summer landed at 6 a.m. at Heathrow one late January morning. It was dark and cold and raining, and immediately I felt bereft.

I got a black cab from the airport to my parents' flat in Kingston. During my time in South Africa, my dad had retired, so they had moved out of the rectory at St Bride's to a place on Kingston Hill. The cab driver did not help my mood.

'Where have you come from, holiday?' he asked.

'No, actually. I'm just back from working for a couple of years in South Africa.'

'Oh, South Africa's a beautiful place. I went there a few years back with the wife.'

I begin to warm to the conversation, and then he says, 'Such a shame the blacks have gone and ruined it.'

I feel like a weight has been dropped on my head. Welcome home to the cold, dark racism of an English winter. I want to tell him to stop the cab, I will get out. Refuse to pay the fare. But it's freezing cold and pouring with rain, so I don't. It appears I am not prepared to pay a very high price for my principles.

Instead, I tell him rather piously that I have lived in South Africa for two years and that I also spent time there under apartheid (I don't specify how briefly), and I can tell him definitively that if South Africa is ruined, it is the whites what done it. My tone does not brook a response. I sit for the rest of the journey in sullen silence, slumped in my seat, angry and depressed, but above all ashamed that I have not stopped the cab.

The UK takes some getting used to after the adventures of South Africa. The general election is coming, and Ed Davey tells me that Jenny Tonge is looking for an agent in Richmond Park. It's something to keep me occupied while I try to work out what to do. 2001 is another massive win for Tony Blair. In Richmond, we manage to nearly double the Lib Dem majority, while in neighbouring Kingston and Surbiton, Ed takes the majority of fifty-six that we scraped together in 1997 and turns it into a majority of 15,676, but overall the political map of Britain does not shift at all.

After the election, Simon Hughes asks me if I will take on a short-term role structuring and recruiting a new office staff for him. It's strange to be back working with Simon fourteen years after I first interned for him, and despite the many frustrations of working for him – it remains as impossible to organise Simon as ever – it's also inspirational to see the commitment and care he has for the community he represents. Gavin Lim is my partner in crime in this enterprise, and when things get a little stressful he can always keep me amused with his monologues of free-flowing outrage at the latest challenge that Simon has thrown up.

Through Rachel, an old friend of mine from my first job in government relations at Westminster Strategy, I hear of a job at the Youth Justice Board, where Rachel works as director of communications. I duly apply and am appointed as a policy and communications coordinator for the chairman, Norman Warner, a self-styled 'Stalinist liberal', whom I click with immediately. Norman has set about reforming the broken youth justice system with an energy and determination that is inspirational.

At this time, Hannah, an old friend from Kingston days, and I are sharing a flat near the Windmill pub, overlooking Clapham Common. It's a beautiful place and we are good flatmates: both out of relationships, we drink and smoke too much and talk about boys even more.

Vijay and Devina live just across the common in the Old Town and are constant companions, and the common serves as an amazing garden in the hot summer of 2003. But in early 2004, I decide it's time to buy a place of my own and I start looking, first around Clapham and then, gulping at the prices, back on my old turf of Kingston and Surbiton.

I go house-hunting with my mum. We view lots of nondescript apartments until eventually, at the top of a Victorian house behind Surbiton's high street, we find one – large rooms with high ceilings and a brilliant location – which clicks immediately with both of us. I snap it up.

In June or July, while the Euro 2004 football championship is in full swing, I meet up with my friend Cathy, another alumna of Westminster Strategy, to watch a game at a pub on Charing Cross Road. Afterwards we walk down to Leicester Square Tube together. I part from Cathy there, telling her I am going to pop into CXR, a gay bar just along from the Tube with a slightly sleazy reputation.

I ostensibly go in to use the facilities, but once I've been to the loo, I decide I will grab a beer while I am here, probably my intention all along. Leaning against the bar, I attract attention from a guy that I don't want to reciprocate, so I move away and as I do so, I see a tall, handsome man, the cliché of the romantic novel, leaning, appropriately enough, against a fruit machine. I am not normally bold in these situations, but I am keen to shake off the guy from the bar, so I walk directly over to the fruit machine man and introduce myself.

He's African American, over here for work, and out and about getting to know the city that is his temporary home. He has a lot going for him, besides the tall and (very) handsome thing. He has the most amazing deep green eyes and a soft rich voice and friendly manner that make me feel immediately at home with him. We share a little information about ourselves. David pretends to like football, a pretence he impressively keeps up throughout the Euro 2004 championships, and I thank my lucky stars that just a few months before I have given up smoking – David hails from California and smoking would definitely have been on a list of prohibited attributes. After an hour or so, we exchange numbers and agree to meet for a coffee at the weekend.

Thank God for mobile phones. I am waiting at a table outside the Caffé Nero on Shaftesbury Avenue where we have arranged to meet, but there is no sign of David. After ten or fifteen minutes, I start to fear he is going to be a no-show, another dashed hope. I text him to ask him if he is coming and he texts back to say he is here already. I go inside and look around, but he is definitely not here. So I call him. He tells me he is sat at a table outside the café, but that is exactly where I am and he is definitely not there. I ask him if he is sure he is at the Nero on Shaftesbury Avenue. I hear him speak to someone and then he comes back on the line, slightly embarrassed. 'Apparently, I am at the Caffé Nero in Old Compton Street. Sorry, for some reason I confused this with Shaftesbury, I will come and find you.'

'No,' I say firmly, worried that if he can't distinguish Shaftesbury Avenue from Old Compton Street, he may get lost on route. 'I will come and find you.'

I find him sitting on a wicker chair facing the street, bathed in June sunshine, and we chat over coffee, getting to know each other bit by bit. As the afternoon turns into evening, we move down Old Compton Street and chat on over dinner at Balans. I have known him just two days and already I feel completely comfortable and at home in his presence.

Often, I think about that geographic misunderstanding and how in the absence of mobile phones to correct it, our lives could have turned out utterly differently. Both of us believing the other to be the no-show.

Both of us chalking up another disappointment. It stops me cold to think about that possibility – that but for the mobile phone I might so easily have missed out on David. It is the most terrifying thought I can have.

Instead, fortune is smiling on us, and me in particular. For our second date we go to see *Fahrenheit 9/11* (my choice, of course) and for some reason this absurdly inappropriate choice of film for a second date does not put him off. Then I take the plunge and invite him to come and stay at my flat the next weekend, and he accepts.

We arrange to meet at the Anchor pub on Bankside, near the Globe Theatre. David is already there when I arrive. It is another idyllic summer's day and he is standing out on the terrace, which overlooks the Thames. I can see him from the street, standing up there in the sunshine, holding a calla lily, which is his house gift to me. We grab a drink before heading to Waterloo and home. I don't know it at the time, and David shows no outward indication of it, but I later discover that whenever he enters a house or flat he is immediately redesigning it in his head. Oh God, this colour is wrong, why on earth would he put that there, what was he thinking with those tiles? It turns out he is going to have a long time in which to correct my very poor taste.

David stays the night, and in the morning we go to breakfast at Gordon Bennett's, once a run-down pub and regular haunt for my friend Hannah and me, now an upmarket bar and café. I can never forget that breakfast and the way David made me laugh: it was the moment I realised that this was the guy; that all the waiting and searching and no one ever being quite right was because this was the man I was waiting for. It feels like I have been playing a poker game all my life and this is the end of it and I have won the jackpot!

In August, my best friends, Vijay and Devina, are getting married in San Gimignano in Italy. This is not only a fantastic event for them, but it is also to bring a piece of good fortune for David and me. Shortly after

I return, I receive a call from the car rental company to inform me that I have been entered into a draw in which I have won the top prize of a £1,000 British Airways holiday. I suspect a scam at first. I have never won anything, let alone a competition that I was not even aware I had entered, but it turns out to be genuine. The *BA Holidays* catalogue arrives in the post shortly afterwards. I browse through it and eventually make a decision. Then I call David and invite him on holiday with me to Venice.

Before our Venice trip at the end of September, David has a friend coming to stay from the States. I am chatting to him on the phone as he waits for her at Heathrow, and he is talking about renewing the short-term lease on his flat as he has decided to stay on longer in the UK. My heart soars at the thought he will not be going back to the States any time soon, but I know that if he signs up for another shorthold tenancy, he will be committed to staying in his flat for a minimum of six months. Without thinking, I jump in and say, 'Instead of signing a new lease, why don't you move in with me?'

There is an ominous silence on the other end of the line, then David says, kindly, 'That's very sweet of you, but I think maybe it's a bit early, don't you? I mean, it would be wonderful, but maybe we should take it step by step.'

'Yes, of course. No, you're right. Of course you're right,' I stammer.

We finish the call awkwardly, both embarrassed by the situation. At home in the bedroom of my flat, I put down the phone and start shouting inwardly at myself. 'What was I thinking? Why am I so fucking stupid? Now I will have frightened him off. Why do I always, always mess things up?'

I am about to move on to the banging-my-head-against-the-wall stage of my despair when the phone rings. It's David. 'Jonny, actually, I've been thinking about it and I think it would be a great idea. I would love to come and live with you.'

Bingo!

The Venice trip is at the end of September and David is due to move in immediately after that, and suddenly I have a panic. What if our five days together in Venice brings to light things we don't like about each other, or we fall out somehow, or we just don't get along? Then we will find ourselves committed to living together, having just discovered it is a bad idea.

One of my brothers warns me, 'You've been used to doing whatever you like ever since you left school. Now you are going to be living with someone, you'll have to change to accommodate another life, another person with different ways of doing things.'

Now I am really nervous.

I suppose Venice could have been a disaster. We could have found ourselves incompatible. But we found the opposite. I knew by the end of the week that in David I had found real treasure, far more valuable than even the finest diamond, and that I wanted, without question, to spend the rest of my life with him.

The following year, in August 2005, in the courtyard of a Barcelona restaurant, I proposed and David said yes. I felt overwhelmed by good fortune. In the year since we had first met, my life had changed out of recognition, lit up with happiness by this wise, handsome, astonishing man.

A few weeks before our civil partnership ceremony, I wrote to Morgan and Alice. I could not take this enormous step in my life without sharing it with them, but I had never discussed my sexuality with them, and I didn't know how they would react. I remember as I pressed send on the email thinking that it was at least possible that I would never hear from them again. Mugabe had been pumping out anti-gay propaganda for years now and I had no idea about how that might have affected attitudes. However, I put my faith in their love and friendship as I waited for a response. This was a time before smartphones had taken off, so emails could take some weeks to get a reply, requiring a trip into town for Morgan and a visit to an internet café. Just as I was beginning to lose faith, an email pinged through from Morgan full of congratulations and love and care. A year or so later, when David and I visited South Africa, I arranged for Alice and Morgan to fly down to Durban and we spent a lovely few days' holiday together.

On a beautiful sun-filled Saturday in June 2006, David and I become civil partners at a ceremony at Kingston Registry Office. The registry office event is followed by lunch by the Thames in Richmond and then an evening party in beautiful hotel gardens backing on to the British Museum filled with our most precious friends, including a number who have travelled across continents to be with us: Ben and Michael from Oakland, Caroline from Cape Town and Elizabeth and Sergei from the US and Russia via Paris. Vijay and Paige, David's best friend, are our best man and best woman respectively, and Ryan, Paige's daughter and David's goddaughter, is our bridesmaid.

Joan, an old family friend and a dedicated member of the Richmond Conservative Association, then in her eighties, tells us with undisguised delight how much she is looking forward to boasting to her Conservative friends that she has been to a civil partnership ceremony. As the civil partnership law has only recently come into force, she is confident that this will be a unique claim that none of them can better. I reflect that the world has changed a lot since 1988.

It is a perfect midsummer's day, the evening light lingering late in the garden and a sense of joy filtering through it and filling my heart. I am at the centre of my own fairy tale here with this beautiful man and all these wonderful friends. From time to time I look up from a conversation and my eyes meet David's and we instinctively give brief nods of confirmation to one another, as if to say, 'Yes, it is true. It is real.'

PART THREE

TOWARDS THE ROSE GARDEN

34

BACK TO POLITICS

My mobile trills into life and I turn from my computer screen to pick it up. It's John Sharkey, a former Saatchi's chief and current counsellor to the Lib Dem leader, Nick Clegg. 'Hello, Jonny. How are you?' he starts brightly, and before I can respond, he adds, 'Of course, I am hoping that you are really miserable in your job...' This said with a warm chuckle. Ignoring my attempt to interrupt him, he goes on, 'Because Nick wants to know if you would consider coming back to work for the party as director of general election communications.'

There is something about the word 'election' that does something to a politico – it dulls your critical faculties. The mental immune system should be crying out, Are you mad? Don't you remember the stress? The hours? The never seeing your family? The base nature of so much of it?

But it doesn't, because already the 'e' word is running riot through the brain, suppressing its immune responses and stimulating those nodes that shout back, 'But remember the camaraderie, the sense of mission, the thrill of the campaign, the euphoria of winning, the importance of fighting for your cause.' So as soon as John Sharkey says the word 'election', I pretty much know what my answer is going to be.

My first national role with the Liberal Democrats was as director of policy and communications, a post I took up in March 2007, in the last months of Ming Campbell's leadership. Before that, my involvement had been as a volunteer, running successful constituency campaigns for Ed Davey in Kingston and Surbiton in 1997, for Jenny Tonge in Richmond Park in 2001 and for Jeremy Browne in Taunton in 2005.

In October 2007, when Gordon Brown cancelled his plans to hold an early election and it became clear that the Parliament would now last until 2010, the relentless media attacks on Ming over his age intensified and the pressure on him to stand down became irresistible. By then, I think his heart was no longer in it anyway. Just over a week after Brown called off the election, Ming decided he had had enough and resigned as leader.

The prospect of a two-year wait until the next general election held little appeal for me either, so I decided I would stay for the transition to the new leader and then I would move back to the private sector. After Nick Clegg was narrowly elected as leader, I did have some second thoughts, but in the end I maintained my resolve, returning to my previous role at Bell Pottinger in October 2008. And that is where John Sharkey found me.

John's proposal is pretty irresistible, but I need to be sure that David will be happy, or at least tolerant of me taking on the role.

David knows a little of what it is like to have a partner embroiled in politics from my days working with Ming. Even out of an election cycle he has witnessed the non-stop nature of the job and the frequent pettiness and nastiness of the political and media world. As a result, he has a natural and understandable reticence about seeing me back in that arena again, but he also knows that it is where my passion lies. After some discussion, we agree that I will take up the role but only for the period until the election is over and I will leave after that.

That's not quite how it turns out.

Before I start the job in September 2009, Nick makes clear that my key objective is to secure his involvement in the proposed televised leaders' debates on the same terms as the Conservative and Labour leaders.

It's a tall order: there have never been TV debates before in Britain, and Labour and the Conservatives are long experienced in cutting out the Lib Dems. But this time there is at least an outside chance. Gordon Brown feels he has nothing left to lose, Cameron, a former Carlton TV PR, is over-confident in his TV skills, and his communications director, Andy Coulson, is a strong proponent. The key now is the not-so-simple task of ensuring that Nick doesn't get cut out of the equation.

Over the summer, I read everything I can find on the subject of negotiating televised debates – not much, it turns out – but there is an invaluable article in *Presidential Studies Quarterly*, an academic journal, on the negotiations for the Ford *v.* Carter debates in 1974, which I manage to unearth. Thankfully, Cameron's team don't. Had they read the same article, they would have run a mile from putting Nick Clegg on the stage on equal terms.

The key lesson that I learn from Carter's negotiation team is to focus on the fundamental principles first and refuse to discuss any of the detail before these principles are established and agreed. This approach makes it much harder for any party to subsequently withdraw, as it would look too petty to quit on an issue of detail when the key principles have already been determined.

The first all-party negotiations take place at the Royal Institute of British Architects, a white stucco building on Portland Place. Our team is made up of John Sharkey, Lena Pietsch, Nick's press secretary, and me. John's gravitas and experience are invaluable, and Lena's attention to detail and sense of how things will play publicly save us from inadvertently agreeing to anything that will later prove detrimental. Despite

John's much greater experience, he is generous enough to insist that as the director of general election communications, I should lead the team.

The Tories are led by Andy Coulson, the Conservatives' director of communications, immaculately suited and booted and supported by Michael Salter, his broadcast officer; Labour, by David Muir, Brown's director of political strategy, and Justin Forsyth, his director of strategic communications.

Muir and Forsyth arrive late to the negotiations, looking harassed and dishevelled. At the time, I regard this as unprofessional, but I later realise from the vantage point of the coalition that this is an occupational hazard of being in government, where events have a habit of taking control. It is also fair to say that while the negotiations were our No. 1 focus, they probably ranked considerably lower on David and Justin's priority list, stacked as it would have been with the unceasing challenges of government.

John, Lena and I have scripted and rehearsed how we will approach the negotiations. Our key tactic will be to block discussion of anything else until all the parties agree that Nick Clegg will take part in the debates on equal terms. Our rehearsals have anticipated an extended back and forth on this issue, but to our surprise, it is conceded immediately. I am so surprised and nonplussed by this that I nearly ask them whether I have heard them correctly. Surely for the Conservatives in particular this is a catastrophic failure of judgement.

Later, when we report back to Nick on this huge negotiating success which has come without any effort from us, he is equally suspicious: 'Why on earth would they do that?' he asks.

John replies in his deep, rich tones, 'Ahm, I think it is most likely that they are just very stupid, Nick, or at least, perhaps they are just very arrogant.'

As a former editor of the *News of the World* who resigned over a phone-hacking scandal, the full details of which are yet to emerge, Andy Coulson is a bogeyman for Liberal Democrats. Nevertheless, I can't help admiring his negotiating approach. He is an artist in the use of obdurate reasonableness. He drives the Labour negotiators to distraction with this technique. He will suddenly put his serious, reasonable face on and say, 'I understand where you're coming from, David, I completely get it and I would love to help you but, I'm sorry, I just can't move off my position.'

His voice is never raised, his face never displays emotion; he conveys utter reasonableness as he refuses, point-blank, to compromise.

I store this technique away for future use.

What is immediately clear is that while the Lib Dem and Tory teams have been given full discretion to negotiate, David Muir and Justin Forsyth are not so lucky. They frequently have to ask for pauses in the discussions to retire to their breakout room for consultations – whether with Brown or Mandelson, or both, is unclear.

Late in the negotiations, which take place over a period of months and have by now moved to an upper room in the Mothers' Union in Tufton Street, David and Justin realise that they have made an error. We have agreed that half of each of the three ninety-minute debates will be themed – domestic affairs (including public services and political reform), international affairs and economic affairs. In practice, it turns out that the themes make no difference to the nature of actual debates, but in fairness to David and Justin, we don't know that at the time. It has also been agreed that the order in which the broadcasters host the debates and the order of the themed debates themselves will be drawn by lot. David and Justin have missed the potential consequence of this decision and they are shocked to discover that the economy has been drawn as the theme for the last debate. When they realise, they call a break to consult their principals.

They return looking more harassed than ever. They tell us that we must change the order. It is unacceptable for the economy to be debated last when it is critical to everything else. Clearly, Brown and Mandelson want the economy to shape the narrative for the election, so they want it to be the theme of the first debate. As a result, David and Justin have clearly been chewed up and spat out for allowing a situation to arise where the economy is scheduled last.

Coulson refuses to budge. His obdurate reasonableness is now turned up to maximum power. David and Justin look like they will spontaneously combust with frustration in the face of it. Instead, they request another break and we retire to our respective rooms. On this occasion, John and Lena are both absent filming a party election broadcast with Nick, so I sit twiddling my thumbs on my own in our breakout room. Suddenly there is a knock on the door and David and Justin enter.

They want to recruit me to their side, arguing that their position in some way benefits the Lib Dems. I can't see it, and anyway I am not going to break with what has already been agreed; the order of the debates is pretty much immaterial to us, as long as we are in them. However, I am alarmed by the potential for this issue to derail the negotiations. My fear is that it will provide the Tories with an excuse to pull out on the grounds of Labour bad faith. It's the Tories I am most worried about, because surely at some point they are going to realise how mad this whole thing is for them. I call John and Lena to check I am seeing it straight, and they both agree. When we return to the negotiating room it is clear that we have reached an impasse, and the talks break up.

Over the next few days, I get increasingly worried that the TV debates are not going to happen. I speak with David Muir and encourage him to concede the point even if they don't like its consequences. Similar pressure, I assume, is being exerted by the broadcasters and eventually, to our huge relief, David and Justin back down.

There is a final meeting between the broadcasters and the negotiating teams in the rooms above the Mothers' Union, where, to the collective astonishment of John, Lena and me, all parties sign up to the final agreement. It seems too good to be true. We almost tiptoe up the street away from the Mothers' Union. We feel like errant schoolchildren who can't believe they have got away with a major transgression and are expecting at any moment to be called back to answer for it. Not until we are safely inside the bar of the Cinnamon Club do we relax. John orders champagne and we toast a first success.

35

ENTER THE OUTSIDER

The 2010 general election campaign kicks off with a statement by Prime Minister Gordon Brown, flanked by his entire Cabinet, outside 10 Downing Street. It is, as Brown concedes, an announcement that surprises no one. Polling day is set for 6 May.

Nick has appointed John Sharkey to lead the election campaign and has made clear in front of the campaign team that John is the boss and his decisions are final. This clarity helps immensely and is essential in ensuring that we fight a disciplined campaign. We are also assisted by the sense of unity and purpose within the team, which is instilled by both Nick and John and is also a product of the fact that most team members have worked together over many months and, in some cases, years.

Nevertheless, the campaign gets off to a frustrating start for us. Media coverage is limited: the broadcasters are defaulting to the usual two-party fight formula – in fairness, it is a much easier story to tell – and we are being squeezed hard. I have invested most of my time in ensuring we are prepared for the debates and fighting with the BBC over their coverage. As a consequence, I have not invested enough time in thinking about how we break through the initial two-party narrative.

The politicians are starting to display modicums of alarm. What can we do to break through? The answer, in retrospect, is to wait. Just stay patient and wait. But patience isn't in huge supply in a general election. Someone comes up with the idea of taking the 'Labour tax bombshell' campaign that the Conservative Party used effectively in 1992 and turning it on them, with a Tory VAT bombshell. An ad is rapidly produced, an ad van is hired and somewhere alongside the Clyde on a desultory Glasgow day, Nick and Charles Kennedy unveil the poster. It gets little coverage at the time, although inevitably it is the broadcasters' favourite image when the coalition government hikes VAT – and 'We warned you they were going to do it' doesn't really feel like a feasible response.

It seems like a lifetime until the first TV debate takes place, but it is only nine days into the campaign. A small team of us repair to a hotel in the countryside outside Manchester that Alison Suttie, Nick's astute head of office, has organised for us. It's the perfect place for Nick, somewhere he is able to walk and think and prepare.

In the late morning, Sean Kemp, the head of the press office, and I head into Manchester to check out the spin room and take one last look at the set and facilities at ITV's Manchester studios. As I am walking from the studios back to the media centre, Chris Huhne, Nick's former leadership rival and big beast of the party, who, with Paddy Ashdown, is to be one of our chief spinners in the post-debate media room, rings me on a poor line.

He is insisting that Carina Trimingham, who is working as an aide to him, is included in the spin room. I tell him that is not possible. Carina is not part of my press office team and I do not trust her to take instructions or carry a message on behalf of Nick and the party. Chris explodes into what at the time appears to be inexplicable fury, shouting down the phone, ordering me to get accreditation for her. I am bewildered by this sudden anger, but adamant. She is not part of the team and that is that. It is a feature of Chris's nature that when I later see him at the media centre that evening, he behaves as if our angry exchange has never taken place.

Lena accompanies Nick from the hotel to the studios and I meet them in Nick's dressing room. We are all aware of what is at stake. At first, we chat and joke, but as the time of the debate gets closer, we allow Nick silence to collect his thoughts. Shortly before the debate is due to begin, I wish him a last, heartfelt good luck and head back to the media centre.

The media centre consists of a large hall with huge screens, where the press is assembled, and a series of small rooms, side by side, which are allocated to each of the parties. Just before the debate starts, the press team and the big beast spinners, Paddy Ashdown and Chris Huhne, assemble in our party room. From the start, it is clear that Nick is going to do well. He is poised and relaxed, hand in one pocket, looking directly down the camera, addressing audience members by their names, delivering his lines seamlessly. Gordon Brown and David Cameron are struggling beside this new phenomenon. Brown resorts to agreeing with Nick, and the phrase 'I agree with Nick' is born.

Then Cameron tells a bizarre story.

'I was in Plymouth recently,' he says, 'and a forty-year-old black man said, "I came here when I was six, I've served in the Royal Navy for thirty years."'

We almost gasp with astonishment at this grating, cack-handed attempt to … to do what? Suggest he is in touch with black people? But while the rest of us focus on figuring this point out, Sean is focused on the facts. He says, 'I know they take people young in the Navy, but ten years old?!'

It's clear the Tory press team are going to be on the backfoot with the media from the start over this story, before they even begin to try to explain Cameron's lacklustre performance. It turns out that the man in question is in fact fifty-one years old. That he served in the Navy for six years, not thirty. And that he is pretty pissed off with the Tories. He takes the opportunity of the media attention to attack them for their immigration policies.

Paddy Ashdown and Chris Huhne are in the media room well before the debate has ended, beaming confidence, success shining in their eyes. There really isn't much spinning to be done. Nick has won hands down. The performance and the polls say it all. The first snap poll is YouGov for *The Times*, which hands the debate to Nick by a staggering margin – 61 per cent to 22 per cent for Cameron and 17 per cent for Brown. The polls that follow are unanimous in calling Nick as the winner by large margins. The margins and the unanimity are vital because it provides no space for the right-wing press to play their usual tricks. They cannot pretend, as they would dearly love to, that anyone but Nick is the winner.

We don't stay in the spin room long, leaving it to the Conservative and Labour teams to explain the poor performance of their respective leaders. Labour decide it is in their interests to play up Nick's success at the expense of Cameron, so they do not contest his victory – 'Clegg won on style, Brown won on substance' is their claim.

Meanwhile, all is not going well on our journey back to the hotel to celebrate. On a dark, narrow country lane, the engine of the cab that I am sharing with Lena and Danny Alexander, Nick's chief of staff, goes bang and the cab shudders to a halt. So it is that we are standing by the side of a dark country lane waiting to be rescued by another taxi when the image of *The Times* front page arrives, bit by bit, on Lena's BlackBerry: a large picture with Nick in the foreground and Cameron and Brown behind him and, below it, the banner headline 'Enter the Outsider'.

I am due to return to London first thing but Lena, anticipating the media storm that is about to engulf us, asks if I will come on the campaign bus for the morning to help her and the team manage the media. I spend an enjoyable morning helping to handle a press corps that, having treated us with studied disinterest in the campaign to date, is now suddenly desperate for copy. Until now, to be assigned to the Lib Dem battle bus was to have drawn the short straw. Not any more: now it is the golden ticket that everyone wants to get hold of. I respond to the barrage of questions and excitement with what is to become the mantra over the next few weeks: 'We are keeping our feet firmly placed on the ground.' Things, after all, can change very easily.

The morning visit completed, I am standing on the platform of Warrington Station, waiting for a train back to London, when my mobile rings. It is an official from the BBC. We are currently embroiled in a battle over the BBC's bizarre decision that, in the week in which the party manifestos are published, there will be no Liberal Democrat representative on the BBC's *Any Questions?* programme, a decision that they have point-blank refused to change.

But now they have a problem. It is going to look pretty odd if, after Nick's triumph last night, there is no Liberal Democrat on the panel. So they are calling to ask for my help in sorting it out – miraculously, the impossibility of switching out the non-party guest, which I had previously proposed, has been overcome. I try to avoid sounding too smug, but the obvious discomfort of the BBC official is just too enjoyable. Rather childishly, I insist that we will only put up a panellist if he guarantees that we will be represented on every subsequent *Any Questions?* or *Question Time* panel throughout the campaign. The official says he would be very surprised, in light of how the election is developing, if that wasn't the case, but he obviously can't sign up to a formal guarantee. I tell him that this is not good enough.

After I put down the phone, I call John Sharkey and we both revel in the BBC's discomfort, but John wisely advises that we will, in turn, look pretty stupid if we don't put anyone up for the show now that we have been invited to take part, which I have to concede is entirely true. So, enjoyment over, I call the BBC back and tell them that someone will appear. Simon Hughes manfully takes on the job with only a few hours' notice to prepare.

Over the next few days, media interest in Nick and the party explodes. The world's media are at our door and for the first time in my life, the Liberal Democrats are being actively sought out for copy – and the resulting coverage is almost universally positive.

On Saturday evening, I receive a call at home from Simon Walters, the political editor of the *Mail on Sunday*.

'Jonny, are you sitting down? I've got some pretty stunning news for you: tomorrow we are publishing an opinion poll. It puts you guys first!'

It all seems very unreal.

But reality is about to catch up with us.

• • •

Before the debates, much of the media and political class regarded the Liberal Democrats as bit-part players in politics. On only two occasions since the Second World War had they really threatened to disrupt the two-party narrative. The first was February 1974, when an inconclusive election had given the Liberal Party and its fourteen MPs a brief moment in the limelight. But the party's travails, not least the trial of its former leader on a charge of conspiracy to murder, had put paid to hopes of building on this base.

The second occasion was the period between the foundation of the SDP in 1981 and the 1983 general election, when the SDP–Liberal Alliance had posed the most significant post-war threat to the two-party hegemony, at one point recording 50 per cent in the opinion polls before the brutality of the first-past-the-post system crushed their hopes in the 1983 election.

Journalists and politicians were therefore understandably sceptical of the significance of the Liberal Democrats. Hung parliaments had often been predicted, most notably in 1992, but in the end had not occurred, and despite a steady increase in the number of seats secured by the Liberal Democrats from twenty in 1992 to sixty-two in 2005, Labour's majorities from 1997 onwards meant the Lib Dems had remained largely irrelevant to parliamentary arithmetic and therefore to political consideration.

The first debate changes all that.

Opinion polls are already predicting a hung parliament, and Nick's performance makes that prospect seem more real than it has in a generation. For some, that is a great opportunity, but for others, it poses a huge threat. Not least the right-wing press, to whom the Liberal Democrats, uniquely among the main parties, owe no favours at all.

As the implications of the debates sink in, Conservative Campaign Headquarters is in a state of panic. If some way of stopping Clegg is not found, the mould of politics may finally be broken and this, most definitely, will not be to their advantage. Not for nothing, however, are the Conservative Party known as the most successful political party in the democratic world. They have a laser-like focus on power and an unblushing ruthlessness in securing it. In achieving this end, they are helped by having some very rich and powerful friends. Foremost among these are the media barons, not unfamiliar to unblushing ruthlessness themselves.

So it is inevitable that the positive coverage of the first few post-debate days, driven by the irresistible story of a new kid on the block, is not going to last. Nor, to be fair, should it. Political parties and their leaders deserve scrutiny, and that goes as much for us as anyone else. We are used to being ignored, so interest, let alone detailed scrutiny, is not usual. Nevertheless, I think we are ready for it. What I have failed to prepare for, in my naivety, is the relentless, personalised, coordinated assault on the party, on Nick and on his family that is about to be launched and which is designed specifically to knock us off our game.

The first inklings begin on Monday, when the press office is deluged with enquiries around a series of negative stories. One example of the ludicrous nature of what is being put to us is the allegation that a Liberal Democrat policy to ban the import of hardwoods exists solely to enrich one of Nick's brothers, whose company imports sustainable timber. The fact that this is a long-standing policy of the party that has existed for many years, well before Nick was even an MP and probably before he was a party member, is not considered relevant by the journalist concerned – or, more to the point, by his bosses. It is just one of a huge number of politically motivated stories that are being put to our press office, consuming precious staff time and forcing us to play defence, as they are designed to do.

The main assault, however, is planned for the morning of the second debate. I am with Nick and the debate team at a hotel near Bristol when I get a call from the *Daily Telegraph*. They have a series of questions about money paid into Nick's bank account by Lib Dem donors to fund a member of his parliamentary staff. I check with Nick, who explains that funds have indeed been made available by party donors to pay the salary of a member of his parliamentary team. Prior to him becoming party leader, this money was paid through his personal account. He concedes that it was a messy arrangement, but nevertheless all the money has been properly declared and properly used.

I get back to the *Telegraph* journalist, explain the facts and warn that we will treat very seriously any allegation of impropriety. It is clear from his response that he intends to publish regardless. I call Tony Gallagher, then editor of the *Telegraph*, who, despite our different politics, until now I have had a high regard for. He does not return my call, and I realise a hatchet job is in the offing.

I ring Tim Snowball, one of Nick's key aides, and ask him to start digging out all the facts: declaration of interest entries, political donation declarations, bank statements – everything. I don't want the whole team distracted from the critical focus on the second debate, so I decide to quarantine the issue and deal with it myself, along with Tim and the team back at our Cowley Street HQ. I explain the situation to Lena and Sean and ask them to take the lead on debate prep.

At around 9.50 p.m., while I am at dinner with Nick and the team, I take a call from Nick Robinson, then the BBC's political editor. He has been confidentially briefed by the *Daily Telegraph* ahead of the ten o'clock news – the *Telegraph* are astonishingly splashing on this complete non-story. He wants to give me a chance to respond before he has to go on air, which I appreciate.

I tell him that the story is nonsense. There is no impropriety whatsoever. Nick received money entirely properly, he declared it fully and it has been used for the purpose that it was declared. Nick Robinson then asks me if I will go on the record and confirm that we will publish the relevant extracts of Nick's bank statements to demonstrate that all the money received from donors was paid out as salary. He is clear that the way in which he will report the story will materially depend on my response. There is no time to consult others, but I know Nick well enough to know that he will have behaved entirely properly, so I give Nick Robinson a definitive yes.

I then head back to my room to call Tim and see how he is getting on with the bank statements. With legendary efficiency, Tim and Ben Williams back at HQ have already assembled them, and Tim and I start the painstaking process of going through every line. But there is a problem: the money received in donations appears to be greater than the amount paid out as salary.

I feel sick. We go through the figures again, but it's by now one or two o'clock in the morning, my brain is addled and my eyes are in open rebellion against the spreadsheet they are being forced to scrutinise. It is going to be critical that whatever information we give to the press is 100 per cent accurate, so I agree with Tim that we should call a halt for the night and resume our efforts first thing in the morning.

I fall into bed desperate for a few hours' sleep, but my mind is turning over the possibility that there has been some error and that Nick did retain some of the money in his account. I can't really compute what this would mean. Would he have to resign? Can a party leader resign in the middle of an election? I know I am not thinking rationally. My body cries out for sleep, but my brain is having none of it, preferring to catastrophise through the early hours of the morning until eventually I fall into an exhausted but all too brief sleep.

By the morning it is clear that the *Telegraph* is not alone in its hostile front page. A coordinated assault against Nick Clegg is under way, led by the right-wing press.

The *Daily Mail*: 'Clegg's Nazi Slur on Britain'.

The *Express*: 'Clegg's Crazy Immigration Policy'.

The Sun: 'Wobble Democrats'.

And then the *Telegraph* with a banner headline so huge that it is reminiscent of the post 9/11 attack headlines. On this occasion, the content seems rather less worthy of the font size: 'Nick Clegg, the Lib Dem Donors and Payments into His Private Bank Account'.

Paradoxically, the all-out assault by the right-wing press gives me hope. It is so transparently a concerted attempt to destroy a political rival that surely it will backfire.

If we were in any doubt, it is now clear that the Conservative Party leadership and its allies in the right-wing press are in headlong panic. We have become their No. 1 threat, a clear and present danger to a system that they are used to controlling.

Tim, Ben and I work throughout the day to get the accounts in order. We manage to locate the payment that we had missed the night before, and I begin to relax a little. However, we still have a huge job to do to get the statements in a state that we can share with media, and everything will have to be checked and double-checked against our spreadsheet to ensure that there is not the slightest possibility of error.

In the meantime, Sean and Lena and the wider press team are fielding calls from all and sundry in light of the morning's newspaper headlines. A sardonic Twitter hashtag, #ItsNickCleggsFault, which takes the mickey out of the press assault, is trending first on Twitter, above Justin Bieber (!), and it keeps me in good humour during an otherwise gruelling day. Eventually, shortly before the 6 p.m. news we are able to release all the material. It kills the *Telegraph* story stone dead.

The second televised debate sees Nick come under much sharper attacks from Brown and Cameron. Adam Boulton, Sky's moderator, also decides to get stuck in, asking Nick about the *Telegraph* story, in complete contravention of the debate rules and despite the fact that the story has by now been completely debunked. Nevertheless, Nick once again performs strongly, with most of the commentators and most of the post-debate polls handing the victory to him. It is by a much smaller margin, however – one or two points maximum – and in two of the polls Cameron is narrowly given the win.

Although the *Telegraph* story has been killed and, together with the other hostile front pages, seems to have provoked a public backlash, dealing with these stories has taken my whole day and a lot of other people's time besides, and they have received significant further coverage. Our comprehensive rebuttal of the *Telegraph* allegations kills that story, but it does not receive anything remotely like the coverage given to the original front page – the broadcasters and print press just quietly drop it from their news lists, where it should not have appeared in the first place. As a result, the public never get to fully understand what a shameless smear it has been.

The drain on the press office team's time is now a cause of acute concern. We have just a fraction of the media staff of the other main parties, and those that we have are all playing defence, tied up in knots dealing with the assault on us; presumably this is the intention. I briefly entertain the hope that today's public backlash may give the press barons pause for thought, but in reality I know that is delusional thinking.

Power is at stake, and they mean to fight for it every inch of the way.

· · ·

Over the following days, the media assault grows more intense. The press office is handling a barrage of stories, each of which has to be looked into, the subject of the story contacted and the actual facts established. The most sensitive stories have to be handled by me and Sean Kemp, usually in a bunker in the basement of Cowley Street.

The party is hugely lucky to have the press team that it does. Their dedication under fire is something to watch, and I am daily grateful to have two people I can trust entirely by my side: Lena Pietsch, Nick's press secretary, and Sean Kemp, the head of press. Lena figuratively, because most of the time she is on the campaign bus with Nick, and Sean quite literally, as he regularly materialises beside my desk in the campaign war room, his presence always a harbinger of doom, indicating another major negative story that has to be tackled. I suggest to him that some time he should come to visit us in the war room when he doesn't have another hostile story for us to deal with, and just bring ice cream instead. That way I won't get to dread his sudden appearances so much. He laughs at the idea and misses the point – I actually want ice cream.

MPs are now reporting that journalists are sniffing around every aspect of their lives, and Sean and I become engaged in increasingly sensitive conversations. Sean provides calm good judgement and absolute discretion. A person to have in your corner when the going gets rough.

The unceasing onslaught, however, is having a heavy impact on the campaign. Regardless of whether the stories are damaging us – and I think they are – even more significantly, the need to deal with them is denying us the space to think creatively and deliver a strong finish to the campaign.

On Wednesday 28 April, the day before the final televised debate, Brown encounters a woman called Gillian Duffy on the campaign trail who heckles him over immigration. There is nothing much to the exchange, certainly nothing particularly damaging for Brown – that is, until he gets back into his car and, not realising that his microphone is still on, describes Duffy as a bigoted woman.

The election campaign explodes into a frenzy and suddenly immigration policy is front and centre. In the debate the following day, both Brown and Cameron round on Nick, attacking our amnesty policy relentlessly, although London's Conservative Mayor, Boris Johnson, backs a similar policy. Brown and Cameron claim that it will allow hundreds of thousands of illegal immigrants to stay in Britain and hundreds of thousands of their relatives to join them. As there are no definitive figures for the number of illegal migrants in the UK, it is impossible to definitively rebut the claims. Nick does well under the circumstances, but all the polls give the debate to Cameron. Nick comes in a strong second in most, with the exception of ICM, which puts him in third place, just behind Brown.

The newspapers follow up the immigration attacks aggressively, and now we are on the defensive on policy as well as the personal attacks that have been unrelenting since the morning of the second debate. We can feel it starting to have an effect. YouGov has us down to 24 per cent in its final poll and anecdotal evidence seems to support this. Ed Davey pops into party HQ in Cowley Street on his way to a media appearance and tells me that, while things seem solid in his constituency of Kingston and Surbiton, there is no sense of the massive groundswell of support that the majority of polls are suggesting.

Nevertheless, we finish the campaign with the strongest poll ratings on the eve of an election since the party's foundation. Only YouGov put us below 26 per cent and many polls have us at 27 or 28 per cent. The euphoria of Cleggmania may have dissipated a little, but I am confident that we are on track to secure our best result ever. I play the expectation game carefully, or so I think at the time, telling journalists that we hope for around seventy seats. Projections from our ground campaign are that we should be in line for around eighty.

The clear likelihood is that on Friday morning the country will wake up to a significantly strengthened Liberal Democrat position in Parliament and the prospect of the UK's first coalition government since the Second World War.

Conscious that there are likely to be some critical decisions to be made the following day, I decide that I will catch some sleep overnight so that I am fresh for whatever the next day holds. Accordingly, at 9 p.m. on Thursday 6 May, I take a sleeping pill and get into bed.

36

UNFULFILLED EXPECTATIONS

The constant beep-beep signal of my alarm breaks through my drug-induced sleep just before 4 a.m. on Friday 7 May. I hit the stop button and switch on the radio, a frisson of excited anticipation hurrying around my stomach as I eagerly await the results in the 4 a.m. news bulletin.

The news is devastating rather than exciting. Despite all the hype and excitement of the election, we are up just one percentage point on our 2005 result and we have actually lost five seats. I feel like I have been punched in the stomach, chest and throat all at the same time. In some ways, though, this is the easier way, receiving the news in one sharp, bitter blow – unlike the staff at Lib Dem HQ, who will have had to sit through an agonising night of disappointment, hoping against hope that the exit poll is wrong and then slowly having those hopes dashed as result after result goes the wrong way.

I pull myself together, put on my best stoic face, well learnt through two decades of disappointing national election results, and walk over to Cowley Street. Despite the disappointment, the Conservatives have failed to gain a majority and there is going to be important work to do today.

Despite my instinctive preference for a centre-left alliance, it is immediately clear that a coalition with Labour is going to be almost impossible to achieve. Labour has lost over ninety seats, a clear rejection by the public – we have lost five seats ourselves – and together we don't make up a majority anyway. A rainbow coalition of all the other non-Conservative parties is another possibility, but is that really feasible?

These are the thoughts that are running around my head as I try to supress sharp stabs of disappointment that keep arriving in waves. I set up shop in a room adjacent to the campaign war room and call Nick, whose count in Sheffield has been massively delayed. Although we are both crushed by the election result, we are aware that the party has just been handed a greater opportunity to make an impact on politics than it has ever had. We also know that we are all about to come under a level of pressure that we have never faced before. This is now a pure tussle for power.

Sean comes upstairs and writes up the numbers on a whiteboard. With our fifty-seven MPs plus Labour, all the nationalists, the Green Party and Northern Ireland's SDLP and Alliance Party, we could just scrape a majority. The fact that this possibility exists will be important to the strength of our negotiating position in the coming days.

Nick arrives back in London about 10 a.m. Helicopters whir overhead as Nick's car makes its way from King's Cross Station towards the media scrum that awaits him outside party HQ in Cowley Street. The car circles Parliament Square twice, confusing the helicopters, as Paddy gives Nick last-minute advice over the phone. Finally, it drives into Cowley Street, where it is immediately surrounded by camera crews and journalists and is forced to come to a halt some way short of the entrance. Nick emerges from the car and, with his protection officers, we try to carve a route to the entrance way, where he will speak to the media. It is complete pandemonium in the street: we are pushed and jostled and I take a blow to the head from a camera as we try to make our way through the scrum. When Nick reaches the door and some order is restored, he makes his statement.

He maintains the position he has held throughout the campaign: that the party with the most seats and votes has the first right to seek to form a government. That means the Conservative Party. Then he comes inside to speak to the staff who are ranged around the grand staircase in the centre of the building and tries to comfort them in their crushing disappointment, although he is feeling it more keenly than anyone.

David calls and offers to drive up with a set of clean shirts for me, as it's clear I am going to have to continue to stay over in London some time longer. It is a massive tonic to see him after the disappointment of the results. We sit in the car together and discuss what it all means. The real truth is that at this moment we have no idea.

The next few days pass in a flurry of internal discussions, public nego-tiations and cat-and-mouse games between Nick and the media as they try to track his every movement, desperate to know who he is meeting.

Our negotiating team of Danny Alexander, David Laws, Chris Huhne and Andrew Stunell holds informal talks with the Conservative team that Friday night. Saturday is taken up with meetings with our parliamentary party, which to our surprise is by a significant margin supportive of a coalition arrangement and sceptical about whether this is feasible with Labour.

On Sunday, formal talks begin in the Cabinet Office. Our negotiators are supported by Alison Suttie, who has coordinated the work of the negotiating team as it prepared for this eventuality; Polly Mackenzie, Nick's policy adviser; Chris Saunders, his economic adviser; and Chris-tian Moon, the party's head of policy. Jim Wallace, the former Deputy First Minister of Scotland, also joins us. His experience and counsel are invaluable over the next few days and throughout the coalition government.

I accompany the team up the steps of the Cabinet Office to be on hand should press statements need to be drafted or other communications advice required. But to be honest there is not a lot for me to do. I spend most of my time relaxing on the soft cream sofas of the Cabinet Office and relishing the space and time to think that this unexpected opportunity for peace and quiet has afforded me.

At the end of the day's talks, a lot of progress has been made but the Conservatives remain unwilling to make any major concessions on political reform. I agree a brief, non-committal but positive statement with Andy Coulson. Fatally, however, we fail to agree a line on how we will describe the sandwiches served during the talks, giving rise to wildly conflicting reports about the fillings. The coalition hasn't even been formed yet and there is division already.

The Liberal Democrat negotiating team, accompanied by advisers, leaves the Cabinet Office and walks down Whitehall to Parliament surrounded by cameras. It is a bizarre experience in which we have to talk to each other so that we don't look like complete idiots, but we can't talk about the one thing that everyone – including ourselves – is interested in. Back in Nick's Commons office, the team set out why, at this stage, a deal with the Conservatives is not possible. Andrew Stunell and I argue strongly that we must not be pressured into rushing the process, but others take a different view, saying the markets will not stand uncertainty.

Over the following days, discussions ebb and flow. On Monday, the Conservatives fail to make any significant concessions on electoral reform and propose instead a confidence-and-supply agreement, which is attractive to no one. At this time Nick and the negotiating team decide it is time to start serious talks with Labour, and Brown now offers to step down, terrifying the Tories that a deal with Labour is possible and bouncing them into a concession on an Alternative Vote referendum. After desultory talks with Labour, who fail to propose anything of substance, and with a number of their own MPs publicly hostile to the idea of a coalition, talks resume with the Tories on their new proposals on Tuesday 11 May.

Paddy is on the *Today* programme that morning, loyally holding the line. He comes into the press office afterwards and asks if we can have a private chat. He hates the idea of a deal with the Tories, but he knows that all the choices are invidious. As we talk, he becomes quite emotional, torn between his loyalty to Nick and his fear of what a deal with the Tories will mean for the party that he rebuilt. I try to reassure him, but I feel completely frazzled and conflicted myself. We are looking down the barrel of two shotguns; we just have to choose which one.

As the negotiations with the Conservatives drag on in the Cabinet Office, the Cabinet Secretary, Sir Gus O'Donnell, is increasingly desperate for a conclusion. He is determined to prevent the UK being left without a Prime Minister. But Gordon Brown, who until now has been holed up in No. 10, has realised the game is up and despite Gus's entreaties is now insisting that he will resign imminently. He wants to leave Downing Street while it is still light.

As this drama unfolds, I slip away thanks to the good offices of a Cabinet Office official who leads me down into the basement of an eerily quiet No. 10 and out the rear exit of Downing Street. I walk briskly back to Nick's office in Parliament, where Alison Suttie and Tim Snowball are desperately playing for time, trying to delay the conversation between Nick and Gordon in order to give our negotiators the chance to conclude their discussions. But Sue Nye, Brown's gatekeeper, is clear: if Nick won't speak to the PM now, he is going to resign immediately. So, as the advisers are finalising the details of the agreement with the Tories, Nick takes the call from Brown, who tells him that unless he ends the discussions with the Tories and focuses solely on coming to an agreement with Labour, then he has no choice but to resign. Nick tries to persuade him to delay his departure, but Brown is done. 'I am sorry, Nick,' he says. 'I can't wait any longer.'

Brown makes his resignation statement as Prime Minister and Labour Party leader outside Downing Street at 7.20 p.m. and departs, with his family, to the palace. Nick holds a final telephone discussion with David Cameron, focused on the approach the coalition will take to the European Union, a critical issue for Nick, and then the Queen summons David Cameron and asks him to form an administration. Shortly afterwards he arrives in Downing Street and announces his intention to form a coalition government with the Liberal Democrats.

A meeting of the Liberal Democrat Parliamentary Party and the federal executive now takes place at Local Government House to agree the terms of the coalition deal. On my way to the meeting, I am on my mobile phone, trying to persuade Philippe Sands, a prominent human rights lawyer and long-term Liberal Democrat supporter, not to appear on *Newsnight* to denounce the deal. It's hard work, so eventually I offer to share a copy of the coalition agreement. He says he will look at it and come back to me. Not long after I arrive at the meeting, Philippe calls me back to say he is amazed by what our negotiators have achieved and offers congratulations all round.

It is midnight before the meeting of the federal executive and parliamentary party concludes, having decided overwhelmingly that it should accept the deal. Paddy makes a barnstorming speech which, while outlining his reservations, gives the agreement his full backing. Charles Kennedy, who is sat just in front of me, is sceptical about the deal. He is notably our only MP who does not back it, although he does not vote against. His reticence gives me my first qualms, because Charles's political judgement is usually pretty astute.

Andy Coulson and I have agreed that we will not share the coalition agreement with the media at this stage, so I am disturbed when a journalist calls to tell me that Andy is handing it out to some of his favoured press contacts. I am aware that this may just be media stirring, trying to create division between the two of us, but nonetheless, I take note.

When the meeting has concluded, the TV cameras are invited in and Nick makes a statement confirming that the Liberal Democrats will form a government with the Conservatives. It is after midnight and Nick is speaking in a dark, empty hall – not ideal optics at the start of the coalition, but perhaps apposite given what the next five years will bring.

After Nick's statement, I return to the hotel where I have been staying, hoping against hope that they will still have a room for me. The receptionist greets me with great ceremony and assures me that, of course, he has a room for me. With that, I am shown to a palatial suite with massive floor-to-ceiling windows overlooking the Thames. I explain that there must be some mistake, I just need my usual standard room. The receptionist explains it is not a mistake. It is the room that they have for me and I will not be charged any extra for it.

I have to be up early to meet Danny in No. 10 before Nick arrives, but, while I crave sleep, I don't think I can go straight to bed – not after such a momentous day and without taking at least some advantage of the stunning suite I have been allocated. I crack open a beer and sit down on the sofa, looking out over the Thames and reflecting on a lifetime of experiences that have brought me here, to the threshold of government.

An hour or so later, I wake on the sofa, my shirt soaked in beer.

37

THE ROSE GARDEN

I may never have been promised one, but I got one anyway.

A full-blown rose garden, complete with brilliant sunshine, 100+ journalists and a Prime Minister and Deputy Prime Minister, to boot.

Like most rose gardens, it also contained a lot of thorns.

• • •

As Nick Clegg and David Cameron emerge from the Cabinet Room and walk down to the podiums set out before the media in a sun-dappled No. 10 garden, I feel a whole range of emotions. The most powerful are pride and relief. That after all the years of effort, and despite the disappointing election result, we have finally achieved what we have been striving for. After an absence of sixty-five years, we have returned a Liberal party to government.

The spring sunshine and the outdoor setting provide the ideal backdrop for the promise of a new kind of politics. The evident warmth between the Prime Minister and Deputy Prime Minister, alongside a bold agreement for government, full of liberal ideas, creates a sense of optimism that is hard to resist. Even the lobby correspondents seem to have been taken a little off their stride by the turn of events.

The sense of warmth between the two men is probably genuine – after all, they are embarking together on an exciting and audacious project – but it is also a calculated display, certainly on Nick's part. His view is clear: the media and the markets need some very visible sense of assurance that the coalition can last, and he is going to give it to them.

Amidst the pride and relief that I feel, there are conflicting emotions too. I am still bewildered and shocked that an election campaign that promised so much has ended in such electoral disappointment. I am also desperately and overwhelmingly tired. That is to be expected at the end of a campaign, but usually – as a Liberal Democrat, at least – one can look forward to a period of restful irrelevance afterwards. Not this time.

Now, instead of enjoying a rest, we are at the heart of government, facing the unique challenge of constructing the first peacetime coalition in seventy years amidst the burning fires of a European debt crisis and a ballooning domestic deficit. We will rapidly have to build the relationships and earn the credibility to ensure that the coalition can survive for the next five years. At the time, few analysts give it five months; few of the hacks give it much more than five minutes.

• • •

Once the press conference is over, the real work has to begin. First of all, we have to sort out how we are going to staff the coalition. Neither Nick nor Danny has said anything to me, but everyone seems to be working on the assumption that I will lead the Lib Dem side of the communications operation in the government, so I go to see Andy Coulson to sort out how we will operate.

We decide, subject to Nick and Cameron's agreement, that we will have a joint Tory and Lib Dem media operation in No. 10, with Andy as the director of communications and me as the deputy director. I am determined that we should have a foothold in No. 10, where the power in government is inevitably centred. Andy agrees, I assume because he doesn't want us running a rival operation elsewhere.

Aware that it will be very easy to become isolated amidst our – sometimes erstwhile, sometimes current – political opponents, I tell Andy that I will need another Liberal Democrat press adviser with me. Andy is resistant – understandably, he wants to keep as many special adviser posts as he can for his own Conservative team – but I insist.

Sean is the obvious choice. I know I can trust him absolutely and also that he has the ability and political maturity to work constructively with the Tory advisers, so although Andy remains resistant, I arrange for Sean to come over and meet him later that afternoon. The meeting goes well: it turns out that both Sean and Andy once worked on the same local newspaper and Andy, like Sean and I, is a Spurs fan, which helps smooth the process.

As I head out of the office that evening for my first night at home in over a week, it dawns on me that I have just let the momentum of events carry me along and I have not really considered whether I even want to be part of the government. More to the point, I have not discussed any of this with David, and I am very much aware of my original commitment: that the job with the Liberal Democrats would not extend beyond the general election.

Tonight, though, I feel too overwhelmingly tired to have a coherent discussion, and by the time we discuss it properly at the weekend, it feels like I am just presenting David with a fait accompli. He is positive and encouraging, but I realise, shamefully, that I have given him little choice over a decision that will have a dramatic impact on both of us.

A few days later, David Cameron asks to see me in his office by the Cabinet Room. In part it is to assert his authority; to be clear that it is he who makes the appointments in No. 10. Nonetheless, he is warm and welcoming, and despite my political reservations I appreciate the personal effort he is taking to make the coalition work.

I am wary of Andy Coulson, but I find he is not a difficult person to work with. I never doubt that he is looking out for the interests of his boss, just as I am looking out for the interests of Nick; nor do I doubt that he will stick the knife into us without hesitation when Conservative and Liberal Democrat interests diverge. In the meantime, however, he is easy enough to get along with, even – whisper it quietly in Lib Dem circles – likeable.

As we try to settle into the alien environment of government, we also have to get used to the alien ways of our Conservative colleagues, and they to ours. These manifest themselves in the very first days of the coalition, when Cameron rather sheepishly approaches Nick on the subject of Dorneywood, a grace-and-favour country home which has previously been occupied by the UK's last Deputy Prime Minister, John Prescott, but also by its last Chancellor, Alistair Darling. George Osborne, Cameron explains, is desperate to have the house, so would Nick mind awfully…? George has particularly set his heart on having his fortieth birthday party there. Nick may never have heard of Dorneywood, and he certainly hasn't spent a moment thinking about what grace-and-favour home he might want to get his hands on, so he is genuinely bewildered that on the first day of this historic coalition Osborne's key focus is on securing a stately home rather than on the considerably more pressing issue of the huge economic challenges that face the country.

He shrugs with astonishment at Cameron's request: 'Sure, if it is that important to George.' His bewilderment is still with him when he shares the story with us later that day: 'Who are these people?' he asks.

38

THE BIG BEASTS AT BAY

Sadly, the optimism of the rose garden doesn't last for long.

Less than three weeks into the government, on a balmy Friday afternoon, I am at a farewell lunch in St James's Park with my former PA, Emma.

We are just finishing the main course when my phone rings. I glance down to see if it's a call I can ignore. It's Andy Coulson, and I conclude that I probably shouldn't. He is short and to the point: 'Jonny, we've got a problem. It's about David Laws. I think you need to come back to the office.'

I have no doubt from his tone that it is serious, so I apologise profusely to Emma, pay up and head back to No. 10. Andy is waiting in his office with Sean, and he quickly outlines the story that the *Daily Telegraph* have put to the Treasury. The essence of it is that David Laws is in a relationship with a man with whom he shares a house, a fact which he has not declared to the parliamentary authorities. This means that he has claimed housing expenses to which he is not entitled. Although, confusingly, the expenses that he would have been entitled to if he had declared the relationship are greater than those that he has claimed but is not entitled to. Work that out if you can; I never could.

Nevertheless, the indisputable points are, firstly, that he has failed to abide by parliamentary rules and, secondly, that the toxic subject of parliamentary expenses is involved. These issues are compounded by the fact that David is Chief Secretary to the Treasury, responsible for the public finances and the spending cuts already under way.

As soon as I hear the story, it seems to me inevitable that David will have to resign. Sean and Andy take the same view. Unhappily, both Nick and David Cameron are in transit, Cameron on a train returning from a visit in the north of England; Nick on the Eurostar, heading for a weekend away with his wife Miriam in Paris, his first break since the election. None of this makes for ease of communications.

Andy gets David Cameron on the phone. I can hear only Andy's side of the conversation, but it is clear the PM is resistant to the idea that David needs to step down. Andy holds out the receiver to me – 'The PM wants to speak to you' – I take it from him and find myself explaining to the Conservative Prime Minister why a Liberal Democrat minister has no choice but to resign from the government.

We hold a similar call, albeit with a worse signal, with Nick, who understandably is even keener than the PM to hold on to David if it is at all possible. We both give him our view that it is not. In any event, it is all academic. David has no intention of trying to stay. As I am about to discover, the real battle now is to stop him from resigning from Parliament as well.

Once we have agreed a holding statement, I head to Waterloo Station to catch a train to Somerset, where David is bunkered down in Paddy and Jane Ashdown's house. Not surprisingly, he is not in a good place. Jane and Cathy Bakewell, then chair of the local constituency party, are trying to support and rally him. Paddy, who is away in Geneva, calls in now and then on a dodgy Skype connection to give encouragement and instruction.

David is dealing not only with the prospect of resigning from his dream job only seventeen days into his appointment but also with the exposure of a life that he has kept private for so long. Neither is an easy thing to handle; together they are overwhelming. We stay up into the early hours trying to reassure him and to persuade him that there is no need to stand down as an MP. Jane knows what it is like to deal with deeply personal issues in public, and her experience and no-nonsense support are crucial.

I am deeply conflicted emotionally. David is one of the most politically impressive members of our parliamentary party. He has an instinct for what is right, and, most importantly for me, he is determined and willing to stand his ground – stubborn as hell, sometimes, but almost always for the right causes.

I feel a desperate sadness to see this bright, intelligent, decent man looking so lost and defeated, but alongside that sadness, I feel a conflicting sense of anger that he can have been this foolish. I want to stand in the middle of Jane and Paddy's cottage and scream at the top of my voice, 'Why?! Why the fuck didn't you just tell people? You are a smart, clever, decent person. Why have you got this so terribly, horribly, stupidly wrong?'

But I don't. Instead, I go upstairs to the bathroom and call Olly Grender, a former director of communications for the party and long-term mentor and friend. I share with her my sadness and my anger. And then, when I have concluded the call, tiredness and emotion overwhelm me and I just stand there, holding on to the sink, tears rolling down my face.

By the morning, David has decided. He will resign as a minister that day but he won't make any precipitous decision about resigning his seat. He will think about it over the coming days. For some reason, he, or we, insists that he must make his resignation statement on camera from the Treasury.

David proposes driving himself, but he has hardly slept a wink and I veto the idea. He suggests that I drive instead, but I have hardly slept much more. Cathy steps in to resolve this problem and heroically offers to drives us to London in David's car. We haven't factored in a rugby match at Twickenham and become agonisingly stuck in solid traffic. We sit silent and tight-lipped for what seems a lifetime, hoping against hope that no one in the cars surrounding us will recognise David. It is a final piece of misfortune on a day already overladen with it.

At the Treasury, Sean is waiting. After a quick run-through of David's statement, Sean takes us down to the room where the TV camera has been set up and David reads out his statement in a room empty except for Sean and I, a member of David's private office and the cameraman.

After it is done and we have left the Treasury, I part from David in Kennington, watching as he walks up the road away from me; desperately worried for him personally and desperately worried for us politically, without him.

By the time I next speak to Nick, he has already appointed Danny Alexander, his chief of staff and current Secretary of State for Scotland, to the vacant post of Chief Secretary to the Treasury. In my view, it is a mistake. Danny is vitally important to us as the coordinating minister for the coalition and as chief adviser to Nick, in addition to his responsibilities as Secretary of State for Scotland. His departure to the Treasury leaves a gaping hole which will not be filled until David finally comes back in from the cold two years later. In view of what has just happened to David and what is about to happen to Chris Huhne and Vince Cable, this gap couldn't appear at a worse time.

• • •

On a Saturday morning three weeks after David's exit from government, I am relaxing on the sofa in my flat in Surbiton when the phone rings. It is Sean, and he has not called to ask me if I want ice cream. 'I've had this weird call about Chris Huhne,' he explains.

Chris, a Sunday tabloid has alleged, is having an affair with Carina Trimingham, a sometime party aide and adviser to Chris. As Sean runs through the allegation, I feel a sense of relief. I have known Carina since I worked as an intern for Simon Hughes when I was seventeen. As Carina is gay – I think in a civil partnership, or certainly she was – it seems the press have really gone barking up the wrong tree this time. Sean shares my incredulity but, he tells me, the journalist is categorical that they can stand up their story.

I finish the call with Sean and ring Chris, expecting a quick dismissal of the allegation, but when I explain to Chris what I am calling about, the expected explosion of hilarity does not occur. Instead, Chris says grimly, 'Jonny, I am with some people. I will call you back very shortly.'

It is not a reassuring response.

Chris calls me back shortly afterwards. He tells me that it is all true and that he intends to leave his wife. As ever, he is unflustered and emotionless, focused laser-like on the next steps. First, the press statement: he starts to dictate, and I grapple physically for my notebook and metaphorically for a mental anchor that will help me take this all in. After less than two minutes of back and forth between us, we have an agreed text. Chris is an ex-journalist and knows what he's about. In purely functional terms, it is impressive. In human terms, it is chilling.

Next, Chris wants to know what view Nick will take. 'Will he want me to resign?' For the first time there is an element of doubt in his voice. Dismissing the thought that has entered my brain for a nanosecond, that perhaps Chris is human after all, I tell him that I very much doubt it but I will speak to Nick.

I ask Chris to stay by the phone until I have made the call to Nick, but when I ring back he has scurried off to the gym, leaving the phone to be answered by his son, who by the sound of his voice already knows too much of what is going on.

• • •

On Tuesday 21 December, the day of a joint press conference between the Prime Minister and Deputy Prime Minister to wrap up the year, a *Telegraph* sting operation on Vince Cable leads their front page. Vince has apparently been sharing his criticisms of the coalition with two undercover reporters and boasting that he retains the nuclear option of walking out and bringing the whole government tumbling down.

It isn't the greatest backdrop for a press conference, but nonetheless, Nick and David Cameron perform well, brushing off Vince's comments and setting out a positive message for the coming year. Consequently, I am in a pretty positive mood as the conference draws towards a close. Then Andy Coulson comes over – he is becoming almost as much of a harbinger of doom as Sean – and as usual he is to the point: 'Jonny, we've got a problem with Vince. Can you come and join Nick and David in his office once this has wrapped up?'

In David Cameron's office, it becomes clear that we have a very big problem. What the *Telegraph* has not reported this morning – but someone has now leaked to the BBC – are the very much more explosive comments that Vince has made 'declaring war' on Rupert Murdoch and threatening to block News Corporation's proposed takeover of BSkyB.

This is a violation of Vince's quasi-judicial role in takeover bids. Nevertheless, neither Nick nor Cameron think it will be helpful to have him outside the tent, so Vince remains and instead his department is stripped of its media responsibilities.

The Vince exposé is followed up with a series of stories resulting from sting operations on various other ministers, all in clear breach of the Press Complaints Commission's code of conduct, which prohibits 'fishing expeditions.'

After advice, we make a formal complaint to the PCC, which finds in our favour. The *Telegraph* prints an apology, which is of course nowhere near the front page, on which they have published most of their damaging copy. In their evidence to the PCC, the *Telegraph* admit that their operation was conceived at the Tory conference in private meetings with Conservative ministers.

So much for a free and independent press.

• • •

Six months into the coalition, David Laws is gone, Vince Cable has been humiliated and his confidence is deeply damaged, and Chris Huhne is distracted by the fallout from the bitter split with his wife, which will ultimately lead to his resignation and to jail.

With his three most powerful Cabinet allies either departed or at bay, the burden that Nick now has to shoulder almost alone at this most critical time in the coalition's life is almost unbearable.

By the time January arrives, the party's position in the opinion polls has collapsed to 8 per cent. It does not recover.

• • •

The first months of the coalition are ones of frustration to me. In No. 10, I feel cut off from the proximity to Nick and the team that I have usually enjoyed, immersed in the detail of the role in Downing Street and struggling to fit into an operation where I have to play second fiddle. Matters come to a head in my mind over the emergency Budget, where I feel excluded from the discussions, the conclusions of which I am then going to be expected to communicate to the public. In retrospect, I should have inserted myself more forcefully into meetings, but Danny was in a strange mood. On one occasion when I popped my head into the Deputy Prime Minister's office, where Nick, Danny and Will de Peyer, Danny's Treasury special adviser, were having a Budget discussion and asked whether it was OK to join them, Danny looked up and said, 'No, sorry.'

I was astonished, as I had always been able to join any meeting Nick held, unless it was a private one-to-one discussion. Nick called me afterwards to apologise for not overruling Danny – he had not wanted to contradict him in front of Will – and to tell me I was welcome to attend any future meetings.

•   •   •

The weeks after the Budget are pretty horrendous: the press and public turn hard against us. Both our integrity and our relevance are under attack. We are accused of having rolled over on Tory demands and failed to gain anything in return. This characterisation is unfair – we have ensured that the income tax bills of millions of low- and middle-income earners will be significantly reduced, while the wealthiest will see a significant increase in capital gains taxes, and we have staved off various Conservative proposals to balance the books on the back of people on benefits. Nevertheless, it is the characterisation that sticks.

After the frustrations of the Budget, I am keen to shift to a role that will allow me to focus on policy and politics and will restore a close working relationship with Nick. So, after discussions with Lena and Nick, Lena is promoted to take on my role as Nick's director of communications and the deputy director in No. 10, and I move over to the Deputy Prime Minister's office as the chief of staff.

The task ahead of me is daunting, but it is great to be back with Nick and the small Lib Dem team of advisers, working alongside the dedicated but equally small team of civil servants led by Calum Miller, Nick's smart and highly capable principal private secretary, with whom I immediately click.

The first job is to secure the resources to allow the office to do its job properly. In a coalition, the workload of the Deputy Prime Minister's office is almost as great as that of the Prime Minister's, as every significant decision has to be cleared by both coalition partners. The staffing of the DPM's office does not remotely reflect this reality in either civil service or political staff. As a result, the office is becoming overwhelmed by the volume of decisions that are coming to us.

Calum and I eventually manage to secure a significant increase in staff resources, but the process is glacially slow and in those crucial early months the resources available to us are completely inadequate to meet the scale of the task. It is during this time that we make many of the errors that are to come back to haunt us. Although, to be honest, quite a few of the mistakes have been made long before we entered government. As Finkelstein's law of political decisions warns, 'You are forever making decisions before you know you've made them. Most choices you make are the prisoner of a smaller choice you made earlier.'

The pressure on Nick and on all of us was immense, yet the team never fractured. Despite the disagreements we often had on policy and the politics of decisions, we fell out badly very rarely. That was largely because of the tone that Nick set. He had an incredible grace under pressure, never seeking to cast the blame at other people's feet, even when it was deserved.

During the Eastleigh by-election, when I offered Nick my resignation after a misjudgement on my part had helped fuel a near-calamitous media storm, instead of expressing his anger or frustration, he refused to accept my resignation and devoted his energy not to castigating my stupidity but to ensuring that I was OK after the maelstrom we had been through.

• • •

Early in the coalition, we face the issue of uprating welfare benefits. It is agreed in the emergency Budget in the summer of 2010 that the basis for uprating will switch from the retail price index to the now more commonly used consumer price index (CPI), which for the government is conveniently lower by a factor of 1.5 per cent. This is tough on benefit claimants, but, as public sector wages have been frozen and private sector wages are also in effect frozen across large areas of business, it doesn't seem unreasonable.

Ahead of the autumn party conferences, 'the Quad' – which consists of Nick, Danny, David Cameron and George Osborne – meets to discuss conference announcements. Despite the agreement at the time of the Budget, Osborne is targeting benefits again. He wants to announce a freeze on council tax at the Conservative conference, which, he proposes, will be paid for by freezing benefits completely. Although a council tax freeze would be welcomed by most people, it would provide a disproportionate benefit to the wealthiest in the land, which under Osborne's proposals would be financed by the poorest.

Nick and Danny reject the proposal out of hand. If Osborne wants a council tax freeze, he will have to find the money from elsewhere. He accepts this reluctantly but tells us through exasperated chuckles that we just don't get it – polling, he says, shows that going after benefit payments would be immensely popular. Although the meeting ends with the outcome we want, I hate every minute of it. It is the Tories at their worst: cynical and chummy at the same time; chuckling over how popular hitting people on benefits is with the public and showing a completely cavalier approach to the lives of other people.

Despite the rejection of his party conference proposal, Osborne isn't about to give up on hitting benefit claimants. The following year, CPI for the relevant uprating period has risen to 5.2 per cent. The Tories argue that it is unreasonable for benefit claimants to get such a large increase when others are facing a squeeze. It is not a simple matter: the savings from a freeze are significant and the Tories have a powerful public argument to deploy.

However, I feel strongly that a freeze is wrong. Benefit claimants are already on the most marginal incomes and most vulnerable to the rise in inflation. Added to that, we have already changed the basis on which inflation is calculated and it seems highly cynical to change the rules yet again. In addition, there is no proposal to freeze other benefits such as pensions – the implication being that those on out-of-work benefits are of less value: shirkers who deserve to be punished.

We are coming under huge pressure from the Tories, the arguments in our team are running backwards and forwards, and I am desperately concerned that we are going to concede. At the weekend, as I run around my local park trying to clear my head, the issue keeps forcing its way back in, until suddenly I have clarity – if we concede to the Tories on this then it will be time for me to move on.

On the following Monday, when the Deputy Prime Minister's team meets to discuss the Autumn Statement, Richard Reeves, Nick's strategy director, and I are forthright on the need to uprate in line with CPI.

Nick is rightly testing the arguments, as he often does before coming to a decision, but I am frustrated with the debate. Afterwards I have a coffee with Richard, and he says that if we abandon the uprating, he is unlikely to stick around. I tell him that I have come to the same conclusion. Subsequently, Danny's special adviser, Will de Peyer, a thoughtful person, not prone to either drama or ego, also tells Richard and me that he is implacably opposed to a benefits freeze and has decided that if it happens, he will resign.

Although all three of us continue to argue strongly against the freeze, to my knowledge, none of us ever mentions our intentions to our respective bosses. We want the decision to be made on the arguments, not on threats. It is just a matter of fact that if our arguments are unsuccessful, we will not want to stay in the government. Nick, as is his practice, listens to all the back and forth between advisers and argues the case both ways to test it for himself, until he is ready to decide. When he does, he concludes that the Tory position is unacceptable. He will block the freeze.

The Tories make one last attempt to persuade him ahead of the Autumn Statement. Frustrated by Nick's intransigence, Osborne waves a chart at him which shows a massive explosion in benefits since the 1980s. (I can't help noticing and pointing out that the majority of the rise is housing benefit, which coincides directly with the Conservative sell-off of council housing.) After a heated discussion in which Nick refuses to shift his position, Osborne exasperatedly, almost spitefully, blurts out, 'Nick, you do know that these people don't vote for you and are never going to vote for you, don't you?'

Cameron gives Osborne a patrician glare, as if to say that is not the sort of thing we say in front of the children.

Nick responds firmly, with an edge in his voice. 'George, I think we have rather wider responsibilities in government than simply who will vote for us.'

Osborne looks genuinely bewildered by this statement.

Of course, on one level he is right. Most of these people will not vote for the Liberal Democrats. Few if any of them will know that Nick fought for them, and none will thank him for it. But on the level that really matters, doing the right thing, it is Nick who is correct.

The meeting breaks up frostily, but Nick's argument has prevailed. I feel a huge sense of relief, having no wish to find myself out of government after we have fought so long to get here.

39

BROKEN PROMISES

As 2011 dawned, we were in a perilous position. The knots we had tied ourselves in over tuition fees were one cause, although our support had already slumped following June's emergency Budget. The policy finally arrived at had merit, but our decision to back a change that raised rather than abolished fees catastrophically destroyed trust in our brand.

We should not have made the decision we did. There is no escaping from that. It was wrong to betray the trust put in us, even if the promise we broke was one we should never have made in the first place. Nonetheless, the motivation attributed to Nick in taking the decisions he did over tuition fees are very wide of the mark.

To Nick's detractors, tuition fees demonstrated that he was an unscrupulous politician, ready to ditch his principles for a taste of power, and in the process happy to betray a generation who had put their trust in him.

The reality is different. Nick found himself in government with a policy commitment of abolishing all student tuition fees that was unachievable, so he tried a different tack and sought to find the fairest solution to student financing that could be achieved.

In reality, it wasn't possible to continue to expand university access and retain the existing funding model, let alone scrap fees altogether.

We should have replaced the policy before the election, as Stephen Williams, then our Higher Education spokesperson, had urged, proposing an alternative very similar to what was finally implemented. But no one, including me, gave us a cat's chance in hell of getting such a change through our party conference. Risking a high-profile defeat immediately before a general election didn't seem wise, so we chose to dilute and downgrade the commitment instead. It was a fatal error.

The coalition agreement compounded that error. It gave us the option to abstain on any vote to raise tuition fees, but as the majority of our MPs had signed a pledge to vote against any increase in fees, it wasn't any help. Exacerbating the problem further, a Liberal Democrat Secretary of State, Vince Cable, led the department responsible for the policy.

After Vince and the Treasury definitively ruled out a graduate tax as bad policy in October 2010, Nick focused on trying to ensure that a progressive contribution scheme was agreed – in effect, a capped graduate tax. The challenge remained that while this was much fairer than the system it replaced, if the funding gap for universities was to be addressed, fees would still have to rise. At this point, we should have overridden the Treasury and insisted on announcing the policy as a capped graduate tax.

This idea, however, was rejected out of hand: by the Treasury, which refused to provide the necessary funding or to allow the scheme to be described as a tax, on the bureaucratic basis that it would add theoretical (although not actual) billions to public sector borrowing; and by the universities and elements within government, who wanted varying fees to be charged to encourage competition – an objection which proved wholly redundant when every university ended up charging the maximum fee.

Despite Nick's success in delivering what was in effect a graduate tax (a policy the National Union of Students itself had favoured), the fact that the mechanism of fees still existed and were to increase threefold meant that all his efforts were in vain. When the plan was finally unveiled, our attempts to explain what had been achieved were drowned out by the howls of betrayal from students and our political opponents. And the trouble was, they had a point. It was true that we had delivered the fairest outcome, but we had not delivered the outcome that we had promised.

As a result, Nick became the central focus of sustained hostility towards the policy. Students and political opponents vilified him, and the following year during the Alternative Vote (AV) referendum on electoral reform, our supposed Conservative allies joined in, with leaflets depicting Nick pledging that he wouldn't vote for an increase in tuition fees and, underneath, the words 'AV will lead to more broken promises.'

On 10 November, a protest against tuition fees brought 50,000 students onto the streets of London, with similar protests taking place in other cities across the country. Placards denouncing Nick for betrayal were ubiquitous, and effigies of him were burnt in the street. The anger boiled over when a minority of extremists among the protesters attacked the building that housed the headquarters of the Conservative Party, smashing windows and occupying the building. This demonstration was followed by similar protest marches on 24 and 30 November, which again descended into violence amidst controversy over policing tactics.

Although Nick continued to believe he had achieved the right progressive policy outcome and remained outwardly calm and resolute, the political and personal pressure on him was intense. On the day of the second London protest, we exchanged emails on the subject and he told me that he was close to despair. Peter Kellner of the pollster YouGov had briefed him on their private polling, which found that the perception that he had sold out and abandoned his principles was widespread among the public. 'I just don't know if it is retrievable,' he wrote.

Protesters again took to the streets on Thursday 9 December, when the motion to approve the new scheme was debated in Parliament. Violence broke out and spread to the West End, where shops were vandalised and a car carrying the Prince of Wales and the Duchess of Cornwall was attacked. When the motion was put to the vote, Liberal Democrat MPs split three ways, and it scraped through the Commons by just twenty-one votes.

With that, trust in our brand was finally shot.

40

EUROPE: THE SLIDE
TOWARDS CALAMITY

One of David Cameron's first acts as Prime Minister is to establish a National Security Council. The public objective is to provide a more strategic approach to foreign policy and national security. I suspect he has just watched too many episodes of *The West Wing*. Certainly, long-term strategy is not his interest. He is all tactics and tomorrow's newspapers. Nowhere is this clearer than on Europe.

As the debt crisis in the Eurozone rumbles on, threatening catastrophic consequences for the European economy as a whole, including the UK, Cameron decides that this is a good time to start lecturing his fellow leaders and banging the table with British demands. On Sunday 23 October 2011, at the conclusion of the European Council, which has been called to discuss economic policy and climate change, Cameron gives a press conference in which he dangles the prospect of a repatriation of powers from the EU to the UK in front of his Eurosceptic MPs, whom he is desperately trying to persuade not to vote for a referendum in the Commons the following day. I happen to catch the PM's statement live on TV. It hasn't been discussed with us and it isn't government policy, but before I have a chance to react, I receive a text from the Prime Minister's chief of staff, Ed Llewellyn, which reads, 'Will call from car, please don't react before we have spoken.' He has clearly understood the difficulty that these words will cause. We speak shortly afterwards and, not wanting to inflame the situation ahead of the Commons vote, we bash out some compromise words between us which Nick and Cameron agree on a call later that evening. The next day, however, Michael Gove, the Education Secretary, goes on the *Today* programme and undoes all our best efforts to dial the issue down, hyping up the idea of a repatriation of powers and souring the mood even further.

That evening, eighty-one Conservative MPs rebel against a three-line whip and support a motion calling for an in/out referendum on Europe. With the support of the Labour Party, it is easily defeated, but Cameron is shaken. The following day, Nick and Cameron meet for their regular bilateral meeting. Cameron tries to tell Nick that the Tory rebellion the previous night was 'my tuition fees'. Nick responds sharply: 'Forgive me, David, if I sound a little sour, but when there are 50,000 people on the streets and you are being burnt in effigy, then come and tell me that it is your "tuition fees".'

In December 2011, the EU Council is discussing the treaty change that the Eurozone countries believe is needed to tackle the debt crisis. But despite the obviously counterproductive impact of his lecturing of fellow EU leaders at the October European Council, Cameron keeps it up. Instead of building alliances, he alienates even our closest European allies.

Ed Davey, the coalition Business Minister, has already shown what can be achieved if you are prepared to put the effort and empathy into constructing alliances, through the 'like-minded' group of EU business ministers he has established, which is allowing Britain to project its interest much more effectively in Europe. But Cameron can't be bothered with the boring intricacies of alliance-building, of listening to the views of others, of showing real understanding of their concerns and issues. He is used to getting his own way, so he has little purpose to learn these skills.

The Swedish minister for Europe later tells me, 'We often agree with Britain, but we can't side with you when you behave in such a high-handed manner.' Even Mark Rutte, the Dutch Prime Minister and Britain's staunchest ally in the EU, tells Cameron that he is demanding too much.

In the early hours of Friday 9 December 2011, I am woken by the No. 10 switchboard. They are setting up a call with Nick and David Cameron. Nick is connected from Sheffield and then David Cameron comes on the line from Brussels. He tells Nick that the negotiations are going badly but, crucially, he assures us that Britain still has two or three allies on board. It is key that we are not isolated.

At 5 a.m., David Cameron calls a press conference and announces that he has vetoed the proposed treaty change. Not a single other European country has supported him. Nick is furious: Cameron has misled us and played his hand atrociously, but we are in the difficult position that we have signed up for the negotiating objectives, if not the negotiating approach. We struggle with this dilemma over the course of Friday, but on Saturday Nick decides he has to speak out. He goes on the Sunday morning programmes and blasts Cameron for leaving Britain isolated in Europe.

For once, Cameron isn't too much bothered by Nick's media response; he is being fêted by the right-wing press and his backbenchers and he seems to get a taste for this. The polls show his veto is hugely popular, and now the papers are turning their fire on Nick.

At their next bilateral meeting, early the following week, Nick warns Cameron not to get carried away by his current popularity. 'It doesn't matter how much red meat you feed the Eurosceptics, David, their appetite is insatiable and they'll be back for more. They won't be happy until we are out of Europe and you are out of your job.'

Cameron says cheerfully and complacently, 'Why don't you let me worry about my party, Nick?'

• • •

The Eurozone crisis continues to develop over the following year, compounded by the political crisis in Greece. On Thursday 14 June 2012, I find myself rowing with the Chancellor's adviser, Rupert Harrison, over the content of Osborne's Mansion House speech. Extraordinarily, just two days before the crucial Greek general election, the Chancellor intends to state that while the Eurozone crisis could be resolved 'it may require a Greek exit to make it happen'. Osborne point-blank refuses to take the words out and they are duly delivered, an astonishing display of arrogant disregard for the interests of our European partners.

On Sunday, the day of the Greek election itself, I belatedly get hold of the text of the Prime Minister's speech to the G20. The Tories are at it again. The draft speech states that 'economic logic' points to the break-up of the Euro. Cameron and Osborne seem determined to run around shouting fire to anyone who will listen while hosing the flames with petrol.

I call Ed Llewellyn, who is in Paris, and he says he will try to sort it out, but he comes back to me soon after to say that the PM won't move. The PM, Ed tells me, is fed up always being muzzled and having to water down what he wants to say. I point out that the PM seems pretty unmuzzled to me. He is saying plenty of things that we object to and we keep biting our tongues, but this is not on: it is completely outside the government's agreed position, it can only cause further difficulties for our European allies at a highly sensitive time, and if the statement is made, we will reject it.

Ed agrees to try again and eventually I get a very grumpy message passed back with new wording which has already been issued to the press. Although the language issued to the press removes the offending phrase and is just about acceptable to us, securing it has required a huge and pointless outlay of time and emotional energy.

But Europe refuses to go away, and disputes over our approach continue to dog the coalition throughout its life. Cameron has fed the Eurosceptic beast and it keeps coming back for more. Finally, on 23 January 2013, in his Bloomberg speech, he concedes the principle of an in/out referendum. The following June, with Cameron's support, a Conservative backbench MP, James Wharton, introduces a Bill which provides for an in/out referendum in 2017. I am having lunch with an old friend when I receive a message from Ben Williams, special adviser to the Liberal Democrat Chief Whip, that the government whips' office has issued a three-line whip to all government MPs, including Liberal Democrats, ordering them to vote for the Bill at second reading. This order has been issued despite the fact that the Bill is completely contrary to the coalition agreement and to agreed government policy. I contact Ed Llewellyn immediately to express my outrage at this abuse of government offices for partisan purposes, but by now the Conservatives are out of control on Europe. They think nothing of ignoring the coalition agreement, although they savagely berate us if we so much as question any previously agreed position.

Nick feels particularly betrayed. The agreement with the Conservatives over the approach to the European Union was painstakingly made during the coalition negotiations. It is the one area that Nick and Cameron discussed at length, and it was the subject of their final call before the formation of the government. The outcome was legislation that guaranteed a referendum should there be any future treaty change which granted significant new powers to the European Union. Now the Tories have publicly torn up that agreement.

We are not entirely blameless ourselves. In 2008, we had introduced the idea of an in/out referendum as a way of dealing with the political pressures around the Lisbon Treaty. Although I was in favour of a referendum on significant constitutional changes – I had called for a referendum on the Maastricht Treaty in a letter published in *The Guardian* in 1993 – I was never completely comfortable with idea of an in/out referendum on the question of Britain's membership as a whole. Why should voters have to make such a stark choice if their objection was to the treaty rather than our membership of the EU as a whole? The answer was that it was thought to be the only way to win a vote on an EU treaty in the face of a hostile right-wing press which had been poisoning the discourse on the EU for decades. Although our proposal went nowhere at the time, David Cameron and his allies subsequently used it to relentlessly attack our opposition after he took leave of his political senses and proposed a standalone in/out referendum. Something we had never contemplated.

•   •   •

My counterpart, Ed Llewellyn, and I have a good relationship despite the amount of time we have to spend disputing issues with one another on behalf of our bosses. Neither of us has a rose-tinted view of our own parties, or indeed our bosses. In one of our first meetings, Ed tells me that when there is a leak from one of their meetings, David is often their first suspect, as he can't help but injudiciously share interesting information. I smile and tell him that when we suffer a leak we also usually look upwards.

Most of the time, Ed and I work well together and are able to sort out difficulties amicably. I like both him and his deputy, Kate Fall, who is also friendly, pragmatic and non-tribal. Together with my deputy, Jo Foster and later Tim Colbourne, we all try to minimise conflict and focus on solutions. Nevertheless, we feel the petty humiliations keenly that are regularly inflicted on us – usually inadvertently – as the junior partner in the coalition. Viewers of the TV show *Veep* will have a good idea of how this plays out: initiatives unnecessarily held up, appointments casually forgotten, the need for joint agreement overlooked.

Although Ed is courteous and thoughtful, he is not immune. My journal records an example from one of our regular meetings in 2012: the predictable confusion over what time we were meeting and where, although as usual we had confirmed the details with his office the evening before. Eventually, Ed arrives in the No. 10 canteen where I am waiting, but shortly afterwards an official appears to ask Ed if he is expecting someone. 'I don't think so,' Ed replies. 'Well,' the official says, 'the US Ambassador thinks he is meeting you – in fact, he thinks he is meeting the PM but he obviously isn't.' Ed excuses himself and I am left to finish breakfast on my own, pondering whether I should be reassured or appalled that our closest ally is treated with the same casual lack of regard as we are.

• • •

As time progresses, the coalition comes under increasing strain across a number of areas, from climate change to Lords reform and the economy.

David Cameron has sought to reposition the Conservatives as a modern party in touch with the concerns of the new century, and as part of this project he has embraced the green agenda. Although in opposition we are highly sceptical that his 'vote blue, go green' mantra extends much beyond a desire to dislodge environmentally conscious voters from the Liberal Democrats, we have high hopes that his prominent profile on environmental issues will help underpin the bold agenda that we have agreed in the coalition agreement. Those hopes are reinforced when, shortly after the formation of the coalition, the Prime Minister announces that he will lead 'the greenest government ever'.

Sadly, it doesn't take long for them to be dashed. From the outset,

George Osborne's Treasury seeks to frustrate the Department of Energy and Climate Change, leading to some epic battles between Osborne and the DECC Secretary of State, Chris Huhne. By the time Huhne departs from government in February 2012, Osborne has been joined on this issue by Cameron. Together they have abandoned almost all pretence of their green credentials.

In September 2012, Cameron appoints John Hayes, a noted right-winger and environmental sceptic, as a junior minister in DECC and Hayes loses no time in seeking to undermine our green agenda from within. On 17 October, without any consultation with Ed Davey, who has replaced Chris Huhne as the DECC Secretary of State – or apparently his own advisers – Cameron announces out of the blue at Prime Minister's Questions that the government is going to legislate to automatically switch energy customers on to the lowest tariffs. It sounds great in principle but would amount to a huge re-regulation of the industry, could undermine investment and possibly push up prices. Ed is incandescent, but the PM refuses to correct what he has said, and no one knows how to answer the deluge of media enquiries about what Cameron is actually proposing. Parliament demands an urgent statement from the government, which Ed point-blank refuses to make, sending Hayes instead to clear up the PM's mess. It is the right decision. Hayes's embarrassingly vague statement is met with laughter from incredulous MPs.

A long-scheduled Quad meeting on energy takes place on the same afternoon as Cameron's PMQs outburst. The mood is already sour, but Cameron turns it toxic by announcing that he wants to completely reopen the Energy Company Obligation agreement – the funding mechanism for investment in energy infrastructure and efficiency – which has been painfully negotiated over the preceding year. His only justification for this about-turn – 'Circumstances have changed' – provokes Nick's anger: 'Do you want me to turn around and say, "Circumstances have changed and I am no longer able to support the government's economic strategy?!" The green focus of the government is central for us and now you are just proposing reneging on a key part of it!' Cameron has no answer for that, and the rest of the meeting is a bad-tempered and unproductive attempt to find a way out of the impasse that Cameron has just constructed.

Relationships within the coalition fray further when, at the end of October, we back an amendment to block the Conservative proposals to change parliamentary boundaries, as we have warned them we will do if they fail to support reform of the House of Lords. No. 10's lack of support for the Lords proposals is graphically illustrated when Cameron refuses to sit on the front bench ahead of a critical vote. Mark Harper, the Conservative minister (later Chief Whip) who serves as Nick's deputy on constitutional issues, is so frustrated that he calls me and asks me to try to intervene with Ed Llewellyn to get him to change the Prime Minister's mind. I tell Mark that I will try but I don't fancy my chances if Mark, a Tory minister, can't persuade him. It is clear when I speak to Ed that the PM will not have himself associated with Lords reform in any way and has effectively abandoned another coalition commitment.

After the amendment to block boundaries is tabled with Liberal Democrat support, the PM demands a call with Nick. He comes on the line as angry as I can remember him, but Nick is resolute. Ed calls me after the PM–DPM call and we have one of our most heated discussions of the coalition. 'Jonny,' he says – a little imperiously to my mind – 'this is not OK.' I tell him that we have been warning them for months that this is what will happen if they fail to back Lords reform: they just haven't been listening.

In January 2013, as the amendment heads towards a vote, Ed and I have another bad-tempered meeting in which he threatens that if any of our ministers vote for the amendment, the Prime Minister will sack them. I point out a little sharply that this is a silly threat to make: if it is carried out, the government will come to an end and it isn't likely that the Tories will be part of the next one. The polls suggest that an election, while not an enticing prospect for us, is hardly more so for them and, in any event, they cannot afford to dismiss the possibility that we might form an alternative rainbow coalition with Labour and the nationalists (though in truth it is unlikely). The threat is quietly dropped and the boundary proposals are duly defeated.

41

THE CANARY THAT KEPT
ON SINGING

It's a Sunday night and I have retired to bed early. Sometime around 10.30 p.m., my mobile cuts through into my sleep-addled brain. I reach instinctively for it.

'Jonny?' It's Nick.

'Hi Nick.'

'Jonny, I've just had a call from Chris Huhne to tell me he's pleading guilty tomorrow morning and is going to resign his seat.'

I am totally awake now. Nothing sleep-addled about me. Not one spot of addling.

'He's what? But just last week he said… Fuck.'

'I know. But that doesn't matter now, I need you to work up a plan for how we handle this tomorrow…'

The media storm the next day is huge, but we weather it and call a by-election in Chris's Eastleigh seat for the earliest date possible, Thursday 28 February 2013.

On 12 February, Nick and I leave on a visit to Mozambique and Ethiopia ahead of the G8 summit, which Britain is hosting. It is my first visit to Ethiopia in twenty-eight years and I have arranged to stay on an extra few days to reacquaint myself with Addis Ababa. I have also discovered that, by amazing coincidence, Father Charles Sherlock will be in Ethiopia at the same time, and we have arranged to meet up. It will be the first time I have seen him in almost three decades.

Despite my excitement at the trip, nagging at the back of my mind is the news we have picked up that Channel 4 is planning an exposé on the alleged sexual impropriety of a former party chief executive, Chris Rennard.

Before I leave, I email our then chief executive, Tim Gordon, emphasising that if we are to tackle this issue effectively, we have to assemble all the facts as swiftly as possible and be as open as we can. I propose that someone is appointed specifically to the role of fact-finder. Knowing that the party staff are swamped with all their focus on the by-election, I suggest that one of our peers should be approached to take on the job.

I arrive back in the UK on Monday 18 February to discover that no fact-finder has been appointed and that we are no closer to assembling the information we will need – although, in fairness, the party is completely under-resourced and all the resources it does have are naturally focused on trying to hold on to Eastleigh, so it is perhaps not surprising that the ball has been dropped. A meeting of senior figures to try to establish, at this late stage, what we actually know breaks up in acrimony, with a distinct element of buck-passing evident. I leave it depressed and angry.

On Thursday 21 February, just before the story breaks, we have a tense meeting of the media team. Olly Grender, who has been drafted in to support the party media operation as it faces the twin challenges of a parliamentary by-election and this looming crisis, and James McGrory, Nick's press secretary, argue that we need to be more open than is evident in the draft statement and Q&A. I fear that without having all the facts together, greater openness is just going to tie us in knots and, scarred by the earlier buck-passing meeting, I angrily ask how we are supposed to be open when we don't seem to have a full grasp of the facts.

With that, I sharply close the discussion down. In doing so, I am acting completely contrary to my own advice to Tim Gordon that this issue has to be tackled as openly and transparently as possible. As the story plays out, it becomes clearer by the day how badly I have got it wrong.

Interest in the story is super-charged by the parliamentary by-election, which is now just seven days away. When the story first breaks on *Channel 4 News*, it is clear that it is damaging, but follow-up from other media is relatively light and it only becomes apparent that we are in a full-blown crisis over the weekend, as new information tumbles out which blindsides us and appears to contradict the statements we have already made in good faith.

Nick is away in Spain – he asks me on Friday morning if it is still OK to go and, not wanting to disrupt much-needed time with his family, I foolishly say yes. Sean is also away for the weekend with Sharan, his new girlfriend, and, again, I don't want to disrupt a much-needed break.

James Holt, the party's communications director – who plays a heroic role throughout the period of crisis – is in Eastleigh; and David is away in Paris with Julia, so on top of everything else, I have charge of our dog, Bentley. Saturday is difficult but manageable, but that night the story explodes with a raft of new revelations.

The media coverage is now relentless and even friendly journalists are savagely critical of how we have handled it. Nevertheless, not once do either James or Olly try to protect their own reputations by breaking ranks and placing the blame on me, which they would have been entirely justified in doing.

The *Daily Mail*, which is now running a hostile front page every day, turns its attention to the BBC, using its leader column to bully them into joining the fray. The BBC resists at first, then caves in. Such is the frenzy that on the day that a Scottish cardinal – who has previously condemned homosexuality as 'moral degradation' – resigns due to inappropriate sexual conduct with men, the BBC News channel is giving higher billing to the Lib Dem crisis.

A number of our MPs and peers are dragged into the story, all need support and a number are understandably stressed and angry, adding to the emotional burden on all of us. On Monday 25 February, I become a focus of the crisis when the *Telegraph* publishes a story about allegations of sexual impropriety against Chris Rennard that they had put to me during the 2010 election. The response I gave at the time was accurate, but I did not volunteer any further information beyond answering the specific points they had asked me to respond to. Helena Morrissey later criticises me for this in her independent report into how the party handled the issue. The report states: 'While it was technically true that Clegg was unaware of the specific alleged incidences as detailed by the newspaper in their correspondence with him, Oates could have made it clear that Clegg was aware of several anonymous, "non-specific" allegations.'

It is true that I could have done so, but the *Telegraph* enquiry came just six days before polling day in the 2010 general election. To have volunteered further 'non-specific allegations' would have begged a series of questions that I would not have been in a position to answer given the issues of confidentiality which even the *Telegraph* conceded it was bound by. What I should undoubtedly have done, however, was to follow up more effectively with the party following the election to ensure that a thorough review took place.

By polling day on Thursday 28 February, the party has been subject to its worst period of sustained negative coverage since former Liberal leader Jeremy Thorpe's trial for conspiracy to murder. I ask to see Nick and offer him my resignation. Nick refuses it and although he is probably feeling even more battered than I am and has good reason to blame me for his predicament, his concern is instead entirely focused on the impact the past few days have had on me.

After the polls close, the news from the election count is conflicting. I have already decided that if we lose, I will resubmit my resignation and this time insist on it. Mind you, if we lose, Nick may not be around to receive it.

The stakes are incredibly high as I sit on the sofa in the early hours of Friday morning watching the television and awaiting the result. I don't relax until, shortly before the declaration, James Holt's unmistakably dazzling white smile flashes briefly onto the TV screen as he turns away from one of the counting tables, indicating that we must be home and dry.

We have scraped through with a majority of just under 2,000, which in the context of the media onslaught is astonishing. UKIP are in second place, the Tories pushed into third. It is a remarkable result in the circumstances, but in retrospect we might have been better off losing.

Eastleigh was the canary that kept on singing, denying us the warning of what lay ahead, allowing us to delude ourselves that if we could win in these circumstances, we could win in any. The party's media briefing note the next day says exactly that. It is an understandable delusion, and one I suffer from too, but it is a delusion nonetheless.

• • •

In early 2011, James McGrory, Nick Clegg's press secretary, approaches me and suggests that we should push the issue of gay marriage on to the coalition agenda. Lynne Featherstone, our minister in the Home Office, is already passionately advocating the idea in her department and winning converts among unlikely allies, and James feels it is time for us to formally take it up from the Deputy Prime Minister's office.

The idea makes me nervous. My mindset is shaped by my experience of the anti-gay atmosphere of the 1980s, and my instinctive reaction is that having achieved civil partnerships, we should perhaps leave it there rather than risk provoking a backlash. James, born a decade or so after me, is not encumbered by such baggage.

My response, therefore, is cautious and sceptical. James, who is the archetypal football-obsessive straight man's straight man, looks understandably bewildered by the lukewarm reception to his suggestion. His brow furrows in confusion. 'Surely that's not right, Jonny. We're in government, we've got a chance to do this. We've got to take it.'

There is something about the simple sincerity with which he says this that strikes me hard. For a moment I see the world through his eyes, where being gay is clearly not a big deal, just who a person is, and that person is as deserving of equal rights as anyone else. It makes me realise how cloudy my vision has remained, still locked in the psychology of the past.

James's simple sincerity finally clears my vision. It's difficult to convey how profoundly that short conversation affects me. The realisation that his generation is free of all that past baggage finally helps free me from its last vestiges and I feel like a burden has been lifted.

Over the following months, with Nick's backing, Lynne presses ahead with her campaign for equal marriage, convincing Home Secretary Theresa May of the arguments in favour, which in turn is crucial in persuading David Cameron to allow a Bill to go forward.

Finally, after a battle with recalcitrant Conservative ministers that goes right up to the wire, Lynne announces at the Liberal Democrat conference in September 2011 that the government will open a consultation on how – not if – the government should implement equal civil marriage for same-sex couples.

The momentous nature of the announcement and Lynne's central role in achieving it, outrageously, does not get the full recognition that it deserves. The day before, Conservative advisers leak the story in order to try to claim it as their own. As is so often the case during the coalition, when the Conservatives see a Liberal Democrat idea whose time has come, they scramble to get on board and take the credit. With an acquiescent media in tow, they are usually successful.

They are helped on this issue by some shameless behaviour from Ben Summerskill, then Stonewall's chief executive. Embarrassed by his own initial opposition to gay marriage, throughout the process he dismisses the Liberal Democrats' role in this historic achievement, later accusing us of 'quite cynically adopting the policy'. This brings forth a swift retort from the prominent gay rights activist Peter Tatchell: 'I am not a supporter of the Liberal Democrats, but on the issue of same-sex marriage the party took an early position, while Stonewall did all it could to sabotage that position. It is unbelievable really.'

The Marriage (Same Sex Couples) Bill is eventually introduced to Parliament in January 2013 and it is not long before the Tories are facing a backlash. At second reading in the Commons, the Bill passes by a healthy majority, but the Conservative Party has split in two on the issue, with 136 Conservative MPs voting against the Bill and only 127 in favour.

Faced with the prospect of a wrecking amendment from a Conservative backbench MP, it takes an appeal to Labour MPs to get the Bill over the line. With their support, the Bill passes its final stages in Parliament on 16 July 2013 and receives Royal Assent the following day. Being part of the government has given us a platform from which to shift the political landscape, exerting real political pressure on the Tories and forcing them to play catch-up.

Delighted though I am that the Bill has become law, I can't help feeling a little cynical as David Cameron so eagerly seeks to claim credit for the success. He is, after all, the leader of the party that did so much to stoke the anti-gay hostility that I encountered as a teenager; he went to work for the Conservative Party at the very height of its anti-gay rhetoric, and as late as 2003 he voted against the repeal of Section 28. A decade later, more of his MPs have voted against our Bill than for it.

It's not that he doesn't deserve any credit for supporting the Bill – he undoubtedly faced down a lot of hostility in his party, and it cost him dearly with his grassroots supporters – I just wonder if a little more humility on his part might not be in order and a little more generosity of spirit forthcoming for the real architect of the reform, Lynne Featherstone.

• • •

London was enjoying one of its periodic heatwaves on the day the Bill passed its final parliamentary hurdles. As I walked across Westminster Bridge that night, a pink carnation pinned to my jacket to mark the event, I paused and leant against the balustrade of the bridge, looking back across the river to the Houses of Parliament, enjoying the balmy evening and feeling a rush of pride at what had been achieved.

At the Scottish party conference the following March, after the Act had come into force, Nick spoke of the difference it had made to how people felt: 'A gay friend of mine told me that, walking past Moss Bros the other day, he saw a window display of two grooms … He said that as he passed that shop window, he literally felt himself walk a bit taller.'

Like the friend Nick quoted, I had also learnt how to walk a bit taller. I had Lynne and Nick and Peter Tatchell and all the campaigners down the years to thank for that.

But I had Nick's press secretary to thank, as well.

• • •

In the autumn of 2014, the conflict in Syria and Iraq is once again at the forefront of the government's agenda. Over the previous year, the fundamentalist terrorist group ISIS has exploited the Syrian civil war and the leadership failures in Iraq to seize huge tracts of territory in both countries. In March 2013, they take the Syrian city of Raqqa and by June 2014 they have advanced into Iraq and seized the northern city of Mosul.

On Saturday 20 September, the Iraqi government formally requests military assistance from the UK. The following day, Cameron calls a meeting at Chequers with Nick and other key Cabinet members to discuss the Iraqi request. Cameron opens the meeting by setting out the background to the request and his belief that we should respond positively. Conservative ministers, particularly Michael Gove, appear reticent, so Nick comes in forthrightly in support, arguing that we have an obligation to come to the Iraqis' assistance.

The Tory ministers are concerned not only about the reaction of their own MPs but also about the position that Labour will take. They feel badly burnt by the government's defeat the previous year over action against the use of chemical weapons by the Syrian regime, attributing it to a last-minute change of heart on the part of Ed Miliband, the Labour leader. I don't share their concern about Labour. I know Miliband and his team reasonably well by now and I am pretty confident that if handled properly – which means Cameron avoiding his high-handed 'now listen to me' approach (no easy ask) – Labour will back the proposals.

As the discussion gets more fretful, I intervene to say that as long as the key arguments are clearly articulated – that there is an unambiguous legal basis for action, that it will be prosecuted by a broad coalition including Arab nations and will be confined to Iraq – then it will be very hard for Labour to oppose, and if they do so in those circumstances, we can win a vote without them anyway.

Michael Gove is not convinced. He is emphatic that Parliament should not be recalled, telling us that the government doesn't have the numbers to win a vote on its own. Only 250 Tories, he claims, can be relied on to back the government, fourteen will vote against, nine will abstain and twenty-three are open to persuasion. Nick is surprised by Gove's assessment of the mood among Tory backbenchers and asks him what the motivation is of those who intend to vote against the government. Gove says, 'They are either Powellites [referring to the isolationist and racist former Tory minister], pacifists or they just hate the Prime Minister.'

Cameron adds, 'Or all three. Some of them would rather depose me than Assad!'

Despite Gove's misgivings, the meeting concludes that we will ask Parliament to agree to the Iraqi government's request. Parliament is recalled the following Friday and votes by 524 to 43 in favour of military action.

•   •   •

A few weeks later, I wake early on the last day of our final autumn conference before the general election and take myself for a run by the Clyde. Running is a relatively late discovery in my life, prompted and encouraged by David; it helps me enormously, clearing my head and keeping me in mental good health.

That final day of our conference is a big day for mental health – not just mine. Norman Lamb, Minister of State for Health, is making a number of major government announcements on the subject, and Nick's conference speech is to build on Norman's efforts to raise its political profile, announcing that additional provision for mental health care will be front and centre of our manifesto for the general election the following spring.

Somewhere along the Clyde, my security pass falls out of my pocket and when I arrive back at the security gate I realise I have lost it, forcing me to retrace my steps until I find it at almost the furthest point I had reached along the river. By the time I am back in my room, Norman Lamb is already on the television news bulletins unveiling a package of mental health reforms, including millions in additional funding and the introduction of binding targets for waiting times for mental health services, putting them for the first time on the same footing as physical health services.

As I watch the bulletins, I find myself suddenly and unexpectedly overcome by emotion, tears in my eyes, thinking of my own struggles with mental health and of all the people close to me and unknown to me who have had to struggle without the support they need. The focus that Norman and Nick are shining on mental health today makes me feel immensely proud.

After breakfast, Nick and I go for a pre-speech walk in Pollok Country Park on the edge of Glasgow. It is a beautiful autumn day, the park sparkling in the cold, clear air. As we walk, I tell him how much it means to me that as a party we have got so firmly behind improving mental health care. I share a little of my experiences with mental health and of the experiences of people I care for, and I tell him that when I saw the new bulletins this morning, I had found myself brought to tears.

Nick says lightly, 'I think you must be overtired if you're crying at the news,' trying in that very English habit to avoid anything that touches too closely on emotion. But this is too important to me to be brushed away, so I press the point. 'Nick, I didn't cry because I was tired, I cried because of how much it means and how proud I am of what you and Norman have done.' He looks at me with a sheepish half-grin and says, 'I know.'

The taboo around mental health that has existed for so long has been slowly breaking down over the years thanks to a host of brave campaigners willing to share their experiences with others, and today Nick and Norman are taking another major step in raising the profile of the issue and committing the government to action.

We finish our walk and return to the conference centre so Nick can prepare for the speech. When he delivers it, it is strong and heartfelt, and cheers of approval erupt from the audience when he announces that further commitments on mental health will be on the front page of our election manifesto.

It is our last full conference before the general election, which is coming in the spring. We are doing important things in government; the mood of the party is resilient, even upbeat, and I dare to hope that brighter days may be coming.

42

BACK TO THE BEGINNING

The words and images from Michael Buerk's 1984 broadcast from the Ethiopian famine have stayed with me all my life. I can picture almost every image, know almost every word by heart. They force their way into my mind uninvited, whenever they feel like it. While I am giving a presentation in a meeting, or talking happily with a friend at a party, or just sat reading a book on a train or a bus. And every time they do, I am gripped by the sadness and the anger that I felt as I sat and watched the news that first time.

In particular, I can't escape the image of that little girl, just skin and bones, or the thought of her mother, who had lost everything worth having. 'This three-year-old girl was beyond any help: unable to take food, attached to a drip but too late; the drip was taken away. Only minutes later, while we were filming, she died. Her mother had lost all her four children and her husband.'

It was that sadness and anger that propelled me into politics. I joined the Liberal Party in 1987 because it was prepared to vocally make the case for Britain to meet its obligations to the world. As early as 1970, the Liberal Party manifesto had committed itself to meeting the target proposed by the Pearson Report for the proportion of national income that developed nations should provide in development assistance. The report's target was ultimately adopted in a revised form as a UN target for developed nations to commit 0.7 per cent of gross national income to overseas development assistance.

At the time I got involved in politics, this seemed like a very distant dream. The Conservative government of the day was cutting overseas development assistance, and the media had little interest. But distant though it appeared to be, I knew it was worth fighting for and so did many other people. Over the subsequent two decades, the campaigners, the churches and the NGOs never gave up, and gradually political opinion began to shift.

In 2005, the Labour MP Nick Brown asked my then boss, Peter Bingle, for some pro bono assistance to support Tom Clarke's Private Member's Bill, which was to become the International Development (Reporting and Transparency) Act 2006. Knowing my passion for the subject, Peter asked if I would lead a small team of colleagues to take it on. It was fascinating working with Tom and Nick, helping them try to informally whip MPs to be in the chamber for the crucial debates to prevent the Bill being filibustered. I was delighted when it became law; it required, among other things, that the government must report annually on progress towards meeting the 0.7 per cent target. It was another step on the long road to securing the goal.

•   •   •

Happily, by the time the coalition is formed, the Conservative Party have fallen into line with both the Liberal Democrats and Labour in backing the target. In fact, the Conservative manifesto goes even further than the Liberal Democrats, promising not only to meet the target but also to legislate that commitment into law, something we are very happy to enshrine in the coalition agreement.

However, despite the coalition commitment to legislation and the Conservative manifesto's explicit commitment that this would be introduced in the first session of Parliament, Cameron and Osborne argue that the legislative programme is already too congested to include an Overseas Development Bill and that the key is reaching the target rather than legislating for it. The International Development Secretary, Andrew Mitchell, is unhappy, but at this stage we are not overly concerned as long as the commitment is met. Legislation, after all, is their manifesto commitment rather than ours.

Meanwhile, steady progress is being made to reaching the UN target, and in 2013 I am sitting behind the Deputy Prime Minister as the Cabinet is informed that expenditure on overseas development assistance has reached 0.7 per cent of gross national income. The UK is the first country in the G7 to meet the UN target established more than forty years previously. It has been a long time coming, but I feel euphoric that a government that I am a participant in is leading the way in discharging the industrial nations' obligations to the poorest people in the world.

Despite this huge achievement, David Cameron is not able to celebrate it too publicly. International development is not popular in many parts of the Conservative Party and particularly not in the conservative press. In the early years of the coalition, we witness the strange phenomenon of a Conservative Secretary of State for International Development submitting proposals to the Deputy Prime Minister's office for announcements at the Liberal Democrat conference, on the grounds that they will find a positive reception there which will not be forthcoming at the Conservative conference.

As the next Queen's Speech comes around in 2013 and David Cameron and George Osborne again resist an Overseas Development Bill, we start to become suspicious. In 2014, when they refuse again, it is clear they have no intention of supporting legislation, which can only mean either that they have become so terrified of their backbenchers and the right-wing press that they are not willing to implement their own manifesto pledge or that they want the flexibility to ditch the UN target if they get into government on their own.

Then we have a rare piece of good fortune. The ballot for Private Members' Bills results in two Liberal Democrat MPs, Michael Moore and Andrew George, being drawn out in first and second place. This guarantees that their Bills will get reasonable time for parliamentary debate. Mike Moore, the former Scottish Secretary, initially intends to introduce a Bill related to Scottish devolution, but he rapidly sees the merit in legislating to enshrine the UN target in law. The Tories will be livid, but they can hardly oppose it; after all, it is a Conservative manifesto commitment.

As soon as Mike's Bill is brought to their attention, they duly explode in private rage and I have the hugely enjoyable task of explaining demurely that we are simply trying to help them achieve one of their manifesto promises, while expressing my surprise that they aren't showing more gratitude for our assistance. They have consistently told us that there is no time in the legislative programme for the Bill, but look, we have found it for them – shouldn't they be delighted?

They are not. But they are stuck with it.

On Monday 9 March 2015, in the dying days of the coalition, the International Development Bill passes its final stages in the House of Lords and is cleared for Royal Assent.

It seems like a fitting end to the coalition and a fitting end to my journey.

43

THE END OF THE AFFAIR

In the first months of 2015, heated discussions are taking place with broadcasters over TV debates for the forthcoming election. Cameron is desperate to avoid a debate between the Conservatives, the Lib Dems, Labour and UKIP, which the broadcasters have proposed – he does not want Farage afforded such a stage. At the end of a bilateral meeting in early February, Cameron asks if he can have a private word with Nick. Afterwards, Nick unusually does not call Lucy Smith (his principal private secretary), Philip Rycroft (his director general) and me into the office for a debrief. I don't press him, as he has another appointment, but later he calls me to discuss his conversation with Cameron.

The PM has offered to get former Conservative MP, Olympic icon and Sheffield local Seb Coe to come out in favour of Nick in his Sheffield Hallam constituency. The quid pro quo for this generous offer is that Nick pulls out of the TV debate with Farage to give Cameron some cover in also refusing to take part. Nick is incensed by the base, transactional mentality of the suggestion and rejects it out of hand. I strongly agree and suggest that we should brief the media on Cameron's offer, in order to expose the cynicism of Cameron and the Tories. Regrettably, Nick is too decent to agree.

Later that month, Lena and I meet with the broadcasters to discuss the TV debates. They spring on us a complete shift from their original proposal for three debates, in which the first would have been a head-to-head between David Cameron and Ed Miliband, the second between the Conservative, Labour and Liberal Democrat leaders, and the third with the Conservative, Labour, Liberal Democrat and UKIP leaders. Now they are proposing two seven-way debates and one head-to-head debate between Cameron and Miliband. This means the Liberal Democrats will be treated no differently from the SNP, who do not contest any seats outside Scotland, and UKIP, who have never won a seat at a general election. It means we will partake on exactly the same basis as the Green Party and Plaid Cymru, who have no UK government record to defend and between them have managed to gain a combined total of 1.6 per cent of the vote and four MPs at the previous election, compared to 23 per cent and fifty-seven MPs for the Liberal Democrats.

The meeting is pretty brutal. Lena and I do not hide our dismay (and in my case disgust) at the way the broadcasters have handled things. They have allowed the biggest parties to dictate terms, just as we warned them would happen following the 2010 debates unless they established transparent criteria on which decisions would be made about participation. Sue Inglish, representing the BBC, who chaired the 2010 debate negotiations brilliantly, seems genuinely distressed by our anger, but it is impossible to hide given the derisory proposal they have come up with.

• • •

The last coalition Cabinet takes place on Tuesday 24 March and the coalition comes to a formal end with the dissolution of Parliament at one minute past midnight the following Monday.

On the Thursday afternoon prior to dissolution, I drop in on Ed Llewellyn, the PM's chief of staff, and his deputy, Kate Fall, to say farewell. We have had many ups and downs in our relationship but they have always been political rather than personal, and we have got on well most of the time. I realise I will miss them as I leave their office and walk up the stairs to the final meeting of Liberal Democrat special advisers.

Our special advisers are gathered in the large dining room in No. 10. They have been an amazing team of people to work with: smart and loyal and utterly committed through an often brutal five years in government. They all know that our chances of returning to government after the election are very slim, but nonetheless, with only a few exceptions, they all agree to work for the party throughout the six weeks of the campaign for free. As I speak to them for the final time in No. 10, I use my personal experiences to outline the pride I feel in what we have achieved.

I tell them about the Ethiopian famine of 1984, about Band Aid and Live Aid and running away from home to Addis Ababa, and I tell them how much it means to me that it is a Liberal Democrat coalition that has ensured Britain is the first G7 country to reach the UN target and that it is a Liberal Democrat MP who has secured that commitment in legislation.

I tell them of my experience as a gay teenager growing up in the 1980s as the drumbeat of anti-gay hostility reached its crescendo, and I tell them of the immense pride we should all feel that it is Liberal Democrat ministers in a Liberal Democrat coalition who have led the way in achieving equal marriage.

And I tell them about the challenges of growing up with mental health problems, of the millions of people who face similar challenges, many of them close to us, and of how proud we should be that it is a Liberal Democrat minister, supported by a Liberal Democrat Deputy Prime Minister in a Liberal Democrat coalition, who has delivered increased funding and the first ever waiting time standards for mental health services.

I thank them all for everything they have done, for their commitment, their resilience, their friendship and their loyalty, and I ask them to do everything they can over the next few weeks to ensure that we can return to government and continue to change the world for the better.

With that, we go back to our respective departments to hand in our passes and to say our farewells to our civil service colleagues, who have provided us with amazing support and friendship over the past five years.

•　•　•

I spend the election heading up a crisis comms team for the party that, with one major exception, is thankfully in much less demand than in 2010. Tim Colbourne, who has been Nick's fantastic deputy chief of staff over the past year, joins me along, with Ben Williams, the Chief Whip's adviser and a friend of nearly twenty years. Sean Kemp, who has by now left government, and Mike Girling, a member of the press team during the 2010 election, generously provide part-time voluntary support.

Although the campaign never takes off and it is clear the outcome is likely to be very bad, I enjoy being back in HQ with all the former special advisers in one place, reunited with our colleagues in the party staff. It feels like we have come home.

I spend polling day in my home constituency of Kingston and Surbiton, delivering early morning leaflets with my friend and fellow special adviser Ruwan Kodikara. Later in the day, when I am knocking on the doors of our alleged voters to encourage them to get out and vote, it is clear that many of them are no longer supporting us.

I am at home at 10 p.m. when the exit poll comes in. It is devastating: predicting just ten seats and 8 per cent of the vote, it is worse than anything I have prepared for. Ryan Coetzee, our strategy director, whom I have known since I worked in South Africa, warns me that it may be even worse than that.

We have a desultory conference call with Nick and Paddy Ashdown, who is chairing the election campaign, but conclude that we can't make any definitive plans until we have more information from the counts.

Around quarter to one on Friday morning, David Laws sends me a text message to tell me that he has lost in Yeovil. I call Nick to tell him that if we are losing Yeovil, the exit poll, which we have desperately tried to dismiss, is almost certainly correct. But Nick is way ahead of me; he has been receiving texts and calls from glum colleagues across the country reporting their defeat.

'It's not just Yeovil, Jonny. It's Cheltenham, Colchester, Southwark, Sutton, East Dunbartonshire. We're losing everything, everywhere.'

There's a pause, and the silence on the phone is leaden with our shock and misery.

Then, quietly and with finality, Nick says, 'Jonny, my heart is broken.'

And after that, there is nothing more to say.

• • •

I am numb as I climb into the taxi to take me to Lib Dem HQ; my mind is finding it impossible to compute the scale of our loss. At HQ, every face is a mirror, stricken like mine with shock and sadness.

Paddy, who took on the role of chairing the campaign very much against his better judgement, and – as I now guiltily recall – as a result of much arm-twisting by Nick and me, is, as always, still on the battlefield, trying to comfort others in the wake of the disaster. But I know how devastating this must be for him also. The party he built from near bankruptcy to a formidable force has just been reduced to ashes. Nick holds his seat in Sheffield Hallam, but I suspect he would prefer to have lost it.

The one positive aspect of an otherwise horrific day is that Hollie Voyce, who has been a close confidante and ally as Nick's political head of office, as usual has in place well-oiled plans for Friday morning, which she now seamlessly puts into operation. As Nick flies down from Sheffield to London, I make my way to the Kensington Gardens Hotel, where Nick will arrive with Miriam, Matthew Hanney, his political adviser, and Phil Reilly, his speechwriter. Here, he will have a chance to shower and change before we are driven to the venue where he will make his resignation speech. Thanks to Hollie, the plan goes perfectly, although I am taken aback when the hotel insists that I pay the bill in advance. It is just a few hours after the election result and the party is already regarded as a credit risk.

While I wait in the hotel room for Nick and the team, my phone rings. It's Nick Dale, a great friend since school days who has a knack for calling at exactly the right time. At that moment he just wants to check I am OK and to say how sorry he is at the result. Three years later, when my mother dies, Nick is again the first to call. On neither occasion does he put it off – as so many of us do in similar situations, wondering whether it is the right time or what the right words are to say – he just picks up the phone, and in doing so says everything that needs to be said. That instinctive friendship touches me profoundly.

Nick and Miriam and the team arrive shortly after and – after hugs and condolences are exchanged – everyone else heads off to the speech venue and Nick and I are left alone. We don't say much about the outcome; we focus on the resignation speech he is about to give. He reads it through one last time and then we go down to the car.

When Nick and I arrive at the venue for the speech, the room is packed with peers, party workers and advisers, many with tear-stained faces. There is not a single seat left, so I prop myself up against the wall as Nick starts to speak and immediately I feel my emotions rising and the exhaustion kicking in. My legs are jelly under me, so it requires use of every ounce of my willpower to stay upright. I cannot allow the importance of what he is saying to be interrupted by me slumping to the floor in a faint.

It's a humble, dignified speech, but it is also a defiant speech, a reminder of what has been achieved in government and a rallying cry for British liberalism. He warns of the threat that the combination of Conservative Euroscepticism and Scottish nationalism now poses to Britain's place in Europe and to the integrity of the United Kingdom itself and then he says:

> Fear and grievance have won, liberalism has lost. But it is more precious than ever, and we must keep fighting for it. That is both the great challenge and the great cause that my successor will have to face. I will always give my unstinting support for all those who continue to keep the flame of British liberalism alive.

At the end of the speech, Nick exits to a standing ovation. The staircase is lined with ex-special advisers applauding him. Nick has kept his composure throughout the speech, but the sight of all his former advisers is too much for him. When the door of the car is slammed shut, his voice cracks and he looks down at the floor of the car.

'Jonny, I have let them all down.'

I put my hand on his shoulder.

'Do you think they were there applauding you because they believe you have let them down? Nick, they were there because they are so proud to have served with you. And so am I.'

• • •

David picks me up from the station and as soon as I am with him, my resolve not to shed any tears vanishes and I dissolve into a sobbing wreck.

The days following the disaster are difficult. All the advisers are now unemployed, and we need to help them find work. The following day, I take the train up to HQ to clear out my desk, check in on advisers and start working out a plan to support people to find other jobs.

Nick calls to ask me how everyone is doing and to offer to meet with any who are particularly struggling. I mention one person and Nick is immediately on to it, inviting them round to his home to provide support and suggestions about possible employment opportunities. It is a mark of who he is that even in the face of such a political and personal catastrophe he is looking out for others.

Lib Dem HQ is mainly empty when I arrive, except for Austin Rathe, who is in charge of party membership, and the former Lib Dem Chief Whip, Don Foster, who sits opposite me. Despite having retired at the election, he is diligently and considerately making calls to each of his former colleagues. At some point in the morning, Austin comes around from the other side of the office and says, 'Something very strange is starting to happen: the website is being flooded with people signing up as party members.'

The numbers are already in the thousands and will build to over 20,000 over the coming days, providing much-needed cheer for those of us left battered and bruised by the election and fearing for the future of liberalism.

On Sunday, I take a long walk with our dog Bentley through Surbiton and Kingston to Richmond Park, where I sit on a bench near Pembroke Lodge looking down on the Thames, thinking of all the hard work that so many people have contributed over so many years which has now gone up in smoke. Kingston and Surbiton, Richmond Park, Taunton, all three seats where I have run election campaigns over the past eighteen years, are now back in Conservative hands. It is heartbreaking, and there is no getting away from the fact that I have to bear at least some of the responsibility. For the many mistakes made, the opportunities not taken, the unforced errors.

I am also beginning to understand what a toll the time in government has taken on David, how much he has had to shoulder as I have struggled through five years, distracted by the pressures of government and increasingly desperate about our political predicament. There has not been a meal when I haven't had a phone, usually two, by my side, blinking with emails and messages demanding my attention, taking it away from him.

On the Monday, I am intending to go up to London to HQ again. Since Friday, David has given me space to try to come to terms with what has happened, and I have responded by being morose and uncommunicative. Now as I head out the door on autopilot, David calls out sharply to me: 'Are you going to even say goodbye to me, even tell me what you are doing?'

I realise that this man who I love beyond words, who has been the kindest, most thoughtful, most understanding person I could have dreamt of, is now at the end of his patience with me. It is time to come home emotionally as well as physically.

The following weekend, we go out for a pub lunch with Julia, my friend from South Africa days. Halfway through the meal, she leans over to David and squeezes his arm and says, 'Oh my God, David, he's back.'

And I understand just how absent I have been.

POLITICAL EPILOGUE

A lot has happened in the seven years since the end of the Conservative–Liberal Democrat coalition government. Five years of stable government under the coalition gave way to three general elections and three Prime Ministers in just four years. A brutally divisive debate over Europe culminated in our exit from the European Union. It was followed by a global pandemic which claimed the lives of over 170,000 people in the UK and well over six million people worldwide; and just as it seemed we were emerging from that crisis, a brutal war erupted at the heart of Europe and shook the foundations of European security.

During our period in government and in its immediate aftermath, it was fashionable to deride the coalition as an arrangement in which the Liberal Democrats played patsy to the Conservatives as unnecessary austerity was imposed upon the country and little of liberal value was achieved. As a narrative, it was compelling in its simplicity. It was also nonsense.

There is a legitimate argument about the pace of the cuts and the balance between spending cuts and tax increases, and it is one that I and many others conducted within the government. However, there is no doubt that when the coalition took office in 2010, major spending cuts were inevitable. The eye-watering deficit bequeathed by the previous government – among the highest of any major industrial nation – meant that no government coming into office at that time could have avoided them.

The other part of the narrative is the suggestion that the Liberal Democrats achieved nothing of value in the coalition; that our MPs sold their souls for seats in ministerial cars and got nothing in return.

Where Liberal Democrat achievements are too clear to be denied, the claim is instead that the change would have been implemented by the Tories without us. This characterisation is demonstrably false, but it has been able to take hold, at least in part, because significant elements of our own party have chosen to believe it.

I am not blind, of course, to the mistakes we made during our five years in government. Some, particularly over tuition fees, were grievous, but they should not obscure what we achieved.

I started my political journey in front of a television screen, watching as the world failed the starving people of Ethiopia. I joined the Liberal Party in 1987, as anti-gay hysteria blazed across the newspapers – a seventeen-year-old seeking the safe haven of a party that valued people for who they were and stood with them even when to do so earned hostility and derision.

I joined a party that believed we should meet our obligations to the poorest people in the world; that demanded equal rights for all citizens; that not only warned of the threat to humanity if we continued to pollute our atmosphere and poison our seas but also proposed concrete practical action to halt the damage.

I was told at the time that these were pipe dreams, which simply evidenced the party's lack of appetite for government. Twenty-three years later, we not only successfully negotiated the first post-war coalition, but we brought to it a detailed, ambitious and liberal programme for government, along with talented ministers determined to implement it.

By the end of the coalition, the vast majority of that programme had been delivered.

Liberal Democrat policies were implemented which reformed the tax system, cutting income tax for over twenty million people and taking millions of the lowest-paid out of paying income tax at all. This would not have happened without the determination of Nick Clegg and Danny Alexander and their willingness to take on the reluctance of their Tory counterparts. At the same time, Britain's vast deficit and spiralling debt were brought under control, ensuring that future generations would not have to bear the full burden of our generation's profligacy.

The detention of children for immigration purposes was ended, the national ID card scheme was scrapped, control orders were reformed and civil liberties were assiduously and intelligently defended, despite the challenging security environment and the state-knows-best tendencies of the Tory Party.

Britain's energy sector was transformed with a dramatic shift towards non-carbon sources of power, thanks to the unprecedented expansion in renewables driven through by Liberal Democrat Climate Secretaries Chris Huhne and Ed Davey, against the trenchant opposition of George Osborne at the Treasury.

Schools funding was protected and the pupil premium, the brainchild of Nick Clegg and David Laws, shook up the school funding system and ensured that extra resources were available to all schools in line with the needs of their pupils.

Pensioner poverty was dramatically reduced as a result of the pension triple lock, designed and implemented by a Liberal Democrat Pensions Minister, Steve Webb.

Mental health care was put at the centre of political debate due to the passion and energy of a Liberal Democrat Health Minister, Norman Lamb, and the first ever targets for mental health services were established.

Same-sex couples were finally able to claim full and equal civil rights when the Equal Marriage Bill, the initiative of a Liberal Democrat Minister, Lynne Featherstone, passed into law.

And the UK became the only G7 country to meet the UN target for overseas development assistance, committing 0.7 per cent of our national wealth to support the poorest people on earth – a commitment enshrined in law thanks to a Liberal Democrat MP and former Cabinet minister, Michael Moore.

That's quite some record for any party in government, let alone a party that had been out of office for three generations.

Sadly, many of these Liberal Democrat achievements have subsequently been reversed in whole or in part, despite explicit Conservative manifesto pledges not to do so. The income tax threshold, which rose throughout the coalition, has been frozen; the national insurance rate has increased for both individuals and businesses; and the pensions triple lock – introduced to ratchet up pensioners' income and address pensioner poverty – has been scrapped, meaning the UK state pension will remain one of the least generous in Europe. Finally, the commitment to spend 0.7 per cent of our gross national income to support the poorest people in the world has been abandoned. The moment in 2013 when the coalition government had finally met this long-standing political aspiration had been a precious milestone for me on a political journey that had started twenty-eight years before, when – aged fifteen – I had stepped foot on that plane to Ethiopia. The callousness with which it was abandoned in the middle of a global health pandemic, when our help was needed more than ever before, broke my heart.

PERSONAL EPILOGUE

It never occurred to me when I started writing this book that my mother would have died before I had completed it. To be sure, she was in her late seventies already, but she was one of the fittest people I knew.

To mark her eightieth birthday, she decided she would swim 2.5km to raise money for Macmillan Cancer Care. She had swum 5km to mark her seventieth birthday, but she thought that was slightly beyond her in her eightieth year and asked me if I would swim the two and a half with her.

So we did, in the outdoor pool at Hampton, on a sparkling April morning. There were some, including myself, who wondered if I would manage to swim that far, but no one ever doubted that my mum would. That's how fit and determined she was.

Just a few months later, she was diagnosed with pancreatic cancer and decided she did not want treatment. The following March, my brother and I sat with her and held her hand as she drew her last breath. In the intervening time between her diagnosis and her death, I had the opportunity to tell her many times how much I loved her and how much I owed to her for all the love and care she had given me over her life. So I don't have any regrets that I failed to tell her the most important things that I wanted her to know. Still, I am sorry she never got to read this book. I hope it might have helped tie some things together for her and that she would have been proud of me for writing it, however difficult it might have been for her to read some of it.

I miss her every day, but most especially on Sunday mornings, when we used to swim together at Hampton and then chat over coffee on the pool terrace about the books we had read, or the beautiful flower she might just have seen on one of her walks along the Thames, or the poetry or plays which we both loved, or something that was happening in our lives that was either challenging or exhilarating.

Whatever mood I was in, she always cheered me up, because the essential principle of her life was that she lived it with enthusiasm and love.

My best tribute to her is to try to do the same.

ACKNOWLEDGEMENTS

I would like to thank all those who have helped me with this book, in particular the fantastic team at Biteback: to James Stephens for agreeing to publish my story; to my amazing editor, Olivia Beattie, who has helped me make the book far better than it otherwise would have been; to Namkwan Cho for designing the cover, which I love; and to Suzanne Sangster and all the team for their help and assistance.

I also want to thank my husband, David, who painstakingly read through my early drafts and made invaluable suggestions for improvements. I would also particularly like to thank Nick Clegg, Sam Green, Sean Kemp, David Laws, Lena Pietsch, Julia Race, Father Charles Sherlock and John Sharkey for their time and advice commenting on aspects of the manuscript.

I also want to record my thanks to the people who ensured I came home from Ethiopia safely. To the late Canon James Robertson, who alerted Charles Sherlock to my presence in Ethiopia and who after my return provided me with kind and wise advice and counselling. To Charles himself, to whom I cannot offer sufficient gratitude. Most importantly, to my mum and dad, who were understanding and forgiving beyond anything I deserved, and to my siblings, David, Jeremy, Becky and Al, who put up with my morose moods and gave me their love every step of the way; and to their partners, Judy, Liv and Scott. Also to my extended family of nephews, nieces and godchildren: Andrew, Claire, Jenny, James, Barney, Lexie, Robbie, Henry, Oscar, Isla, Darcy, John, Kira, Kit, Phoebe and Roddy, and to my wonderful godmother, Margaret Appleton. I am lucky to have inherited family and friends in the United States, and my thanks to them for all their love and friendship: David's dad; his brother Michael and sister Cheryl; the amazing Roberts-Giglio clan – Sharon, Paige, Greg, Bridger, Ryan and Ava – and our wonderful friends Ben, Elizabeth, Howie, Lisa, Mark, Michael, Revola, Sal, Sergei, Theresa and Tracy, and our late friends Alonzo and Stephen.

I owe a huge debt of thanks to all my friends in the UK who have helped me along my way, often without realising it. From my school days: Will, Sarah, Nick, Becca, Kelly, Allan, Marguerite, Polly, Nicky, Justin, Harry, Seb, Emeka, Jon and Dave; from university: Sarah, Jonathan, John, Sam, Dilip, Dom, Richard, Yvette, Sonia and Steve; from other parts of my life, less easily defined: Ruth, my friend and second sister from earliest childhood; my best friend, Vijay; and my amazing friends who are not mentioned elsewhere: Alison, Anthony, Cath, Devina, Erica, Fran, Guy, Hannah, Hugh, John, Julia, Kat, Laura, Liz, Mark, Melissa, Rachel, Susie and Wyn.

I am hugely grateful to the late Jim Cogan, who established Schools Partnership Worldwide, which gave me one of the most formative experiences of my life in Zimbabwe; to Ken and Polly Anderson, whose home in Marondera was always open to me; and to Alan de Saram and Joe West for their friendship and for putting up with me as a colleague and housemate. My immense gratitude and love to Morgan and Alice, who looked after me during my time at Zongoro and whose love and friendship over three decades is a most precious treasure to me. My thanks also to all the pupils I had the privilege to teach and to learn from. I hope, for all of them, that brighter days come to Zimbabwe.

I am immensely grateful to Simon Hughes and Richard Caborn,

without whom I would never have had the chance to work in South Africa at such a key moment in its history, and to Prince Mangosuthu Buthelezi for supporting and encouraging me in my work. While in South Africa, I was privileged to be in receipt of a wealth of kindness and friendship from a wide range of people, including the late Inka Mars, who looked after me from start to finish and kept me endlessly enthralled with fascinating tales from her life; Nicky Lucas, my sister in Africa, who was always ready to sink a beer with me and whenever necessary – quite often – puncture my pomposity; and Eric and Daphne, her very special parents. I am also immensely grateful to Reverend Musa Zondi, whose good sense, calm judgement and friendship were always on hand; to Velaphi Ndlovu for the friendship and trust he put in me; and to Alex Hamilton, whom I spent many hours arguing with about politics but who was always a good and true friend.

Craig Clark, with whom I shared an office in Cape Town, wisely counselled me against sending the most incendiary of my letters to Koos van der Merwe and has been a friend ever since. In Cape Town I also had the privilege of working with Joshua Mazibuko and Joyce Moretlwe, who were always kind and supportive and great colleagues to work with. Richard Calland and Lawson Naidoo introduced me to cricket and, along with Gaye Davis, guided me through South African politics, usually accompanied by copious quantities of beer and fantastic food.

To Caroline Bagley, whose fabulous restaurant, the Savoy Cabbage, was a fixture of Cape Town for me (I still dream of the chocolate pancakes) – thank you for all your wonderful friendship over the past twenty years. Thanks also to Frank and Peter and all the innumerable staff at the Savoy Cabbage who made every visit a pleasure. And particular thanks to Gavin for his friendship and the times we spent together. Above all, my thanks to my dear friend Ebrahim and his sons Ashraf and Zakeer, who made me feel a part of the family from my earliest days in South Africa.

My thanks to the amazing team of people I had the privilege of working with while at the Children's Investment Fund Foundation: Abbi Knell, Clarissa Rumbidzai Radebe, Gopi S-R, Joanna Mikulski, Lilies Njanga, Lina Estlind, Linda Weisert, Dr Mairo Mandara, Matt Gould, Monica Allen, Rajat Sindhu, Sukhmani Bajwa and Yemurai Nyoni. Particular thanks also to Kate Hampton for employing me and for all her support during my mother's illness.

A huge and heartfelt thank-you to the team of special advisers I worked with in government. You were the smartest, hardest-working, most loyal people anyone could ever hope to work with: Monica Allen, Duncan Brack, Peter Carroll, Julia Church, Ryan Coetzee, Tim Colbourne, Zena Creed, Conan D'Arcy, Alex Dziedzan, Myrddin Edwards, Jo Foster, John Foster, Emily Frith, Emma Gilpin Jacobs, Olly Grender, Matthew Hanney, Paul Hodgson, James Holt, Veena Hudson, Christine Jardine, Sean Kemp, Joel Kenrick, Ruwan Kodikara, Steve Lotinga, Ashley Lumsden, James McGrory, Polly Mackenzie, Shabnum Mustapha, Chris Nicholson, Will de Peyer, Lena Pietsch, Vanessa Pine, Elizabeth Plummer, Adam Pritchard, Richard Reeves, Phil Reilly, Matt Sanders, Chris Saunders, Neil Sherlock, Tim Snowball, Alison Suttie, Hollie Voyce, Emily Walch, Katie Waring, Ben Williams, Giles Wilkes.

Special thanks to Zena Creed, who gave me a copy of the manuscript music of 'I Never Promised You a Rose Garden' when she left government, one of the most thoughtful gifts I have ever received. Also to Ryan and Jessica Coetzee, who first met each other when Ryan – whom I had known from South Africa days – came to work for the coalition and Jessica was a civil servant working with me in the Deputy Prime Minister's office, thanks for all your friendship over the years.

I worked with a number of amazing civil servants, including: Ros Allen, Michael Anderson, Michael Bourke, Sarah Byers, James Clarke, Jessica Coetzee, Jonathan Crisp, Jane Cunliffe, Caleb Deeks, Jack Fulford,

Sue Gray, Steve Hall, the late Sir Jeremy Heywood, Rachel Hopcroft, Siobhan Jones, Stephen Jones, Suzanne Kochanowski, the late Chris Martin, Ciaran Martin, Samantha Massey, Calum Miller, Laura Lutkoski, Sam O'Callaghan, Gus O'Donnell, John Owen, Peter Ricketts, Christina Roberts, Jamie Ross, Philip Rycroft, Lucy Smith, James Sorene, Mark Sweeney, Sarah Thacker, Katy Weeks, Kate Whitty-Johnson, Shelley Williams-Walker, Chris Wormald and Bilal Zahid.

I have had the privilege of working with some wonderful people at party HQ, on the leader's office staff and in Parliament, including Humphrey Amos, Ernest Baidoo-Mitchell, Sam Barratt, Lucy Billingsley, Ruth Brock, Emma Cherniavsky, Rachel Clarke, James Drummond, Emma Foster, Chris Fox, Laura Gilmore, Mike Girling, Tim Gordon, Tim Hobden, Naimah Khatun, Steven Lawson, Gavin Lim, Melissa Lynes, Paul Maloney, Bess Mayhew, Christian Moon, Sian Norris Copson, Sarah Pughe, Austin and Ben Rathe, Ian Sherwood, Ed Simpson, Tom Smithard and Beau Wilson.

Thanks to Nick Clegg for giving me the job as his chief of staff and always keeping his faith in me, even when I got things spectacularly wrong; to the late Paddy Ashdown, a force of nature who inspired me every day; to my good friend Ed Davey for always fighting the cause with such passion and dedication; to Jim Wallace for his wisdom and kindness to me; and to David Laws and Danny Alexander for their sharp minds and friendship.

Finally, I owe a particular debt of gratitude to Dr Philippa Whitford, who listened to my story on a bumpy minibus ride through Ethiopia and gave me the courage to tell it more widely; and to David Laws, whose introduction to his publishers brought me to this place.

ABOUT THE AUTHOR

© Barney Oates

Jonny Oates was born in 1969 and educated at Marlborough College. He was the director of communications for the Liberal Democrats for the 2010 general election and chief of staff to Deputy Prime Minister Nick Clegg through the coalition government of 2010–15.

Inspired by Michael Buerk's world-famous broadcast from the Ethiopian famine, he ran away from home to Addis Ababa in 1985, hoping to help the victims – an endeavour that, unsurprisingly, proved unsuccessful. He subsequently worked as a teacher in a rural school in Zimbabwe and as a political adviser in South Africa's first post-apartheid parliament.

He has been a member of the House of Lords since October 2015, where he focuses on climate change, international development and mental health.